CHALLENGING THE THIRD SECTOR

Global prospects for active citizenship

Sue Kenny
Marilyn Taylor
Jenny Onyx
Marjorie Mayo

First published in Great Britain in 2017 by

Policy Press
University of Bristol
1-9 Old Park Hill
Bristol
BS2 8BB
UK
t: +44 (0)117 954 5940
pp-info@bristol.ac.uk
www.policypress.co.uk

North America office:
Policy Press
c/o The University of Chicago Press
1427 East 60th Street
Chicago, IL 60637, USA
t: +1 773 702 7700
f: +1 773 702 9756
sales@press.uchicago.edu
www.press.uchicago.edu

British Library Cataloguing in Publication Data
A catalogue record for this book is available from the British Library

Library of Congress Cataloging-in-Publication Data
A catalog record for this book has been requested

ISBN 978-1-4473-1694-7 paperback
ISBN 978-1-4473-1691-6 hardcover
ISBN 978-1-4473-2142-2 ePub
ISBN 978-1-4473-2143-9 Mobi
ISBN 978-1-4473-1692-3 ePdf

Cover design by Robin Hawes
Front cover image: www.alamy.com
Printed and bound in Great Britain by CPI Group (UK) Ltd,
Croydon, CR0 4YY
Policy Press uses environmentally responsible print partners

Contents

About the authors

Sue Kenny is Emeritus Professor in the Community and International Development programme at Deakin University, Australia. She was previously the director of the Centre for Citizenship, Development and Human Rights at Deakin University. Her research includes comparative studies of active citizenship, community development and the third sector. Recent publications include *Developing communities for the future* (2011), *Challenging capacity building: Comparative perspectives* (2010) (co-edited with Matthew Clarke) and *Post-disaster reconstruction: Lessons from Aceh* (2010) (co-edited with Matthew Clarke and Ismet Fanany).

Marilyn Taylor is Emeritus Professor at the University of the West of England, Bristol, UK, and visiting research fellow at the Institute for Voluntary Action Research. Her research covers community development, neighbourhood governance and voluntary sector policy. Recent publications include a fully revised second edition of *Public policy in the community* (2011) and, with Alison Gilchrist, *A short guide to community development* (2011). Marilyn is a member of the editorial boards for the *Community Development Journal* and *Voluntas*.

Jenny Onyx is Emeritus Professor of Community Management in the Business School at the University of Technology, Sydney, Australia. She is co-director of Cosmopolitan Civil Societies research centre, and former editor of *Third Sector Review*. She is particularly concerned with issues of advocacy, social capital, social impact, volunteering and civil society, and has published widely in these fields with over 100 refereed publications, including *Comparative third sector governance in Asia: Structure, process and political economy* (2008) (co-edited with Samiul Hasan); *Spinning straw into gold: Social capital in everyday life* (2004) (with Rosemary Leonard); *A dynamic balance: Social capital and sustainable community development* (2005) (with Ann Dale); *Emergence, social capital and entrepreneurship: Understanding networks from the inside* (2011) (with Ellen Baker and Melissa Edwards).

Marjorie Mayo is Emeritus Professor of Community Development at Goldsmiths, University of London, UK, where her research has included a focus on learning for active citizenship and access to justice in disadvantaged communities. Previous publications include *Global citizens* (2005) and *Cultures, communities, identities* (2000). Recent publications include *Access to justice for disadvantaged communities* (2014) (with Gerald Koessl, Matthew Scott and Imogen Slater).

Acknowledgements

Dedicated to all those in far-flung places across the globe who have given their valuable time to share their varying experiences and challenges with us, pointing to ways forward and promoting active citizenship based on the values of cooperation, social solidarity, human rights and social justice.

Preface

Why this book?

The idea for this book emerged as the four of us sat in the sunshine, sharing reflections, during breaks between sessions at the International Society for Third Sector Research's conference in Siena, Italy, in 2012. The third sector was facing many challenges in the context of neoliberal globalisation, challenges with major significance in relation to our shared interests in the promotion of democratic participation, equalities and social justice. Was globalisation opening up new spaces for active citizenship, locally, nationally and/or internationally? Or was the third sector becoming increasingly incorporated into neoliberal agendas? How far could the third sector's own claims for its contributions be justified by the evidence? What about the 'dark side' to the third sector and to wider social movements, the side that excludes outsiders and practises discriminatory approaches to active citizenship? And in what ways might the third sector be reinventing itself, more generally, in response to changing circumstances?

Between us, we began to share reflections from our own empirical research, comparing and contrasting experiences from a wide variety of contexts, across continents. We started to identify the theoretical implications, taking account of differing definitions and varying perspectives. And we began to reflect on the possible ramifications for developing policies and practices to promote active citizenship. While we set out to unpack contested concepts and critically examine the evidence, this did not in any way imply that we had no starting positions ourselves. Far from being totally neutral, we share common commitments to the values of equality, social solidarity, human rights and social justice, together with respect for diversity and differences within and between communities. These shared commitments have underpinned our approach to the third sector and active citizenship.

This has not meant, though, that we have been in total agreement. Given our own particular backgrounds, from different continents, and given our varying theoretical approaches and experiences, as researchers and activists, it would have been somewhat surprising if we had found ourselves in unanimous agreement about each aspect of every chapter. So how have we managed the process of writing this book together?

Sue Kenny took the lead in developing the proposal in outline. Once this had been agreed we each took responsibility for drafting specific chapters.

Sue Kenny produced the first drafts of Chapters Two, Three, Four and Seven. Jenny Onyx produced the first drafts of Chapters Six, Ten and Eleven. Marilyn Taylor produced the first draft of Chapter Five. In addition she produced the first draft of Chapter Eight jointly with Marjorie Mayo who also produced the first draft of Chapter Nine. Marjorie Mayo took the running with the introductory chapter while Marilyn Taylor produced the first draft, with Jenny Onyx, of the concluding chapter. These drafts were then discussed and revised, taking account of each other's comments, adding examples from our own research and experiences, respecting each other's insights without necessarily accepting every suggestion or agreeing on every particular point. Marilyn Taylor then completed the process with a final edit, for overall coherence (with some assistance from Marjorie Mayo), exploring the links between the different chapters to highlight common themes. Similar processes were put in place, at the next stage, in response to the reviewer's helpful feedback.

From the outset we have aimed for a common terminology. For example, we have, as far as possible, standardised our use of terms such as 'the third sector', along with the term 'third sector organisations'. This was more problematic in some cases than others, however. For example, we struggled with the most appropriate ways to refer to the countries that are often described as the global 'North' and compared and contrasted with the global 'South', or 'developed' and 'developing' and 'Western' and 'non-Western' countries. The terms global 'North' and global 'South' seemed particularly inappropriate from an Australian perspective. In the end we decided that as far as possible we would refer to the countries of the global 'North' as OECD countries (i.e. countries included within the Organisation for Economic Co-operation and Development, which includes Australia and Japan), except when referring to local sources or quoting from secondary sources that were using other terminologies. Overall the intention has been to achieve as much consistency as possible, while taking account of the differing ways in which terms have been applied in varying contexts. The extent to which this has been achieved, though, is, of course for you, the reader, to judge.

Sue Kenny
Marilyn Taylor
Jenny Onyx
Marjorie Mayo
January 2015

ONE

Introduction

Active citizenship and the third sector have come to the fore in policy debates internationally, as well as in a variety of national contexts. As John Gaventa was already arguing at the turn of the new millennium, through 'community organizations, social movements, issue campaigns, and policy advocacy, citizens have found ways to have their voices heard and to influence the decisions and practices of larger institutions that affect their lives' (Gaventa, 2001, p 275). Over several decades there has been growing interest in the capacities of citizens to take responsibility for their own destinies as civil society actors, if for a variety of reasons, as we explore subsequently. And one of the key sites that has been identified as having the capacity for nurturing as well as for expressing active citizenship has been the third sector. Yet 'active citizenship' and the 'third sector' have been contested as concepts and both have been affected by processes of change, including neoliberal globalisation.

There are those who argue that the expansion of active citizenship provides significant opportunities to promote democracy and human rights both locally, nationally and globally (Held, 1995; Archibugi, 2008), while globalisation offers possibilities 'for a new sense of solidarity and new opportunities for engagement' (Gaventa and Tandon, 2010, p 5). In an increasingly interconnected world, changing patterns of power and governance have been emerging and, with these, new and reconstructed spaces for public action together with changing, multilayered and multidimensional identities of citizenship (Gaventa and Tandon, 2010). Citizens and their organisations have been invited to engage with policy makers at local, national and, increasingly, at international level – in the latter case through opportunities such as the UN Human Rights Committees and the Global Platform for Disaster Reduction. They have also been creating their own discursive spaces

However, critics argue that, far from extending democratisation and the promotion of human rights, deepening neoliberal globalisation policies have been undermining the role of the state along with the independent role of the third sector. Thus Gaventa and Tandon question the extent to which globalisation does actually offer a 'real opportunity for expanded solidarity', suggesting that it 'weakens the possibilities for human agency' and concluding that 'In sum there are winners and losers in this process' (Gaventa and Tandon, 2010, p 5).

In OECD countries, critics argue, some third sector organisations have been colluding with neoliberal agendas, increasingly focusing upon providing public services as agents of the state, potentially squeezing out smaller, community based organisations in the process as well as opening up potential markets and spearheading opportunities for privatisation. Meanwhile, international NGOs have been accused of promoting the agendas of the most powerful (Hulme and Edwards, 1997), under the guise of government agendas for spreading democracy (by force) in countries such as Afghanistan and Iraq.

This prompts a number of questions. Is the concept of the third sector being redefined and re-evaluated and, if so, in what ways? And how might the notion of active citizenship be undergoing contestations and challenges, whether by agencies of governance from above and/or by active citizens, third sector organisations and social movements, from below? Are such processes of neoliberal globalisation being experienced very differently – and responded to in very different ways – as people exercise their capacities for human agency in varying contexts? How might the third sector be promoting active citizenship in these varying contexts, taking account of the accompanying opportunities and challenges at different levels?

Given the significance of these debates, it is timely to engage with the issues critically, linking the discussion of these contested concepts and competing perspectives with evidence that has been emerging from empirical research. Our overall aim is to further stimulate critical debate, exploring ways of developing strategies for the third sector and active citizenship in the light of these contemporary opportunities and challenges.

Perspectives

So to begin, we set out to unpack the varying definitions and the competing perspectives that underpin contemporary discussions of active citizenship and the third sector. Active citizenship can be promoted for a variety of reasons, as subsequent chapters explore more fully. The aims may be related to the extension of neoliberal agendas, which seek to roll back the state, and encourage self help and the provision of public services on the cheap via increasing the use of unpaid, 'voluntary' labour, while opening the way to more comprehensive marketisation over the longer term. Active citizenship may also be promoted for the purpose of maintaining or securing a market or cultural foothold in a newly industrialised country. Alternatively however, the aims may be related to motivations of altruism, mutual caring and social solidarity, including engaging active citizens in advocacy and campaigning for increasing equalities, social justice and human rights. These different definitions and perspectives need to be disentangled, taking account of the varying ways in which they may – or may not – be manifested in differing geographical contexts, whether locally, nationally and/ or internationally. In the latter case, it is also necessary to unpack the contested concept of 'global citizenship'.

In parallel, we set out to consider the varying definitions of the third sector itself and the differing ways in which the sector has been delineated. Subsequent chapters go on to develop the case for conceptualising and critically examining the claims about the third sector's contributions to nurturing active citizenship.

The book explores the potential value of the third sector (however defined) together with its potential contributions to the promotion of active citizenship. However, this is not to idealise the third sector or to accept the accounts of its champions uncritically, rather than examining the evidence, in varying contexts, over time. We are only too aware that there is a dark side to the third sector, just as there is a dark side to active citizenship, to communities and to community based organisations and social movements, which can exclude outsiders and practise discrimination against 'the other'. Popular movements for social change can contain socially reactionary and culturally fundamentalist elements, just as third sector organisations and social movements can promote widely differing agendas.

In this book, we set out to examine arguments and evidence, drawing upon our own research in varying contexts. In doing so, we aim to explore the different ways in which third sector organisations have been responding to the all too real challenges that face them in the contemporary policy context. Human beings have agency to make choices, even if in varying and potentially decreasing degrees.

The structure of the book

Part 1: Exploring concepts and contexts

The first chapter in this part, Chapter Two, introduces meanings and practices of active citizenship, beginning by locating the idea of active citizenship in the wider theoretical discussion of citizenship. It identifies different forms, levels and dimensions of active citizenship and develops two ideal types: active citizenship as civic commitment and active citizenship as social and political activism. Chapter Three then moves on to explore differing approaches to the concept of the third sector, starting from the historical context of the revival of interest in the notion of civil society in the late 1980s and early 1990s. This sets the framework for considering how third sector organisations may provide sites and actions that nurture active citizenship.

In much of the literature concerned with the relation between the third sector and active citizenship, third sector organisations are placed in a privileged position as key nurturers of active citizenship. Chapter Four sets out the claims concerning this relationship and arguments supporting these claims, drawing on the writings of de Tocqueville, Putnam, Hirst, Turner and Warren, among others. This chapter introduces concerns about the veracity of these claims. These include, for example, the paucity of empirical research dealing with the claims, the unidimensional notions of the third sector and active citizenship upon which some such claims are based and the failure to grasp the fluidity of both the third sector and active citizenship.

Part 1 concludes by setting the contemporary context for current debates about the third sector and active citizenship. Thus in Chapter Five the relationships between the state, the market and the third sector are critically explored, taking account of different ways of understanding these relationships and varying typologies as these have been developed over time. It draws on institutional and governmentality theories to consider the implications of blurring and hybridisation for the sector's role in promoting active citizenship and considers how different historical and cultural contexts affect the way third sector organisations experience and respond to these challenges.

Part 2: Forms of active citizenship

Part 2 moves on to explore different forms of active citizenship. The first concerns citizenship as civic commitment, that is, where citizens actively work together to preserve and protect, to enhance and improve the community in which they live, generating social capital and encouraging social cohesion. In this way they provide services to those who would otherwise do without; they keep the 'wheels turning'. Chapter Six explores these forms of active citizenship, starting by examining research concerning volunteers: where they come from, what motivates them, how they benefit, and what they achieve. They may be seen as at the core of social capital generation. However, they are not simply passive and obedient subjects, but display considerable agency, not only in maintaining existing services and organisations, but on occasion in challenging existing practices.

The next chapter in this part, Chapter Seven, explores the varying ways in which such forms of active citizenship have been understood and applied in very different cultural contexts. This chapter draws upon original research, including research based in Indonesia and in Russia. This leads into the discussion of active citizenship and political engagement through the third sector.

Chapter Eight considers how different forms of active citizenship take shape as social and political activism, reflecting on the varying roles that third sector organisations can play in nurturing civil commitment and activism. While recognising potential limits and constraints, this chapter also explores ways in which third sector organisations can support marginalised groups in finding their voice and organising resistance to discrimination and oppression. In tracing the changing landscape, the forms of activism that dominated the last decades of the twentieth century are contrasted with new forms of activism launched through social media.

This leads into the discussion of social movements and social transformation in Chapter Nine. Social movements have been defined in terms of their powers of independent disruption, their ability to push beyond the limits of compatibility with the system in question, breaking the rules in ways that question the legitimacy of power and proposing alternatives. How can formal organisations, including third sector organisations, support social movements, such as anti-poverty movements or global campaigns for the right to education, for example, without undermining their independence – and without diluting their disruptive potential? And how can they promote such campaigns without substituting for the voices of the poor themselves? Although there is an increasingly extensive literature addressing these types of question, there remain continuing dilemmas for those concerned to strengthen active citizenship and the third sector in the context of strategies for social transformation.

Part 3: New forms of active citizenship: Emerging forms and challenges

The third and final part discusses recent shifts in the thinking and practices of active citizenship, including how citizens are finding new ways of dealing with social and environmental problems and how they engage in civil society. The first chapter in Part 3, Chapter Ten, considers ways in which citizens come together to create new forms of organisation, focusing upon the emergence of social networks. The chapter investigates the dynamic processes by which these new types of social form emerge within communities. Sometimes there is evidence of a central initiator, often the state or sometimes another external agent. Sometimes there is evidence of entrepreneurial activity within the community, perhaps with the leadership of an individual or group of people, or third sector organisation. And sometimes there is evidence of collective action arising spontaneously without any obvious external leadership. The actions of many small local climate action groups provide illustrations, along with a range of other examples, in varying contexts, internationally.

As previous chapters will have already argued, the third sector and the nature of active citizenship are both changing rapidly. Chapter Eleven explores the nature of these changes in greater depth. With the increasing dominance of neoliberal ideology, many third sector organisations, whether by choice or necessity, have been turning to market driven models of organisational structure and function, operating more like entrepreneurial businesses. However, this is only part of the story. At the same time much is also happening under the surface, out of the mainstream media gaze, until a major crisis or event occurs to make these new types of third sector activity visible. Examples include the actions of social media, Facebook and Twitter, but also more targeted forms of civil activism such as GetUp, Avaaz and Wikileaks. Such unruly, apparently unmanaged actions nonetheless may have an (emergent) organisational base, and indeed often operate through transnational networks. This chapter explores the implications of these dramatically different emergent forms of organising.

The concluding chapter, Chapter Twelve, summarises the key challenges that have been examined in previous chapters, raising questions as to how the third sector might respond and returning to the central questions of the book: the role of the third sector in promoting active citizenship and the implications for the future.

Part 1
Exploring concepts and contexts

TWO

Active citizenship

Introduction

To understand the contemporary idea of active citizenship we need to note the intellectual shift that was taking place in the social sciences during the 1980s, which focused attention on the importance of human agency in social change. At one level this shift was reflected in the growing interest in new social movements (Melucci, 1989; Touraine, 1988). At another level it found expression in new approaches to welfare. Giddens, for example, writing in Britain, argued for a 'positive welfare' approach (Giddens, 1994, p 152), which would recognise the role of self development and the importance of reflexive engagement with life chances and social security systems. This approach can be understood as setting the scene for self determination. However, it also provides a policy platform for 'self responsibilisation', requiring individuals to rely on their own resources and take individual responsibility for their own livelihoods. Indeed, Fuller et al (2008, p 157) argue that the emphasis on the self responsible, active citizen emerged in explicit contrast to the earlier needs-/rights-based notion of citizenship. Arguments for self responsibilisation and self help are easily crafted to accord with the principles of neoliberalism – a recurring theme throughout this book.

The refocusing of thinking about the role of human agency in social change has not been limited to Western societies. In other parts of the world, the failure of anti-poverty strategies organised around top-down structural economic adjustment policies led to a rethink of aid policies by international agencies (Chambers, 1983; Bhatnagar and Williams, 1992; Eade and Williams, 1995; World Bank, 2013). By the late 1990s many international development programmes were being reworked, emphasising new programmes for capacity building to 'empower' local people to develop and act upon their own policies to improve their lives.

Citizenship in theory

While we can trace the intellectual interest in human agency to the 1980s, the specific theoretical construction of human agents as *active citizens* has mainly come about through the field of citizenship studies. Much contemporary discussion and debate in citizenship studies has been informed by the writings of T. H. Marshall (1992) in the immediate post World War II years. For Marshall, citizenship denoted membership of a political community, with members entitled to equal rights and participation. He identified different dimensions of citizenship, which, he argued, became institutionalised in Britain in three stages, with a gradual extension of citizen rights from civil rights, to political rights, and then to social rights (Marshall, 1992, p 8). Thus, the eighteenth century saw the establishment of civil rights, including the right to freedom of speech and access to the legal system and justice. In the nineteenth century political rights, such as the right to participate in the political process, were developed (and extended in the twentieth century when women gained the right to vote). In the twentieth century social rights were established, such as the right to welfare and social security in times of sickness and unemployment, culminating in the development of the post war welfare state. The development of these three kinds of rights, which were to apply equally to all members of society irrespective of social differences, provided a means of mitigating the inequalities of social class.

Marshall's concept of citizenship has been subject to considerable analysis and critique and some have called for a post Marshallian concept (Evers and Guillemard, 2013). Nevertheless, the following six aspects of Marshall's treatment of citizenship are particularly important for the arguments in this book. These are: the need to distinguish between formal and substantive rights; the evolution assumption; the emphasis on individual rights; the stated-bounded framing of citizenship; the framing of the citizen as a passive recipient of rights; and ethnocentricity.

The first aspect for review is Marshall's focus on citizenship as consisting of legal rights (Roy, 2005). Legal definitions and approaches to citizenship can be exclusionary. For example, those defined as non-citizens, such as asylum seekers and migrants *sans papiers* can be, and typically are, treated in discriminatory ways. But critics also argue that the Marshallian formulation failed to understand the importance of distinguishing between formal/legal equality and substantive equality, the latter required for the practical exercising of rights (Delanty, 2000). While they are equal members of a society under the law, many citizens do not have equal substantive membership of society and therefore equal access to rights, because of the structural disadvantages associated with their identity or circumstances, such as those based on gender, ethnicity and class. This has led to a questioning of the assumption that citizens can enjoy rights independent of context or identity. Feminists, for example, have criticised a failure to understand the ways in which women have been either excluded from citizenship entitlements or incorporated on the basis of their services in a patriarchal society (Dietz, 1987; Lister, 1997).

The second aspect for review is Marshall's focus on an evolutionary framework of citizen rights (Turner, 1992). This linear evolutionary perspective ignores the often disjointed and contradictory nature of change and development. History shows that rights can be claimed and won only to be subsequently clawed back. Third, it could be argued that Marshall's evolutionary view has paved the way for liberal interpretations of citizenship that are organised solely around individual rights and interests, as we discuss later in this chapter. However, Marshall himself defined citizenship in broader terms (Marshall, 1992, p 18), which incorporated the duty or obligation of civic participation. This understanding of citizenship has been taken up in the civic republican tradition, which is concerned with public political life and civic virtue. In this tradition, citizenship provides a common bond, a process through which individuals from diverse groups can practise civility. A major way of developing and sustaining citizenship today, in this view, is through associational life and, in particular, through involvement in third sector organisations (Turner, 2001; Warren, 2001).

The fourth aspect under review is the state-bounded framing of citizenship and its corollary, the idea that citizenship involves membership of a set *political* community. The conventional historical reference point in citizenship studies is the Treaty of Westphalia in 1648, this being the origin of the modern nation state. Citizenship relations have thus been primarily conceptualised as interactions between the state and the individual. However, people are now also beginning to think about and act out their social obligations as *global* citizens (Schattle, 2008, pp 3–4). Yet global citizenship is deemed to be problematic because there are no legal entities that have clear global authority to identify and fulfil rights and set out obligations in the same way as a nation state (a potential exception may be the International Court of Justice in The Hague). Turner (2001) argues, in regard to citizen rights within the nation state, that the three traditional routes to legal entitlements – participation in employment, military service and reproduction – have been eroded. However, there are ways of practising obligations and claiming rights other than with reference to legal authorities or through the legal edifice of the nation state. Substantive citizenship rights can be claimed and practised through people participating at different levels of society as local, national and transnational citizens, claiming the right of recognition and practising obligations based on a common humanity. Yaln-Heckman (2011, p 435) further points out how struggles over access to social rights, state resources and inclusion take many different shapes, based on the 'multiple, political, and economic processes in post-socialist, post-colonial, post-totalitarian states and transnational fields'.

The fifth aspect of Marshall's approach to citizenship for consideration is the construction of the citizen as a subject who passively receives privileges of citizenship that are bestowed from above (Marshall, 1992, p 28). Critics of this approach argue that the development of citizenship rights is a ruling class strategy for hegemonic control (Mann, 1987). As Turner (1992, pp 38–9) points out, Marshall failed to account for the role of conflict and struggle in the development of citizenship, in effect denying a role for active agents in these developments. A more dynamic approach to citizenship focuses on how people actively engage in society and how citizens are active and reflexive agents (Evers and Guillemard, 2013, p 48). From this perspective it is their engagement that makes people full members of society. In this view, much of the discussion of citizen engagement constructs the citizen agent as a person who is involved with political and social institutions in collective struggles, both to gain new rights and to give substance to existing rights (Lister, 1997, p 5). Active citizens participate in the identification of, and practices relating to, their obligations to both society and other citizens, just as they engage in claiming new rights.

The final challenge to Marshall's legacy relates to its ethnocentricity, with citizenship conceptualised in terms of unified and homogenous sets of (Western) social arrangements (Giddens, 1982). As such, the Marshallian analysis fails to grasp the context-specific nature of citizenship. Citizenship studies have tended to focus on either the English-speaking world or Western societies, almost completely ignoring questions of citizenship elsewhere in the world. It is only recently that international studies have begun to investigate the wider applicability of this Western-framed notion of citizenship (Gaventa and Tandon, 2010). It does seem that, regardless of whether the term 'citizenship', or similar terms, are in common usage, notions of the rights and obligations of members of a society, however limited, do seem to have universal currency. What does change across time and different cultures is the *content* of rights and obligations and their applicability across gender and social groups.

Further empirical studies are needed to test the applicability of Western concepts of citizenship. However, noting the ethnocentrism embedded in much of the existing research into citizenship, some researchers argue for an approach that not only understands citizenship as a dynamic process, but also analyses the ways in which it takes shape, without reverting to the idea of citizenship as a singular or universal object, principle or desire (Neveu et al, 2011, p 945).

So, what are the implications of these debates for contemporary citizenship studies? First, they draw attention to the problems of conceiving of citizenship as a stable, singular object. Indeed, an important argument for a post Marshallian conception of citizenship rests on the observation that economies, societies, cultures and ways of being citizens in contemporary society are different from those at the time that Marshall was writing (Evers and Guillemard, 2013). Identity and difference have emerged as key issues in the social sciences, adding new dimensions to earlier preoccupations with issues of inequality in relation to social class (Delanty, 2000). The contemporary world has been affected by significant policy shifts, including, as noted earlier, the erosion of traditional means of claiming citizenship entitlements (Turner, 2001) and the changing roles of women (Lister, 1997). A key challenge, therefore, is to grasp the complexities and changing nature of citizenship (Gaventa and Tandon, 2010). Membership of a political community involves more than just simply claiming rights and fulfilling obligations. It involves complex sets of relationships between rights, duties, participation and identity (Delanty, 2000). These sets of relationships are affected by dominant ideologies, changing political configurations and in recent years, the forces of neoliberal globalisation. It is necessary, therefore, to probe configurations of active citizenship and ask how constructions of citizenship and perceptions of rights and obligations differ according to context.

Second, much of the discussion and debate in citizenship studies has been conceptual and theoretical. A wider appreciation is necessary, moving beyond the abstracted constructions of citizenship rights and obligations to empirical studies of substantive forms of citizenship in their varied settings. Indeed, the very idea of active citizenship underscores a substantive approach to the study of citizenship insofar as it takes the view that citizenship is concerned with the concrete practices of active citizens: how individuals and collectivities, as agents, construct their membership as citizens in any particular society; how they are supported and resourced (their rights); and how they contribute as active citizens (their obligations and duties). As well as understanding the contexts of active citizenship and acts of citizenship (Isin and Nielson, 2008, p 2), the study of citizenship also involves discerning the factors that facilitate and hinder acts of citizenship (Jochum et al, 2005; Robins et al, 2008; Brodie et al, 2011), as well as investigating struggles for recognition and redistribution (Isin and Turner, 2007, p 13).

What is needed is an approach that involves investigation of the ways in which people participate as members of society, defining and practising their rights and obligations, within subnational, national and transnational contexts. It is an approach that sees citizenship as an historically evolving concept (Gaventa and Tandon, 2010, p 10; Neveu et al, 2011), expressed through different practices that can be defined and handed down from above but are also constructed through active engagement in society from below. In this book, therefore, we are concerned with the practices and processes of active citizenship in different settings and levels, including at the subnational, national or transnational levels. Our focus is citizenship in its substantive sense. And we use a working definition of (active) citizenship, while at the same time we acknowledge the contested nature and changing meanings, concepts and manifestations of this term. In the remainder of this chapter, we move from theoretical understandings of citizenship to the ways in which it is manifested in policy and practice.

The practices of active citizenship

Two particular aspects of policy and practice are of concern for this book. The first is to understand the different forms that active citizenship takes or that are promoted. The second is to address the tendency to bestow a normative gloss on active citizenship and judge the active citizen to be more virtuous than the 'passive' or 'apathetic' citizen. Each of these aspects is now explored in turn and we end by illustrating some of the issues raised, through the example of humanitarian aid.

Forms of active citizenship

For the purposes of our analysis here and in following chapters, we can begin by distinguishing between the two broad manifestations of citizenship that seem from our earlier discussion to have universal significance: citizenship as obligation and citizenship as rights. Citizenship studies have often focused on political activism, locating citizenship in historical struggles or describing acts of citizenship as those comprising political rupture and political claims for new rights (Turner, 1992; Isin and Nielson, 2008; Gaventa and Tandon, 2010). But in the policy discourse, it is citizenship as obligation that has featured most prominently in policies and programmes to promote active citizenship.

Active citizenship as obligation

This type of active citizenship involves people as agents identifying and fulfilling what can be considered as *obligations* to society. Obligations are sometimes linked with an altruistic intent to 'do good' without reward, although 'doing good' can also have an instrumental purpose, such as volunteering practised for the purpose of improving a *curriculum vitae*. In this book we use *civil commitment* as the generic term to describe this form of active citizenship as obligation. However, a further distinction can be made on the basis of whether active citizenship as obligation is focused on the idea of *civility* or *civicness* (see Jochum et al, 2005, pp 13–14). While *civility* and *civicness* overlap, it is possible to distinguish the idea of civility, comprising manners, attitudes and acts that are manifestations of mutuality, tolerance and selflessness and that can take place in both private and public realms, from civicness, which is more directly associated with involvement in institutional settings and processes (Evers, 2009, p 242).

Active citizenship based on *civility* is evident in horizontal relations organised around recognition and respect for others, reciprocity and equality in public life. For example it involves 'treating others as equals on the condition that they extend the same recognition to you' (Kymlicka, 1998, p 189). Such citizen obligation is based on solidarity with other citizens and driven by a sense of 'giving back to my community'. Examples of civil commitment include local community groups in OECD countries setting up support groups for refugees and retired people or organising literacy classes for those with low literacy skills. Such groups are sometimes known as public-serving third sector organisations (Lyons, 2001, p 23). People working together to maintain an arts club or community garden in member-serving organisations (Lyons, 2001, p 23) are also expressions of civil commitment. In other parts of the world, the pooling of cooperative resources in a village for the purpose of funding young people's attendance at school and a support group for widows would be examples of active citizenship based on civil commitment. Active citizenship as civil commitment is discussed in further detail in Chapters Six and Seven.

Civic commitment is a particular form of civility. It is associated with public institutional settings as spaces for dialogue (Evers, 2009, p 242), into which citizens are invited by the state. These may, for example, be government advisory committees or partnership forums, where citizens can advise on policy and planning matters. In such contexts, relations between the state and citizens tend to be vertical in nature.

A more recent addition to conventional ideas of obligation based on principles of mutuality and altruism is the notion of the obligation for active citizens to take individual responsibility for their own wellbeing and direction – the self responsibilisation discussed earlier. The idea of the responsibility or obligation of people to look to their own decisions and own resources is sometimes expressed in the term 'individualisation' (Beck, 1992, p 135). Individualisation involves the view that the destiny of individuals lies in their own hands, dependent on the decisions they make and the resources they have (Beck, 1992, p 135). Stories of the self construction of our identities and life chances are played out in all aspects of life. In ways never experienced before humans are obliged to be informed about the conditions in which they live, to respond to events, and to calculate and monitor risks. From this perspective, as people practise active citizenship, they are continually caught up in a reflexive process of gathering information, decision making and responding. What has come to be known as consumer citizenship, where active citizenship is defined as the right of a citizen to have consumer choice and the obligation to act in one's own interest on this choice, is an example of how individualisation works.

For Bauman (2000, p 37), however, rather than being a form of citizenship, individualisation 'spells trouble' for citizenship. It is certainly a much more stunted notion and one which has been central to the advance of neoliberalism. In this conception of active citizenship individuals are prompted to venture into the public arena as active citizens not in the search for common causes or for ways of negotiating the meaning of the common good, but on the basis of individual interest such as the need for instrumental networking. In this way, according to Bauman (2000, p 37), the public is colonised by the private. Similarly, in her study of the promotion of active citizenship, Gaynor (2011) argues that contemporary forms of active citizenship in Ireland are depoliticising processes, glossing over state responsibilities for deficits in infrastructure and substituting self help for redistribution, self reliance for state accountability.

Active citizenship based on rights

For all the assumed linkages between active citizenship and political activism there is a lacuna when it comes to discussion of the specific meaning of activism in citizenship studies. Indeed, there is a wide range of actions that can be identified as activist. For example, one view is that, to be fully active, citizens should strive for the power to name and construct meanings and to exert control over the flow of information (Stevenson, 2001, p 2). Others argue that active citizenship involves 'collective or individual deeds that rupture social-historical patterns' (Isin and Nielson, 2008, p 2). However, not all activism is so expansive or ambitious. It might be expressive of alternative values, or involve modest struggles around more limited issues of activism for local empowerment.

For the purposes of this book, an action is identified as activist if it challenges or changes the dominant power relations and structures, regardless of whether it is small scale or large scale in scope. Practices can be activist in intent, method or outcome. For example, a petition to a local government authority to democratise budget decisions, so that all members of the community have a say, is clearly activist in intent but the petition method itself is a conventional one. A violent demonstration in favour of a government bill to rescind special taxes on the mining industry is clearly activist in method but with the intent of returning to the status quo. A local demonstration that begins as a protest against a local event can grow into a powerful mass movement. This was the case in Tunisia in 2011, where a protest against the death of a fruit vendor led to the fall of the Ben Ali government (although the outcomes of the 'Tunisian revolution' are still unfolding). Of course, much of what is understood as activism is activist in both intent and method, and sometimes in terms of outcome as well. Discussion of activism in this book is concerned with each of these aspects of active citizenship as activism. In one way or another, of course, they are all underpinned by discourses pertaining to the identification, articulation and claiming of rights on the basis of membership of a group. These rights claims are expressed in demands for self determination, recognition, freedom of expression and association, and political and social change designed to redistribute resources and promote social justice agendas more widely.

In today's globalised world, activist citizenship ranges from local issues to transnational action. Examples of local issue activism include protests against cuts in funding for community projects and sit-ins in working class neighbourhoods protesting against high-rise apartment developments. They also include regionally based anti-fracking campaigns and boycotts of multinational companies exploiting local labour. The list of transnational activist efforts is growing, as people commit to supporting actions around any number of issues, such as demonstrations against elite land grabs in poor regions of the world, activist movements to support women's rights, and activism around the power of capitalist elites, such as the Occupy movement. These forms of activism, particularly virtual transnational activist groups, are sometimes distinguished by their loose and emergent organisational forms. These different forms of citizenship as activism are discussed further in Chapters Eight and Nine.

Normative views of active citizenship

Our second concern in relation to the practice and promotion of active citizenship relates to the normative gloss that so often characterises citizenship studies and debate. This normative gloss is manifested in the view that people who engage with society and participate as civilly and civically minded citizens or as activists, are 'better' citizens than those who do not. Yet beyond this favourable assessment, active citizenship is not always benign. Nor does it necessarily contribute to civility. Calhoun (2000) points out that civility is linked to social norms that might not correspond to morally virtuous actions. For example, when active citizenship involves breaking the law it is usually deemed unacceptable. Yet the criterion of unacceptable active citizenship is not always clear cut. A critical (re)assessment of existing social norms of civility can lead to their rejection. Many of our rights have actually been won by collective forms of resistance, including law breaking – as in past and more recent struggles to gain the vote, for example.

Then there are the 'uncivil' active citizens who are members of hate and racist groups, such as neo-Nazi organisations and the Ku Klux Klan. The actions of 'uncivil' politically active citizens such as these challenge conventional normative approaches to active citizenship, in terms of both moral virtue and the norms of civility. While these are often directed towards malevolent ends, acts of citizenship in many more groups may be organised around parochial and/or narrow self interest.

Active citizens can also, at the extreme, be involved in acts described as terrorism. The descriptor of terrorist can be complicated insofar as 'one man's terrorist is another man's freedom fighter'. The implications of the changing nature of the designation of 'terrorist' are illustrated dramatically in the way that descriptions of the Muslim Brotherhood in Egypt have shifted between 'terrorist organisation' and 'legitimate government'. From the perspective of members of terrorist organisations, their struggles for self determination are entirely legitimate civic ones, aiming towards a better society for themselves and their followers. Members of such groups often describe their activism as based on a moral, political or religious obligation to defend (or extend) their social, cultural and religious space, through any means available.

Active citizenship in practice: the example of humanitarian aid

The normative framing and the contested nature of acts of active citizenship are both illustrated in the 'virtuous' acts of citizen obligation involved in humanitarian aid. The origins of Western humanitarian aid can be traced to two aid-giving traditions: religion and the European Enlightenment (Terry, 2003, p 281). The Christian religious tradition found expression through the idea of charity. The charity framework is organised around the discourses of moral discipline, service, moral virtue and obligation (Brown et al, 2000) and clearly expresses ideas of active citizenship as obligation, traceable to Christian organisations in the Middle Ages. The Enlightenment tradition is organised around humanist and rights discourses such as those expressed in the anti-slavery movement that began in the late eighteenth century.

Aid giving is not, of course, the prerogative of Western cultures alone. For example, humanitarian aid has a strong tradition in Muslim countries, deriving from injunctions in the Koran and the Hadiths (reports of the deeds and sayings of Muhammad). The main origin of Islamic humanitarian aid lies in the injunction to almsgiving (*zakat*) and the establishment of religious endowments of foundations (*waqfs*) (Benthall and Bellion-Jourdan, 2003, pp 7–10).

At the core of humanitarian aid is the delivery of assistance to those in need, as a moral virtue and/or religious obligation. The broad aim of humanitarian aid is to save lives, alleviate suffering and maintain human dignity in times of emergency and disaster (Riddell, 2007, p 312). However beneath this broad aim lie many contested issues about means, ethics and values as well as numerous dilemmas facing those involved in humanitarian aid. In addition, critics have drawn attention to the less benign objectives of aid and development. For example, aid may be provided to promote a particular religious dogma and/or ideological, political and/or commercial interests. And the selection of who is to receive aid may be based on marketing or strategic (including military) imperatives rather than need (Bob, 2005; Riddell, 2007; Moyo, 2009).

Perhaps most important today are the challenges to the founding principle of modern humanitarian aid, that is, the principle of political neutrality – and this is where concern with citizenship as obligation flows into concern with citizenship as rights. The principle of neutrality involves commitment to helping all who require assistance, regardless of 'which side they are on'. In some ways the practice of political neutrality epitomises the idea of altruistic active citizenship based on the obligations to fulfil duties to society. Yet political neutrality might not always be the most effective approach to saving lives in disasters and emergencies. One view is that neutrality can prolong misery and suffering by ignoring the very causes of a conflict and through its preparedness to 'patch up' all sides (Anderson, 1996; Terry, 2003, p 282). The civil commitment of humanitarian agencies can also be compromised when humanitarian organisations inadvertently or indirectly provide aid to militants, thus aggravating violence, as well as potentially putting their own lives and those of other aid workers in jeopardy (Anderson, 1996; Lischer, 2005). Recently some aid agencies, such as Oxfam and Medicins Sans Frontieres, have been prepared to abandon strict adherence to political neutrality in what has come to be known as the 'new humanitarianism'. New humanitarianism is based on the view that complete neutrality is impossible – any assistance has political inputs and effects (Weiss, 1999; Terry, 2003, p 283; Duffield, 2005, p 75). In such cases civil commitment as obligation may develop into the activist form of active citizenship, as when an aid group aligns with local women struggling against oppression, for example.

Subsequent chapters will investigate further how forms of active citizenship are manifested in different contexts and third sector settings. But before we do this we need to elaborate the other key concepts in this book: civil society, the third sector and third sector organisations. Such elaboration is the task of the next chapter.

THREE

Civil society and the third sector

Introduction

To understand the relationship between the third sector and active citizenship we now need to consider the ways in which the concept of the third sector is constructed and how it is framed theoretically. The third sector is located in what has come to be known as civil society. But the concepts of both the third sector and civil society have been subject to contestation and changing emphases. This chapter begins, therefore, with discussion of the varying approaches to, and uses of, the idea of civil society with reference to specific sociopolitical contexts. This is followed by consideration of the issues raised by these different approaches. The second part of the chapter introduces the concept of the third sector, identifies ambiguities and tensions, and explains how the concept is used in the book.

Civil society

The roots of the idea of civil society lie in Western classical antiquity and the modern history of the concept can be traced back to the 17th and 18th centuries (Keane, 2005; Alexander, 2006). While the concept has slipped in and out of fashion in both academic and policy circles, there is now a plethora of literature on the subject, which includes extensive debate about its meaning and role. Of particular interest for the purposes of this book is the renewal of interest in civil society since the 1980s as a focus of intellectual curiosity, social transformation and political endeavour, since this can throw light on the way in which third sector organisations have come to be understood as central to what Salamon et al (1999) have identified as an 'associational revolution'. Three themes stand out in this respect: first, the scope and definition of civil society activities; second, the normative dimensions of civil society; and finally, the question of how to test the claims of civil society theorists.

Scope and definition

Contemporary discussion of the scope and definition of civil society is often framed by the idea that civil society is a social sphere (or arena, realm or domain) within the wider society, with its own rationales and logic, separate from the state or the market. For example, Cohen and Arato (1994) discuss civil society as a sphere of social interaction that is located between the economy and the state, composed of the domains of intimate relations, associations, social movements and forms of public communication. In this view, civil society is the sphere where people associate freely, where they can identify shared interests and where groups can shape their norms and articulate their purposes (Rosenblum and Post, 2002). Relationships in this sphere are constructed around the principles of mutuality and equal social exchange, meaning that, in theory, it is a sphere where humans can present their viewpoints and reconcile private and public interests (Seligman, 1992). Importantly, civil society is self constituted and self mobilised.

However, there is a longer history of ideas concerning civil society that offers a wider understanding. Before the 18th century, it was used as a more generic term referring to a secular constitutional order, based on the rule of law and not clearly distinguished from the state (Kaldor, 2003). With the consolidation of the nation state in the late 18th and early 19th century, however, state power was centralised and widened but also circumscribed by the beginnings of democratic practice and ideas of citizen rights. It was during this period that the idea of civil society as separate from the state took hold.

Gramsci, in contrast, took a different view of the relationships between civil society, the state and the market. Rather than seeing them as separate spheres with their own logics, he identified civil society as an arena for the reproduction of the norms and ideologies that underpin existing power relations – and alternatively, as an arena for the development of challenges to these dominant ideas, an arena in which other cultures and ideologies could be promoted in opposition to the those of the dominant class (Gramsci, 1971). That is, he envisaged civil society as the site for both compliance and resistance. Gramsci developed the concept of ideological 'hegemony' to investigate the role of the power of culture and ideas, focusing upon the ways in which relatively less powerful people come to accept – or to challenge – the legitimacy of existing, and unequal, social relationships. His work, and particularly the idea that civil society comprises an arena of contestation, has been an important influence upon the ways in which we understand the ideological roles of civil society today (Bebbington et al, 2008).

Habermas' major contribution to our understanding of civil society lies in his discussion of the public sphere (Habermas, 1989). The public sphere is the sphere for open deliberation, where people can discuss matters of mutual concern, exchange views and ideas and negotiate differences. To fully grasp the significance of the public sphere, it is important to understand Habermas' distinction between the 'systems-world' and the 'life-world'. The systems-world is the world of the state and the economy. It operates on the basis of instrumental rationality and is driven by power and money. In contrast, the life-world operates through communicative rationality. It is driven by a commitment to mutual understanding through dialogue. In a penetrating critique of late capitalism, Habermas argues that the systems-world is colonising the life-world and, in so doing, is constructing citizens as passive consumers of the market and of newly professionalised services. From this perspective the very future of democracy and the public sphere depend on the renewal of civil society.

Following Gramsci's contention that civil society is a site of contestation and Habermas' notion of the importance of a public sphere for reasoning and debate, Kaldor (2003, pp 44–5) defines civil society as 'the medium through which one or many social contracts between individuals, both women and men, and the political and economic centres of power are negotiated and reproduced'. In her book *Global civil society: An answer to war*, she argues that global civil society 'offers possibilities for emancipation on a global scale' (Kaldor, 2003, p 12). Civil society has the potential to minimise violence in human relations and to champion the use of reason as a way of managing human affairs, in place of submission based on fear and insecurity, ideology and superstition.

Our approach in this book is to define the concept of civil society broadly, as a sphere in which people come together freely and independently to discuss, debate and negotiate issues and work collectively to influence and shape their society. It is also a contested sphere in two senses. In one sense, it is a space where people exchange and contest ideas and challenge practices. But the sphere itself is contested, for example as groups in society and with competing agendas jostle for control.

Civil society as a normative project

Civil society involves normative interpretations as well as sociological description and analysis. As indicated earlier, we can trace current constructions of civil society as a normative project to the period beginning in the 1980s, in which civil society came to the fore as a key site for extending democracy and developing self determining citizens. It has also been hailed for its role in fostering civility and civic commitment, as a challenge to Western approaches to international development and as an alternative to the state. We consider each of these in turn.

Civil society as an explicitly political project

Civil society activism has been a central player in many of the challenges to authoritarian regimes in both the 1980s and 1990s, and more recently in a number of Mediterranean and North African countries. Civil society action based on 'people power' was also evident in the relatively peaceful overthrow of the government of Ferdinand Marcos in the Philippines in the early 1980s and was identified as a force in the collapse of authoritarian regimes in Latin America. One of the most remarked upon manifestations of civil society, however, was the citizen action that occurred during and immediately after the collapse of the Soviet Union in 1989. As citizens learnt the power of citizen action, Russia experienced an explosion of civil society activity (Leitch, 1997; McFaul, 2000; White, 2002). By the 1990s, many Latin American countries also witnessed a rebirth of civil society institutions following the release of citizens from the ironclad hold of state military regimes (Kirby, 2003).

The role of civil society as a political project in Russia and Latin America has been complex and is still unfolding. But there are now several new theatres of civil society activity where the outcomes are even less clear. In a number of Middle East and North African (MENA) countries there has been a parallel and profound shift in the position of civil society activities from a long held location as marginalised and often underground phenomenon in society to centre stage (Gelvin, 2012). These many struggles have differed in aims and scope, but on the surface, they all originally involved a quest for 'people power'. Analyses of the uprisings and assessments of the longer-term sustainability of the 'Arab Spring' vary and are affected by changing configurations of power (Aouragh and Alexander, 2011; Bradley, 2012; Isakhan et al, 2012). It would now seem, however, that the optimistic prognoses concerning the rise of civil society in the MENA region that were expressed in 2011 were profoundly misplaced. Indeed following a coup in 2013, Egypt has returned to a military backed government and the original protests against the Assad Government in Syria have turned into a full scale and violent conflict, split by internecine struggles between warring groups of rebels.

At another level, the 21st century has also seen the rise of activist struggles that have become global in scope, giving rise to the idea of 'globalisation from below' (Falk, 1997; Kellner, 1999). These struggles include protests such as the World Social Forum and the Occupy movement, to which we shall return in later chapters. Along with struggles against authoritarian regimes, these new manifestations of civil society raise two questions for scholarly analysis: first, to what extent are we witnessing new forms of civil society in these activist eruptions; and second, if the events and activities are manifestations of new forms of civil society, what are the implications for social and political organising and the generation of active citizenship?

Civil society, civility and civic commitment

There is another way of thinking normatively about civil society, which, while having political implications, does not express civil society as a political endeavour. This involves an understanding of civil society as associationalism. The associational base draws attention to the ways in which citizens practise collaboration and contribute to collective wellbeing. Civil society 'solutions', such as 'community participation' and 'community strengthening', have been championed as strategies for integrating people into local affairs. Through association, citizens demonstrate civility and civicness. In civil society discussions, civility is linked with social concern, tolerance, mutual respect, selflessness, altruism and a sense of responsibility (Billante and Saunders, 2002; Evers, 2009). Anheier (2007) points out that civility is embedded in the social and cultural codes of society and is learned. These codes set out processes and practices that value the dignity of others and, while civility is generated in a range of social institutions, it is clearly a feature of civil society. As discussed in the previous chapter, civicness tends to be conceptualised as an attribute of citizenship as a formal practice. It is linked with activities taking place in the public realm and is most clearly expressed in vertical relationships where citizens engage the state and local political institutions, articulating obligations for example. As Dekker (2009) and Evers (2009) discuss, the two notions are intertwined. For example, a civic culture of practised cooperation and participation sets the context for civility but, in turn, a civic-minded community requires civility.

Civil society and international development

By the end of the 1980s, policy makers, researchers and practitioners in the field of international development were beginning to question the development agendas and organisations that had been established after the Second World War. A focus on civil society opened up prospects for reconstructing international aid and development, and a way of conceptualising ordinary people as active agents, who were capable of self organisation or self direction, rather than passive recipients of aid. Civil society solutions offered 'bottom-up' approaches, methods and processes that were organised around participatory processes and were thus better suited to effective, sustainable development than 'top-down' development projects, such as the structural adjustment approach programmes offered by the World Bank and International Monetary Fund (Chambers, 1983; Ayittey, 1991; Bhatnagar and Williams, 1992; Eade and Williams, 1995; Stiglitz, 2002; Easterly, 2003, 2006).

Civil society as an alternative to the state

Since the 1980s, the project of neoliberalism, which found its first exponents in the UK and the US, has been embraced in many parts of the world, profoundly influencing government policy, albeit in varying ways and at different levels. Under neoliberal policies, governments have been committed to shifting, as far as possible, the control and functions of economic and social activities away from the state, primarily to market forces but also to individuals and communities (Harvey, 2007, p 33). What are of interest in this chapter are neoliberal approaches to civil society. Perhaps most importantly from a neoliberal perspective, civil society offers an alternative to dependency on the state. Here, individuals and community organisations, in seeking their own interests, can participate in society as free agents entering into contracts with other individuals, business and the state, taking responsibility for individual and local welfare. For example, in the UK, under both 'Third Way' and 'Big Society' policies, community programmes have been introduced to enhance civil society capabilities and to increase the potential for the organisations within civil society to take on services previously provided by the state.

Contestations within civil society

Much of the foregoing discussion focuses on the emancipatory potential of civil society humans collaborating for the purpose of the creation of a better world. It would be naïve, however, to think that the concept of civil society is unproblematic and foolhardy to suggest that the progressive potential of civil society is self evident (as the discussion of neoliberal approaches has already suggested). There are several pitfalls in approaches that focus upon civil society's emancipatory potential. The first relates to the potential cooption of the very notion of civil society. For Cohen (1999, p 211), for example, the opportunistic use of the normative baggage of civil society by politicians, journalists and public intellectuals alike means that the whole idea of civil society has become idealised, backward-looking and one-dimensional. She argues that such a theoretically impoverished conception of civil society focuses exclusively on traditional, but now waning and anachronistic, models of civil association. From the perspective of commentators who identify with a social democratic or Left position (see Powell, 2007), the cooption of civil society as a mechanism for self responsibility in neoliberal regimes erodes state responsibilities. It undermines public policies based on a commitment to social justice, equality and rights along with attempts to deepen democracy and progressive social and workers' movements, all of which are necessary for a robust civil society. From this standpoint neoliberalism depoliticises the meanings and processes of civil society.

There is a paradoxical congruence between the increasing policy focus upon strengthening civil society and the neoliberal commitment to reducing the role of the state. In Brazil, for example, Dagnino (2008) describes how the enlargement of democracy in Brazil involved the extension of citizenship, the creation of public spaces and increasing participation in civil society. At the same time, however, she draws attention to the withdrawal of the state from social responsibilities, as it shifted these to civil society institutions. She argues that both the democratic and neoliberal projects, while pointing in different directions, use a common discourse. And both require an active role for civil society. In a similar vein, Kenny (2002, p 295) describes how the 'market discourse' of neoliberalism promises empowerment and choices for citizens, using much the same language as community development, while ignoring the competitive agendas in which individuals and organisations now operate, and their unequal resource bases.

Second, the application of civil society solutions to international development endeavours is not without challenge. There is a well-rehearsed critique of the presumed universality of the notion of civil society, which questions the applicability of the 'Western' values and ontologies on which the notion of civil society is constructed to non-Western societies. One view is that Western discourses of civil society have established an ideological framework for reshaping Western foreign policy and legitimating inappropriate interventions. This discourse presents Western countries as moral gatekeepers and speakers for victims of poverty in 'developing countries' and, in the process, denies local agency and disempowers local people (Chandler, 2002, p 35). Obadare (2012) and Fowler (2012) comment on the tendency to use Africa as a battleground for foreign-derived concepts and theories, often allied to externally-driven knowledge agendas. A third challenge to the emancipatory discourse surrounding civil society is the recognition that there are 'dark sides' to civil society. These dark sides are manifested in activities that fit the description of civil society, because they exhibit strong associationalism and they aim to influence and shape society. However, as we saw in Chapter Two, these apparent civil society actions lack the 'civility' characteristics many attribute to civil society. We suggested there that such manifestations of the 'dark sides' of civil society include the activities of neo-Nazi and racist organisations, along with Mafia and terrorist groups. More ambiguously, there are also organisations based on religious and political fundamentalist beliefs, which in some ways fall within widely accepted definitions of civil society but are exclusive, undemocratic and sometimes oppressive. In closing off options for debate and challenge and demonstrating intolerance to outsiders, these organisations certainly do not fit comfortably with the dominant civil society narrative presented earlier.

These challenges highlight the importance of testing the claims of civil society theorists. Given that civil society is the site of so many normative claims, agendas and political projects, a critical discussion of the empirical evidence supporting such normative claims is a necessary part of a comprehensive understanding of civil society. As Edwards argued in 2004:

> civil society must be able to be described and understood in terms accessible to the sceptic, tested rigorously and successfully against the available empirical evidence and converted into practical measures that can be deployed in real-world contexts. (Edwards, 2004, p ix)

Before such an investigation can take place it is necessary to identify the concrete manifestations of civil society. That is, if we are to examine fully the promises of civil society it is necessary to have clear empirical referents. One fruitful way of examining the promises of civil society empirically is through the study of third sector organisations. While these organisations are only one part, albeit a significant part, of civil society, an investigation of third sector organisations and the active citizens who participate in them can offer important insights into the role of civil society and the promise claimed for it.[1] However, the concept of the third sector is itself contested. It is to this that we now turn.

Third sector organisations

Much of the discussion of the third sector today assumes that there is agreement in regard to the meaning, terminology and scope of third sector organisations. For example, in a recently published compendium of third sector research, Rupert Taylor (2011, p 1) refers to a general acceptance of the term 'third sector' as a 'catch-all' term for the organisational space between the government and the market. It has an empirical presence in third sector organisations, whose characteristics, as we shall see, have been set out in the seminal research undertaken by the Johns Hopkins Comparative Nonprofit Sector Project (Salamon et al, 1999). At one level it would appear, therefore, that issues of definition and terminology in third sector research have been settled. Yet even a cursory probe of the idea of the third sector and the various terms used to describe the sector suggests that the 'loose and baggy monster' described by Kendall and Knapp in 1995 remains nebulous, with ongoing tensions in the scoping of third sector research. The remainder of this chapter, therefore, identifies both points of agreement and continuing tensions in the discourses of the third sector. It also considers the question of whether it actually matters if issues concerning the definition, meanings and terminology of the third sector are settled or not.

[1] For example, the International Society for Third Sector Research, the leading international network of third sector researchers identifies the sector as a discernible entity that can be studied empirically. It defines the third sector broadly and includes NGOs, nonprofit organisations, voluntary associations, social economy organisations, community organisations, self help and mutual organisations, civil society organisations, foundations, philanthropy, and other manifestations of civil society operating globally and locally, for example in networks and social forums, unions, religious organisations, cooperatives, and volunteering.

Definitions

We can begin with some broad areas of agreement. A good place to start is with the term 'sector' itself. This can be understood as a structural concept referring to a space, arena or sphere in society in which certain activities take place and in which relations, including relations of power, are constructed. The idea of a third sector, of course, implies that there are other sectors. Generally, as our more general discussion of civil society demonstrated, two other sectors are identified, the state and the market, each with its own rationale and dominant forms of relationships. An additional fourth sector, consisting of the informal or household sector, has sometimes been identified, although the term fourth sector has also been used to describe a problematic hybrid 'social entrepreneurial' sector that merges elements of the market and the 'community' sector (Alessandrini, 2010).

The third sector has come to be widely identified as an intermediary or mediating sector located between the other sectors. For de Tocqueville (2003), for example, the third sector of intermediary groups can stand between the individual and the state, protecting dissent and diversity in a democratic society. For Durkheim (1957), the sphere of associations can regulate economic transactions and contain individual egoism. Anheier and Seibel (1990) locate the third sector between the private, for-profit world and government. Evers and Laville (2004, p 11), meanwhile, have emphasised the intermediary nature of the third sector within a 'pluralist welfare framework'.

The designation of the third sector as a mediating field brings with it the notion of negotiation for the protection of the interests of ordinary people. This notion fits well with the normative reading of the third sector, in a similar vein to the normative reading of civil society. Yet, terminological confusion haunts the term third sector. If the third sector is not to be conflated with civil society, which is the position taken in this book, then the third 'sector' is only one part of the 'sphere' of civil society. Both the sector and the sphere are widely assumed to be separate from other sectors and spheres. But this raises the issue of the boundaries between the specific sectors and spheres, which are neither clear-cut nor unchanging. The international Nonprofit Sector Project (Salamon et al, 1999), mentioned earlier, takes a structural/operational approach (Kendall and Knapp, 2000, p 2) to definition, which in turn has also been identified as the American approach (R. Taylor, 2011, p 12) and the 'American definition' (Evers and Laville, 2004, pp 13–14). This project, carried out by the Center for Civil Society Studies at Johns Hopkins University, set up a framework for third sector studies and has generated considerable discussion concerning the nature of the third sector. It aimed to: document the scope, structure, financing and role of third sector organisations in empirical terms; explain variations in the third sector; and evaluate the impact of these organisations (Salamon et al, 1999, p 5). The research began with a definition of the third sector based on five defining characteristics, which are based on the following descriptors:

- organisations, i.e., they have an institutional presence and structure;
- private, i.e., they are institutionally separate from the state;non profit distributing, i.e., they do not return profits to their managers or to a set of "owners';
- self-governing, i.e., they are fundamentally in control of their own affairs; andvoluntary, i.e., membership in them is not legally required and they attract some level of voluntary contribution of time or money.(Salamon et al, 1999, pp 3–4)

However, the distinctiveness of the third sector and third sector organisations is not as straightforward as this list of characteristics suggests. Four issues stand out.

First, the criterion of 'nonprofit distributing' is not clear cut. The intent of the term nonprofit is, of course, to describe an organisation that does not generate private profit. Generally this means that any 'profit' or surplus that is made through the activities of the organisation is not distributed to individuals but is ploughed back into general revenue for the organisation. This is problematic, however, because it excludes cooperatives and mutual aid societies, which are key components of the broad third sector in Europe (Evers and Laville, 2004). In the European context, where it is part of what is known as the 'social economy', a third sector organisation can both generate and distribute profit to private individuals (Laville, 2011). Cooperatives and mutual aid societies have played important roles in other countries as well, including the UK (Kendall and Knapp, 1996, p 87), Australia (Lyons, 2001, p 82) and many developing countries, where village-based cooperatives are critical forms of mutuality, voluntarism, self government and social development (Kenny et al, 2013). One response to this is to use the term not-for-profit rather than for-profit to signify that third sector organisations are created out of mutual interest and focus on generating collective wealth rather than individual profit making.

This leads to the second major issue – the notion of boundaries. Can third sector organisations always be clearly differentiated from organisations in other sectors? A number of writers argue that the state and market sectors overlap with the third sector (Evers, 1995). For example, market or business rationales are evident in the third sector when, as mentioned earlier, mutual aid societies and cooperatives distribute profit to private individuals. They are also evident in varying degrees when social enterprise organisations seek to meet unmet community needs by trading goods and services in the market place on a nonprofit basis (Barraket and Archer, 2010, p 14) and adopt business lexicon and methods of operation, including establishing competitive enterprises and marketing their products.

Similarly, overlap between the third sector and the state sector occurs when agendas are set by the state and when service delivery is outsourced to third sector organisations, to the extent that they act as agents of the state. Indeed, as long as the state acts as a regulator, even at arm's length, it will always be implicated in the operation of the third sector. In some third sector organisations there are different operating rationales that provide a mix of business and government elements (Etzioni, 1973, p 315), either working together or pulling against each other. In response to this blurring of sector boundaries, there has been growing interest in thinking of the third sector as a hybrid sector (Lewis and Kanji, 2009; Billis, 2010; R. Taylor, 2011) and a tension field of mixed logics (Evers, 1995). This approach is discussed further in Chapters Five and Ten.

The third challenge in adopting the Johns Hopkins definition of third sector organisations concerns the criterion of having 'an institutional presence and structure'. What does institutional presence actually mean? In the case of large activist groups and charity and welfare organisations there is a definite institutional presence in the sense of formal structures, explicit operational processes and clear lines of accountability. Yet there are many small groups of people with loose and fluid organisational structures that are not normally thought of as having an institutional presence and structure. Their organisational structure might be no more than a list of people who come together for several months to protest about a local development, or collaborate around cultural activities, such as in a reading group (see Chapters Six and Ten).

Finally, the meanings of the term 'voluntary' can be confusing. For example, what is the object of the descriptor 'voluntary'? Is it an organisation, activities, participants or all of these? A third sector organisation, qua organisation, is established voluntarily but this does not tell us much about it. Mostly the term seems to be a descriptor of the activities of participants, as voluntary, and as the descriptor of participant volunteers. In the context of volunteerism, a minimal definition of a voluntary act is that it is not coerced or legally required, is of benefit to the community and the volunteer, and is for no financial payment. These three criteria are applied to the definition of volunteering used by the National Council for Voluntary Organisations (NCVO) in the UK (www.ncvo.org.uk/ncvo-volunteering) and Volunteering Australia (www.volunteeringaustralia.org/research-and-advocacy). Certainly involvement in third sector organisations by unpaid members and participants is not legally required or coerced; it is established voluntarily on the basis of common social, cultural or political interests, and entry and exit to the group is presumably voluntary. But how should employees in third sector organisations be described? Paid workers seem to be in an ambiguous category between voluntary and non-voluntary. Dekker and Halman (2003, p 2) point out that the 'unpaid' requirement is not clear cut and suggest a modification, namely that the work is not undertaken primarily for financial gain. Once the issue of motivation is considered there are further complications. Even where participants join an organisation voluntarily, there can be several motivations. For example, in a volunteering organisation, a person might be involved both as a commitment to raising funds for victims of a disaster and for her or his own instrumental reasons, such as developing a network of people who could provide a reference for a job. This definition is further complicated by the fact that volunteers can be found in both of the other sectors.

Terminology

In addition to complexities in the assumed characteristics of the third sector, there are also terminological issues. There is a wide array of terms which are at various times used interchangeably with the term 'third sector organisation', each set within different traditions, narratives and locations (Lewis and Kanji, 2009). Four major terms stand out in the international lexicon. These include: voluntary association; nonprofit or not-for-profit organisation; nongovernment or nongovernmental organisation; and civil society organisation. There is another term, found particularly in Australian research, which is sometimes used interchangeably with the term 'third sector' or is identified as a central part of the third sector: community organisation. Each of the first three terms focuses on one of the characteristics of third sector organisations identified by the Johns Hopkins Center for Civil

Society Studies. The fourth term – civil society organisation – draws attention to the identification of the third sector with civil society and thus carries with it a forceful normative meaning.

To make sense of these terms we can link them to specific histories. We begin with the term voluntary association. This term, which has strong currency in the UK, draws attention to the fact that third sector organisations are established voluntarily on the basis of principles of cooperation, mutuality and self government (Hirst, 1994, p 15). They can thus be understood as communities of choice (Hirst, 1994, p 52). But also, as noted earlier, the voluntary nature of voluntary associations does not mean that all activities are undertaken by volunteers or that all volunteers are found in the third sector and thus the term volunteer can be confusing.

We have already discussed the terms nonprofit organisation and not-for-profit organisation and commented that the term not-for-profit can highlight how the mission of the organisation is not to generate and distribute profit. It is also important to note that identification of third sector organisations in the typology of for-profit and not-for-profit is embedded in economic terms of reference, thus leading to a focus on economic categories pertaining to size, cost, financial contribution, function and impact of the sector (Salamon et al, 1999, pp 9–17; Brown et al, 2000, pp 120–1). This focus has dominated much of the research agenda of the third sector. One criticism of the characterisation of the descriptors nonprofit and not-for-profit, however, is that they are residual categories, rendered as 'the other' to for-profit organisations (Corry, 2011, p 11). Similar criticisms are levelled at another 'residual' term: nongovernment/nongovernmental organisation, or NGO.

The term NGO is applied mainly to third sector organisations in the so-called developing world or global South. There is an historical reason for this. The term NGO gained currency in the post Second World War period as a description of types of organisations offering 'people-centred' approaches to development, largely independent of government, although often working within the orbit of the United Nations (Lewis and Kanji, 2009, p 8). There is a particular normative undercurrent in this way of thinking about third sector organisations. The appeal lies in the idea of NGOs working with local people and offering authentic bottom-up approaches to development. However, the actual practices of development often belie the rhetoric, because of both entrenched local hierarchical and patriarchal structures and the too often patronising attitudes of international funding agencies – not to forget the wider influences of neoliberal globalisation. For some critics, the establishment of NGOs has been no more than a 'mechanism for the production and management of the third world' (Escobar, 1992, pp 413–4), to the extent that they have often blocked the nurturing of ordinary people's own capacities (Nair, 2003). For this reason NGOs are sometimes contrasted with 'people's organisations', which are regarded as more genuinely grassroots. Indeed, the practice of reserving the term NGO for third sector organisations in developing countries highlights the troubling persistence of the Western habit of classifying societies on the basis of their apparent level of development. In this world view, the terms voluntary association and nonprofit/not-for-profit organisation are reserved for third sector organisations in the 'developed world' and the term NGO is reserved for the 'undeveloped world'. This habit has always been problematic, but as Lewis (2014, p 1136) argues, 'the changing global conditions of the twenty-first century make binary distinctions at global and sector levels even less sustainable than they once were'.

The term civil society organisation, or CSO, which emphasises the civil society location of an organisation, is perhaps the most value laden of the terms discussed here, especially when it draws on a notion of civil society equated with emancipatory politics (Edwards, 2004, p 6) and civic virtue (Powell, 2007, p 7). Yet the meaning of the civil society designation is often ambiguous. Indeed, the term CSO is used interchangeably with the term NGO in reference to organisations working with large international agencies operating in a top-down manner, particularly those concerned with the economic development of various countries (World Bank, 2011). The World Bank, for example, carries heavy institutional baggage, which is far removed from encouraging emancipatory politics. Nonetheless, the normative resonance of this third sector descriptor is a reminder that, as with the term 'civil society' itself, there is slippage between descriptive and normative uses.

The same applies to the final term that is considered in this brief discussion of descriptors of third sector organisations. The term community organisation is commonly used in Australia with reference to the third sector. Yet community organisations are actually subgroups within the third sector. They represent geographic or common interest groups and they can operate as community activist organisations, advocacy organisations or community service groups, including those undertaking service delivery for government. The descriptor 'community', loaded as it is with nostalgia for the presumed good life of a past epoch (Bauman, 2001), like the term 'civil society organisation', thus ascribes positive meaning to an organisation.

Dominant discourses

There is another lens through which tensions in third sector research can be identified. This lens filters areas of focus and orientation. It highlights certain aspects and theories of third sector practice while sidelining others. For the purpose of this book this lens can be identified as a discourse lens. Following Fairclough (1992), the term 'discourse' is used simply to describe the structuring of knowledge and social practice. While discourses frame our understanding of an object under investigation, they often remain implicit in research agendas.

It is possible to draw out three main discourses from the array of definitions and terms in third sector research discussed earlier. The first discourse, which is indicated in our earlier discussion of the Johns Hopkins Comparative Nonprofit Sector Project (Salamon et al, 1999, p 5), is economic discourse and is concerned with the economic contributions of third sector organisations. Economic discourse focuses on metrics (such as the number and size of organisations), the contributions to the economy and the wealth of the sector. The second, related discourse is concerned with organisational forms in the sector, including management, regulatory and employment structures, and the organisation of activities sustaining third sector organisations, such as volunteering, welfare services and philanthropy. Accountability issues, leadership, governance and organisational effectiveness are examples of third sector topics considered within organisational discourse. The final discourse, and the primary focus in this book, is the one that has been discussed already – that of civil society. Although the third sector is only part of civil society, the emphasis on agency in this discourse is evident in notions of the third sector nurturing active citizens, who define and fulfil social and civil obligations and claim rights. Civil society discourse thus draws attention to the third sector as a site for citizen mobilisation and an arena for the deliberation of issues of public concern (Edwards, 2004).

Does it matter?

The purpose of this chapter so far has been to discuss the relatively recent revival of interest in the idea of civil society and elaborate the ways in which the concepts, meanings and terminology of third sector research seem to have been settled or, alternatively, remain unsettled. But does it really matter if concepts or definitions or language are never precise? Is it indeed ever possible to ultimately define such complex spheres of human interaction? Do blurred boundaries, mixed logics and the residual characterisations mean that the concept of a third sector loses conceptual integrity? And, as a result, is the explanatory value of third sector research eroded or is this inherent in the nature of the sector as a tension field?

At one level it does not matter. Words change meanings in subtle ways all the time. Indeed, the history of third sector research is one of critical probing and new insights. There is continuing discussion about whether it is actually possible or desirable to have a singular definition of the third sector or agreed terminology (Kendall and Knapp, 1996; Evers and Laville, 2004; Corry, 2011). At the same time there is a conventional response to these questions – that definitions do matter because of the need for conceptual clarity. And where empirical research takes place, it is important to be as precise as possible about what is and is not included in the phenomenon under study.

In regard to the third sector, as Lewis (2010, p 236) points out, ideas about sectors continue to shape people's ideas and expectations and play an important role in the ways in which people operate. A dominant view is that while there is some blurring at the boundaries, the third sector operates primarily according to values that are quite different from those underpinning the state and the market. It has its own social forms based on a different practical logic (Corry, 2011, p 11). For example, organisational principles based on solidarity and cooperation and decisions taken through democratic processes are highly valued in principle, if not always in practice (see Warren, 2001). The third sector aims to empower people and give voice (Blake et al, 2006, p 7). Resource allocation is more informal in the third sector than in the state and the market (Anheier and Seibel, 1990, pp 12–13). Third sector rationales can be differentiated from market logics in other ways as well. Edwards (2008, p x) argues that business and markets are not designed to build those third sector rationales that are concerned with the cohesion of communities and strengthening the ways in which people care for each other. Following Billis (2010, p 3) then, there is a view among researchers that most organisations, including those in the third sector, have primary allegiance to distinctive operational principles, which are primarily associated with this one sector. The extent to which such views can be confirmed is of course subject to empirical study.

For our purposes, therefore, we commonly use the term 'third sector' to identify the broad phenomenon and type of organisation that is the topic of our investigations. We include social movements as part of civil society and we argue that they overlap with the third sector (see Chapter Nine). In some research settings it makes sense to adopt the term used by commentators and referred to in local debates. NGO and nonprofit organisation are two such terms and there are occasions in which we describe an organisation using these or other conventional lexicon. At the same time there is a need to be continually assessing the usefulness of conventional lexicon and probing core ideas. In fact, it is clear from the discussion so far that a considerable amount of effort has gone into specifying these core ideas.

Another reason why definitions and terminology matter relates to the emerging imperative to re-examine key social science concepts. As the social and political world changes, it is important to ask whether the concepts that were established in the late 20th century and earlier are still useful for describing and explaining the world in which we live today. Take, for example, the nation state as a 'natural' socio-political form in the modern world. Beck (2006) argues that globalisation has thrown the explanatory power of this concept into question and that a more appropriate way of understanding the world today is through a cosmopolitan outlook, characterised by boundarylessness, global interconnections and cultural mixtures. The new social and political forces of the 21st century are not always satisfactorily explained through the categories and understandings of concepts that became embedded in social science discourse decades ago. It may be time to consider whether we are witnessing changes in the ways in which we 'act out' and 'think about' social connectedness, political engagement, and increasingly complex social and environmental problems. For us, this means that, while the concepts and terminology of the third sector have never been settled fully, it might well be timely for third sector researchers to carry out a stocktake of the different conceptual tools that are still used to describe and explain the role of third sector organisations.

Conclusion

In conclusion then, if we are to critically investigate the contemporary contribution of the third sector and third sector organisations to active citizenship, it is necessary to begin with working definitions. However, we also need to have a double gaze, in which we have one eye on existing parameters and working definitions, and the other eye acknowledging the fluidity of the sector and continuously reviewing conceptual tensions and shifting frameworks.

Our working definition of a third sector organisation begins from the five characteristics of the third sector set out originally in the Johns Hopkins study, which are explained in the body of this chapter.

In this concluding section, we take each of the five characteristics in turn. First, for the purpose of this book, we have modified the idea of an institutional presence. An institutional presence is clearly evident in a third sector organisation which has a formal structure, such as a large charity or professional occupational association. However, our study is also concerned with the third sector in a broader sense, which includes informal groups, such as a small community choir and a local protest group, and the emergence of embryonic forms of organising (rather than organisations), such as discussion groups concerned with understanding climate change. The authors of this book are also interested in traditional social movements and more recent forms of network organising, including those which may occur entirely virtually.

Second is the characteristic of separation from the state. The state will often be involved in the activities of a third sector organisation, through governance processes and its regulatory powers, through partnership projects and, where government funding occurs, through financial control. Nonetheless, third sector organisations are formally separate from the state and it generally remains possible for a third sector organisation to have a significant degree of autonomy, even when funded by the state. However, this means, thirdly, that the characteristic of self governing needs to be evident in the sense that an organisation is largely in control of its own affairs.

Fourth, to be included in as part of the third sector, a group or organisation must be not-for-profit in the sense that it is created out of mutual interest and its focus is on generating collective wealth rather than profit for individuals. Finally, there are several ways in which the descriptor 'voluntary' can be applied. For the purposes of our discussion, a third sector group or organisation must be established voluntarily for a common purpose, rather than being set up as an arm of government or for individual reward. And involvement in the organisation should be voluntary, in the sense that there is no legal requirement concerning entry and exit.

In regard to terminology, our preference is to use the term 'third sector organisation'. However in the spirit of sensitivity to context, in some chapters we use the conventional terms that describe the third sector in the empirical studies to which we refer, such as voluntary association and NGO. Use of the term NGO does not mean acceptance of the bifurcation in the distinction between third sector/nonprofit terminology on one hand, and nongovernmental organisation or NGO terminology on the other that is evident in the discourse of the third sector, however – a reminder of the colonial past which is still to some extent embedded in Western development discourse.

There is a final, and sensitive, issue that should be acknowledged here. This is the issue of whether we include in our understanding of the third sector those activist groups with largely uncivil messages and violent methods, such as hate groups and 'terrorist' organisations. As we emphasise, much of the literature on the third sector is normative, in the sense that this sector is assumed to make a positive contribution to society. If third sector organisations are located unambiguously in the normative concept of civil society and based on civility and the commitment of citizens to contribute to collective wellbeing, then, as Anheier (2007) argues, such organisations cannot be included. However, from a value-neutral perspective, many such organisations fit some of the third sector organisation criteria listed above. And such organisations certainly nurture certain forms of active citizenship. We return to this in later parts of the book.

For the moment it is important to remember that third sector organisations can be based around strong feelings of mutuality and solidarity, while at the same time having a dark side. Indeed, in some regimes civic duty is practised in a way that is uncivil. Take, for example, the civic duties of militia groups supporting uncivil regimes. Militias are often deeply committed to fellow believers and practise a civic culture of cooperation and participation. In such situations the types of intense bonding social capital (Putnam, 2000, pp 350–8) and 'hot' solidarity (Turner, 1999) that result can mean that such organisations are exclusive, intolerant and destructive. While such characteristics sit uncomfortably in third sector research, this does not necessarily exclude such organisations from inclusion in an examination of active citizenship in the third sector. In our next two chapters, therefore, we set out the claims about the ways in which the third sector nurtures active citizenship and discuss further the changing boundaries between state, market and third sector.

FOUR

Third sector organisations nurturing active citizenship: the claims

Introduction

Previous chapters have argued that a robust civil society requires active citizens. In turn, active citizenship requires nurturing settings, with facilitating processes, practices, structures and norms. Over the past three decades there has been a growing body of literature championing the role of third sector organisations in cultivating citizenship. But what is it about third sector organisations that might make them special sites for the development of active citizenship? A detailed answer to this question involves a number of elements: identification and appraisal of the theoretical claims; investigation of the types of active citizenship under consideration; analysis of the different forms of third sector organisation; consideration of the context in which they are operating; and examination of the evidence available. A comprehensive study of this kind is beyond the scope of this book. However, we can begin to unpack these elements. This chapter begins therefore by discussing theoretical arguments about four major features of third sector organisations that can nurture active citizenship – or can be claimed as doing so. Later chapters then consider examples of different types of active citizenship in various third sector settings.

Features of third sector organisations

The four main features of third sector organisations that we have identified as nurturing active citizenship are: agency; association; democratic processes; and the development of cosmopolitanism. These features are interrelated and not necessarily of equal strength in any one organisation. Nor are they evident in every third sector organisation. But they provide cultural frames that can induce people to think and act in certain ways. The first part of this chapter discusses each of the features or claims we have identified in turn. The second half of the chapter highlights some of the complexities in understanding the roles of the third sector.

Agency

Third sector organisations are a vehicle for citizen agency – which, for this book, is perhaps their most important feature. They are the means through which citizens can actively engage with each other and with society at large to discuss issues of mutual concern and then take further action around this engagement. They foster initiative and reflexive action. As centres of uncoerced activity they act as the communities of choice mentioned in Chapter Three, in which people can participate, or from which they can exit of their own volition. They provide social spaces for political action and, when a third sector organisation is established around a social and political issue, members can learn how to articulate concerns, challenge dominant views and develop strategies of their own.

The idea of agency as an explanatory concept gained momentum in the 1980s and 1990s and was characterised by an emphasis on the autonomy of the political subject as an active and self-determining being (Delanty, 1999, p 22), as well as a rhetoric of participation and empowerment. In the context of the particular political upheavals at this time, agency was often understood as a collective activity and associated with social and political activism, including mass mobilisation for large-scale social reorganisation or change, the construction of a visionary utopia and ongoing protest movements. Yet collective agency can also be more modest in scope, such as in small-scale activism around a village or neighbourhood issue aimed at influencing public policy. These activities are all expressions of active citizenship as activism. But when third sector organisations are involved in setting up volunteering activities and local community programmes, they develop a form of agency constructed around civil commitment based on social obligations. Village cooperatives and women's microcredit groups are examples of the latter. Robert Sampson describes how collective efficacy, which he defines as a community's shared belief in its ability to realise the common values of its residents, enables communities to respond to social problems like crime or humanitarian disasters (Sampson, 2007; see also Chapter Six).

In contrast to ideas of collective agency and efficacy, the neoliberal notion of agency focuses on individual self determination, incentive and leadership. These can be fostered within a collective approach. However, our previous discussion of citizenship noted that neoliberal policy favours the promotion of agency through an individualist mould of enterprise and self responsibilisation. In this construction of agency, it is through individual enterprise that individuals practise their agency and earn their right to be citizens, with the privileges and entitlements that citizenship involves. Social entrepreneurial organisations, insofar as they are linked with notions of the individual entrepreneurial citizen, economic initiative and self determination, are expressions of this version of active citizenship. Later chapters will explore further the ways in which both collective and individual agency are expressed through third sector approaches to citizen action.

Associationalism

Collective agency involves association. Over the past two decades we have witnessed the development of an extensive body of literature articulating and examining the assumed benefits of association for a harmonious society (for example, see Hirst, 1994; Gutmann, 1998; Putnam, 2000; Warren, 2001; Jochum et al, 2005; Powell, 2007). Yet reflections on the significance of associationalism can be traced back to de Tocqueville in the 1850s and Kropotkin at the beginning of the 20th century (Kropotkin, 1902). More recently, Hirst has championed the value of self-governing communities through what he identifies as associative democracy. His argument is that:

> ... if human actors are given the greatest possible freedom to associate one with another in voluntary bodies to perform the main tasks in society, then the affairs of that society will be better governed than if they are left either to the isolated activities of individuals or to the administrative organs of a centralised state. (Hirst, 1994, p 44)

Much of the discussion about the contribution of association to a 'good' society draws on the ideas of communitarianism. While communitarianism consists of a range of views, the communitarian idea that a cohesive and productive society is based on cooperative endeavour is particularly important for understanding associational claims concerning the role of the third sector. For its advocates, organising a society around communitarian principles offers a way of overcoming the erosion of social solidarity in modern societies and the *anomie* engendered by neoliberalism. The construction of active citizenship as obligation also draws on the communitarian argument that to have cooperation it is necessary for members of society to accept their mutual responsibilities (Etzioni, 1996; Tam, 1998).

The significance of associationalism for the third sector and active citizenship is manifested in several ways. The most obvious link is found in terminology, wherein 'third sector organisation' is used interchangeably with the term 'association' (Warren, 2001) or 'voluntary association' (Hirst, 1994). As Chapter Three noted, third sector organisations are placed at the centre of what has come to be known as the 'associational revolution' (Salamon et al, 1999, p 4). Another link is evident in the rationales of third sector organisations. While associational relations can take up residence outside the third sector (Warren, 2001, p 55) and there are many spaces that encourage people to practise collaboration, the distinctive claim of third sector scholars is that the very purpose of these organisations is to facilitate practices, processes and opportunities for people to associate and cooperate with one another (Delanty, 2000; Warren, 2001). The pervasiveness of associational processes and norms in third sector organisations, together with their location outside the state and the market, makes third sector organisations ideal sites for nurturing an active citizenry of people identifying their rights and obligations and acting upon these. As Warren points out in making this case, unlike state organisations which are structured around legal–administrative power and market organisations which are structured around the power of money, associations (third sector organisations) 'are constituted primarily by shared purposes and interests, and the dominant means of organisation is influence' (Warren, 2001, p 54). Through involvement in associational life, citizens develop the capacities for sociability and are able to act and work cooperatively together (Warren, 2001, p 225).

This theme is reflected in Putnam's work on social capital. Social capital was defined by Putnam et al (1993, p 167) as 'those features of social organisation, such as trust, norms and networks that can improve the efficiency of society by facilitating coordinated actions'. For Putnam and others following this approach, social capital focuses on the productive aspect of association whereby people are able to work cooperatively and collaboratively (see also Putnam, 2000). In his work, third sector organisations are seen as a significant indicator of social capital. When people associate with each other in the context of mutual respect they can develop capacities for sociability and cooperation (Warren, 2001, p 225). They can become more tolerant and trusting and this smooths the way for collective active citizenship.

We saw in Chapter Three how association was linked to civility and civicness. Associational life is said to afford a way of displacing narrow self interest and provoking civil and civic consciousness (de Tocqueville, 1969; Warren, 2001, p 30). Some scholars emphasise how third sector organisations generate an associationalism that is characterised by the provision of 'non-violent zones' for learning the practices of civility and cooperative citizenship (Kaldor, 2003; Anheier, 2007). Rehearsing the sentiments of Kropotkin (1902), who advocated a society built on mutual aid and cooperation, and de Tocqueville (1969), who argued famously that intermediary associations are essential 'springboards for civic virtue', Rosenblum (1998, p 44) emphasises the power of what she calls the 'morality of association' to cultivate the 'disposition to cooperate'. A much-noted manifestation of the value of associationalism for civil commitment in society is found in the extensive literature on volunteering, which we discuss in Chapter Six.

Active citizenship in third sector organisations is also increasingly valued as a means of generating shared understandings and perspectives on the public interest (Jochum et al, 2005). Because of their contacts and networks at the grassroots, participants in third sector organisations often have considerable knowledge of the needs, interests and concerns of the communities where they work as well as experience of developing activities, services and campaigns in response to these needs. The importance of grassroots networks in the development of active citizenship is taken up further in Chapter Ten.

Democracy

One of the most persistent normative claims for third sector organisations has been based on the connections between democracy and associational life (Almond and Verba, 1963; Hirst, 1994; Warren, 2001; R. Taylor, 2011). Warren, for example, argues that democracy – taken to mean 'collective self-rule under conditions that provide relatively equal chances for citizens to influence collective judgements and decisions' – is boosted by a correct right mix of associational attachments (Warren, 2001, p 60). In its turn, it is clear that democracy requires active citizens. However, democratic organisation is not a necessary condition for active citizenship and, while democracy has many shapes, third sector organisations are not always clearly democratic in their operations (see Coelho and von Lieres, 2010). Active citizenship practices, in both their civic commitment and activist forms, can happen outside a democratically organised third sector organisation. Yet it is possible to argue that a democratic habitus in a third sector organisation provides a major way of inspiring and invigorating active citizenship.

We revisit the arguments that third sector organisations provide exemplary sites for cultivating and expressing a democratic active citizenry in our examination of empirical settings and third sector literature in Chapter Eight. In this chapter our aim is to outline the claims. A central claim relates to their importance as 'schools for democracy', insofar as they give citizens skills in the 'democratic arts' by teaching them to deliberate and reach compromises (de Tocqueville, 1969). Because people 'learn by doing', the everyday involvement of members in forms of cooperative group action and collective decision making in third sector organisations can provide an exemplary political education for democratic conduct.

Third sector organisations also have a number of public sphere effects that render them appropriate sites for generating and nurturing active citizenship. They can operate as public spaces in which people can come together to express different and common viewpoints, where they can deliberate on issues as equals, and seek out and publicise information on issues that concern them. They provide networks for communicating information and, in so doing, facilitate participation in agenda setting and the formation of public opinion by active citizens.

Another way in which third sector organisations can contribute to democracy is through their oppositional and advocacy roles, sometimes referred to as 'giving voice'. 'Giving voice' refers to the articulation of people's viewpoints, and often those that are not commonly heard or which are alternative to the mainstream. Minority groups whose members are disadvantaged and marginalised have historically often had limited or no public means by which they could express their identities, their views and their claims. Third sector organisations, Rosenblum argues (1998, p 206), are able to nudge their alternative viewpoints into the public consciousness. In offering sites and processes for giving voice, third sector organisations can also recognise and authenticate the struggles of those who are disadvantaged and offer a home for those groups identified by Fraser (1992) as subaltern counterpublics. In this way they can provide sites for resisting power. They can also provide sites, in both their civil commitment and activist forms, for dispossessed and marginalised groups – such as unemployed people, disabled people and asylum seekers – to find the encouragement and support necessary to become active citizens.

Third sector organisations have been credited with doing more than just equipping their members to participate in representative democracies, thereby increasing the effectiveness of such democracies. They can also open up possibilities for the development of deeper forms of democratic governance, including deliberative democracy (Dryzek, 2002) and associative democracy (Hirst, 1994; Cohen and Rogers, 1995). Deliberative democracy requires a commitment to listening to others and deliberating on issues, either through informal processes or through more formal modes of alternative governance (Fung and

Wright, 2003; Cohen and Rogers, 1992). Because membership and involvement in third sector organisations is voluntary, people can leave if they feel they are not respected, thus encouraging the use of open discussion and persuasion rather than force to keep people's commitment. From the perspective of active citizenship, the appeal of the idea of associative democracy lies in its commitment to the principle of subsidiarity, where accountability is downward. For Hirst (1994, p 20) this means that, where at all possible, decision making in a society would be devolved to the lowest level, and voluntary and self-governing associations would become the primary means of democratic governance of economic and social affairs (see Chapter Five). Third sector organisations are often managed by a committee representing the community or communities they serve. They are sometimes resourced entirely by volunteers or by finances drawn from the community. These characteristics mean that, in principle at least, such organisations can be accountable to their base rather than to government or to a business enterprise (Edwards, 2004).

Cosmopolitanism

Before concluding this review, there is one other claim to consider concerning the role of third sector organisations in nurturing active citizenship. This is the claim that in some circumstances, third sector organisations can contribute to the development of cosmopolitanism. Like the other major concepts discussed in this book, the meaning of cosmopolitanism is far from settled. However, it is useful to identify three dimensions of cosmopolitanism: as an object of study; as a distinctive methodological approach to the social world; and as a normative standpoint committed to the primacy of world citizenship (Beck, 2006; Beck and Sznaider, 2006; Delanty, 2006), the latter involving both ethical and political aspects (Skrbis and Woodward, 2013). Central to all these dimensions are premises relating to: global interdependencies (Beck and Sznaider, 2006); the reflexive and dialectical nature of cosmopolitanisation (Beck, 2006); and transcendence of the nation state (Beck, 2000; Stokes, 2000). Skrbis and Woodward argue (2013, p 2) that cosmopolitan citizens share a disposition of openness to the world around them. They are thus able to form meaningful attachments to issues, people and places beyond nation states (Vertovec and Cohen, 2002, p 2), all of which can be cultivated in cosmopolitan-oriented third sector organisations.

Beck (2006) and Skrbis and Woodward (2013, p 3) argue that a cosmopolitan perspective requires a new form of analysis that goes beyond the assumptions of the nation state framing of society. For Beck (1999), humanity now faces global risks that cannot be settled by way of activities in sovereign nation states alone. An appropriate response to global risks requires an understanding of the interconnectedness of all life on the planet and universal solutions. Beck (2006) argues for a methodological cosmopolitanism constructed around an epistemology that suspends the assumptions of the nation state and the correlation of society and nation. Yet while cosmopolitanism is based on a universalist concept of society, the challenge for the cosmopolitan citizen is to recognise and celebrate difference, while at the same time understanding our interconnectedness and supporting the universality of both human rights and human destiny.

Ethically, cosmopolitanism is based on principles such as the equal worth of each person, mutual respect among all humans, tolerance of differences and acceptance of multiple and overlapping identities. These principles underpin a global perspective on the obligations owed to others, including the principle of hospitality (Skrbis and Woodward, 2013), regardless of ethnicity, religion or social status (Stokes, 2000). The obligations of cosmopolitan citizens are constructed around human rights and the obligation of care and stewardship for other cultures. For Turner (2006) the basis of the obligation of care and stewardship for other cultures that is embedded in cosmopolitan citizenship stems from an outlook which involves a sceptical and ironic view of one's own traditions. While concern for others beyond the nation state is not new, cosmopolitanism is characterised by increasing awareness of the borderlessness and interconnectedness of people's lives globally, a common responsibility for the future of the planet and a new intensity in scepticism, particularly in regard to the supposed goodwill of governments of nation states.

While cosmopolitanism is normally addressed to actions that are transnational in intent, more recently the concept of 'everyday cosmopolitanism' has refocused attention on the local. Within studies of Australian multiculturalism, there has been a marked shift in the last two decades towards the 'everyday' as a focus of research. Scholars of 'everyday multiculturalism' or 'everyday cosmopolitanism' (for example, Wise and Velayutham, 2009; Butcher and Harris, 2010) have turned their attention to the grassroots, ordinary interactions that occur between people in their daily lives, focusing on social sites such as neighbourhoods, schools, workplaces and the like. These interactions can be understood as a form of lived cosmopolitanism, which sees individuals of different cultures routinely negotiating across difference in order to coexist within a shared social space.

How then can the third sector foster cosmopolitan citizenship? Currently the potential for the third sector to cultivate cosmopolitan citizenship is still very much in the making. However, third sector organisations have the potential to provide a major site for the development of a cosmopolitan outlook (see for example, Edwards, 1999; Turner, 2006; Beck and Sznaider, 2006), through engagement with transnational activities and involvement in social and political action that aims to protect rights and livelihoods across local, national and global levels. Later chapters discuss the ways in which many third sector organisations already cooperate transnationally and seek to learn from alternative ways of organising within and across national borders. However, notwithstanding the growing corpus of publications discussing cosmopolitan citizenship per se (see Linklater, 1998; Brown, 2000; Delanty, 2000, 2006; Osler and Starkey, 2003; Furial, 2005; Isin and Turner, 2007; Joppke 2007), further research into the links between third sector organisations and cosmopolitan active citizenship will be important if we are to make sense of the implications of new forms of transnational and global citizenship for the future of the third sector.

Challenges

While we might be able to identify the major features of the third sector and argue that these features, when they are in evidence, can nurture active citizenship, it is quite another matter to conclude that there is a simple causal relationship between the third sector and active citizenship. We need instead an approach that begins from the premise of the reflexivity and fluidity of social and political life, and frames the relationship as a symbiotic and complex one. Accepting this premise and framework for analysis, there remain several issues that demand further attention if we are to advance our understanding of the connections between the third sector and active citizenship. The first of these issues concerns the tendency to make broad generalisations when expounding on the features of the third sector. The second set of issues concerns the normative claims that stem from high expectations of the capacities of the third sector and the tendency to overstate the claims of positive effects.

In regard to the first issue, there exists a significant body of literature pointing out the problematic nature of overgeneralisation in third sector research (Rosenblum, 1998; Warren, 2001). For example, some commentators highlight the way in which the distinctiveness of the third sector is overdrawn (van Til, 2000; Warren 2001). Thus, in a discussion of civicness and civility in third sector organisations,

Dekker argues that, rather than use the construction of the discrete third sector organisation:

> We would do better to focus on the civicness of the hybrids at the margins of the civil society sphere, or places where voluntary commitment and discursive coordination are imported into other spheres. (Dekker, 2009, p 235)

A broad-brush approach to the characteristics of the third sector also ignores the various types of organisations and the different forms of active citizenship that can be found there. For example, as van der Meer and van Ingen (2009) comment, the extent to which a third sector organisation might be linked with agency organised around political activism depends on the nature of the organisation. Sports organisations are less likely to cultivate activist forms of citizenship than those with explicitly political commitments, such as Greenpeace, for example. Conversely, active citizens who are interested in sports issues may be likely to establish different types of organisation from those interested in environmental issues – although individuals and organisations can and do shift their interests and focus of activities over time. Drawing on their research in Brazil, Favoreto et al (2010) discuss how different types of citizen activism may therefore have different forms of democracy

With regard to the second issue, Tamir (1998) warns against seeing third sector organisations as 'a panacea for all the main illnesses of modern society' (Tamir, 1998, p 214). Such enthusiasm for the emancipatory promises of the third sector has led to many quite extravagant claims. There are blind spots in which the less benign effects and weaknesses in the roles of the third sector are ignored. These blind spots are found in all of the claimed features discussed previously. For example, while there has been extensive positive comment to the effect that participation in the third sector enhances agency and is a form of empowerment, this commentary fails to acknowledge or account for the power differentials and inequalities that exist within and between third sector organisations. Third sector organisations are not immune from exclusivity and parochialism. Thus, rather than offering an open space for association, a space where people can enter freely and debate issues as well as practise civil commitment oriented to redressing social disparities in society, third sector organisations can also offer the reverse. At times they can be little more than closed interest groups, with little or no interest in challenging social inequalities (Unsworth, 2005). Even within organisations, leaders can act in ways that are not representative of their members (Coelho and von Lieres, 2010, p 4). As Gaventa and

Tandon (2010, p 18) point out, most mobilising groups get caught up in the politics of representation, including the issue of 'who speaks for whom'. Indeed, despite their passion to reinforce their virtuous bona fides, active citizens can form solid social cliques (Rosenblum, 1998). This potential for ignoring power differentials within third sector organisations has implications for claims concerning their capacity to enhance democracy. Tamir suggests, on the contrary, that third sector organisations are not inherently democratic. Nor does a commitment to democratic decision making necessarily emerge from people associating freely (Tamir, 1998, p 219). Aspirations for democratic practices must be understood as context specific, often hampered by wider cultures of authoritarianism, clientelism and patronage (Coelho and von Lieres, 2010, p 3).

Conclusions

This chapter has identified some of the principal claims made for the relationships between active citizenship and the third sector. In doing so, it has drawn attention to the risk of overgeneralisation and overambitious claims. To give a more balanced account, research is needed that acknowledges the multidimensional, contingent and shifting features of both the third sector and active citizenship and that provides perhaps more modest normative accounts of the features of the third sector. It is important to acknowledge that third sector organisations and active citizenship are socially and historically constructed. There are different meanings and forms for each and these come together in a variety of configurations, with differing effects (including harmful as well as benign ones). There are varying forms of relations between the third sector and active citizenship and, perhaps most importantly, these are context specific. Sometimes third sector organisations present as hybrid entities, for example, being voluntary and not-for-profit organisations but adopting market models of operation and working in partnership with the state to deliver welfare. At other times they fit a fairly straightforward model of an activist group that is separate from the state and eschews both state funding and market mechanisms to generate resources. The remainder of this book explores such complexities in the relationships between the third sector and active citizenship, drawing out varying perspectives and contestations and focusing on the ways in which context matters.

FIVE

The third sector in context

Introduction

Chapter Three highlighted the ambiguities inherent in defining the third sector. This chapter explores further the changing boundaries between the state, the market and the third sector, discussing different ways of understanding the relationship between the sectors over time and space and the implications for third sector organisations as channels for civil commitment and activism. It then draws on institutional and governmentality theory to consider the implications of blurring and hybridisation for the sector's role in promoting active citizenship.

Models of the state–third sector relationship

Several attempts have been made to formulate typologies of the relationship between the state and the third sector (Kramer, 1981; Gidron et al, 1992; Salamon and Anheier, 1998; Wagner, 2000). Salamon and Anheier, for example, drew on Esping Andersen's (1990) welfare regime theory to suggest four models of third sector regime – liberal, corporatist, statist and social democrat. Such attempts are open to challenge in three respects. First, they tend to focus on the OECD countries and take for granted ways of understanding the world in relation to the state and market that may not always apply elsewhere. Second, they take insufficient account of change over time and variations within sectors and countries and between welfare fields. Third, they tend to focus on service delivery – or the 'welfare mix' and hence on civil commitment rather than activism. Nonetheless, they provide a useful starting point for our discussion. With such reservations in mind, therefore, we draw on these and other sources to identify a number of 'ideal types', characterised by different ideological perspectives, and explore their implications for the role of the third sector in promoting different types of active citizenship.

The ideal types we have identified are presented in Table 1, along with a description of the ideologies that underpin them, the relationship between the sector, the role of the state and the role of the third sector – first in promoting citizenship as civil commitment and second in promoting citizenship as activism.

Table 1: A typology of state–third sector relationships

Description	Ideology	Relationship	State role	Third sector role: civil commitment	Third sector role: activism
Dual	Liberal Laissez faire	Parallel bars Laissez faire	Basic provision (for undeserving poor)	Meeting needs largely unmet by state; Catering for diversity	A route into public life; Campaigning for social change
Welfare state	Statist Socialist	Government dominated	Main responsibility for welfare funding and delivery	Catering for special needs (extension ladder)	Watchdog; expressing emergent and special interests, but largely to make the state work better
Corporatist	Social democracy	Corporate partners – joint responsibility for meeting need	Funding	Providing (often through a pillarised system)	Incorporated
Collaborative	Social democracy	Partners – joint responsibility for meeting need	Enabling, coordinating, providing	Partners in delivery	Partners in policy making
Associative democracy	Communitarian	Third sector dominant	Marginal	Providing for the diversity of need	Expressing plurality of voices
Quasi-market	Neo-liberal	Market dominant	Marginal	Competing in the market; Compensating for market failure through family and community provision	Consumer advice; otherwise seen as 'strangling serpents'
Southern/Mediterranean			Weak	Providing through family and community ties and NGOs	

Embedded in a liberal *laissez faire* ideology, the **dual model** is one in which state and third sector roles develop largely independently of each other and are seen as separate spheres. Pre-20th century Britain proves a strong example of this model: the Charity Organisation Society at the time promoted the idea of 'mutually exclusive spheres', with charity providing for the deserving poor while the state, through the Poor Law, regulated the undeserving poor. There was little or no concept of a third sector as such at this time and most historical accounts tend to focus on charity or mutual aid as obligation and as civil commitment. But, in pre-20th century Britain, and elsewhere, charity and mutual aid also offered groups excluded from the establishment – certain religious groups, working class men and women, indeed women in general – not only a way of meeting needs not met by the state, but also a route into public life (Taylor and Kendall, 1996). A liberal commitment to freedom of speech also meant that, in practice, campaigning was a significant feature of third sector activity. The Society for the Abolition of the Slave Trade in the early 18th century – whose reach extended far beyond Britain – provides an early example of global activism.

The **welfare state** or **statist model** is one where the state takes the major responsibility for welfare. In part, this could be seen as a pragmatic response to 'voluntary failure' (Salamon, 1987) – the past failure of voluntary provision to provide a healthy and educated workforce or military force, for example (Taylor and Kendall, 1996). In part, it reflects a socialist ideology – at the extreme, in communist countries, third sector organisations and associations were often actively discouraged unless under the control of the state and/or acting as a vehicle for state policy. But this model does not necessarily prohibit voluntary action. Scandinavia, where the state plays a major role in welfare, has a strong tradition of associations – Norway and Sweden being among the highest ranking countries in the world when it comes to active membership in associations (Jepson Grassman and Svedberg, 2007; Lorentzen, 2010). Here, third sector organisations have acted as a channel through which to voice demands and mobilise networks to foster the delivery of services by public organisations. They also have a strong presence in the field of leisure and cultural activities, as well as housing cooperatives (Pestoff, 2004). In the UK, in the post war period, when this model was in the ascendant, third sector organisations retained some specialist niche roles and offered complementary services, as well as developing new roles as 'watchdogs' on the state (Brenton, 1985). In the latter role, they provided advice, information and advocacy to help citizens navigate complex state systems but they also campaigned for improved services and rights, acting as a channel for both civil commitment and activism. In either case, however, the third sector contribution was intended to make the state work better.

Across some parts of Europe, a somewhat different pattern emerged, which assigned a much stronger role to the third sector. In the **corporatist model** (Schmitter, 1974), potentially conflicting interests in society are institutionalised along religious, political or economic lines through peak organisations that are incorporated into the system of government (for example, trades unions, employers). In Germany, Belgium and the Netherlands, for example, welfare peak organisations – organised along predominantly religious and political lines – became the predominant providers of welfare, in line with the Catholic principle of subsidiarity, which holds that human affairs are best handled at the lowest possible level (see Chapter Four).

Proponents of what we have labelled the **collaborative model** distance themselves from any discourse that claims the supremacy of a particular sector. In this model, briefly termed 'the third way' (Giddens, 1998) but increasingly common over the 1990s, welfare draws on all three sectors, which are expected to act as partners with joint responsibility for meeting needs. Here, in theory at least, the state is first among equals with an enabling and coordinating role. The third way promotes the role of the third sector as a counterbalance to the state and market. Citizens are partners and coproducers. Third sector organisations – along with for-profits – are seen as significant players in both policy making and the delivery of welfare but are also seen as having an important role in mobilising and representing citizens. Influenced by the work of Robert Putnam (Putnam et al, 1993; Putnam, 2000), third sector organisations are seen as a way of democratising democracy.

In the next two models, the role of the state is considerably reduced. Earlier chapters have indicated the importance of the idea of **associative democracy** in understanding the democratic potential of third sector organisations. Proponents of associative democracy argue for a model in which the third sector is dominant. Thus, as we saw in Chapter Four, Hirst proposes 'a new democratic welfare system based on provision through self-governing associations' (1994, p 16), expressing the plurality of interests and preferences that exist in society. This is a system that resonates with a communitarian ideology, as propounded, for example, by Amitai Etzioni in the 1990s (Etzioni, 1998), which was critical both of the expansion of the state and of the individualism associated with neoliberal philosophies (although the indications are that Etzioni himself would have favoured a collaborative model; Lorentzen, 2010).

There are also parallels here with libertarian socialist approaches. For example Colin Ward, as an anarchist/libertarian socialist, has lauded the role of self help rather than state interventions in housing in developing countries (Davis, 2006). However these approaches have been much criticised to the extent that they may end up – whether intentionally or not – supporting the roles of powerful local leaders and underpinning patron-client relationships. Davis' study, *Planet of Slums*, refers to what he describes as 'Illusions of Self Help', demonstrating ways in which such initiatives can be hijacked. For example, when squatters convert apparently barren hillsides into housing land, they may end up 'leveraging up land values for owners who can then evict residents or rack up their rents' (Davis, 2006, p 89). The associative model reflects Hayek's concept of 'spontaneous order' (Macmillan, 2013), with its emphasis on 'dispersed agents using their local knowledge to pursue their interests within a single framework of general rules which prescribe just conduct' (Gamble, 1996, cited in Macmillan, 2013, p 7). Such a system should, so the argument goes, work though self-organising adjustments to local conditions. The associative model gives primacy to the third sector. But this argument could also be applied to neoliberal models that give primacy to the market.

What we have called the **quasi-market model** is informed by a neoliberal ideology and seeks to shrink the state, opening up welfare to the free play of market forces. The basic assumptions are that the individual citizen/consumer should exercise his or her free choice in accessing goods and services and that quality is ensured by competition between providers. The citizen is thus redefined as an individual consumer. Welfare provision is based on the privatisation and outsourcing of public sector agencies and services, procurement through a purchaser–provider split, and competition policy. In this model, the opportunities for the third sector are two-fold. On the one hand it can be a competitor in a social welfare market alongside the for-profit sector, acting as an agent for service commissioners. On the other hand, it can be a substitute for the state, with associations, 'communities', volunteers and families as a first line of support at local level. However, advocacy and campaigning are delegitimised as distorting the market (Acheson and LaForest, 2013).

Esping Andersen originally suggested three welfare regimes – statist, corporatist and social democrat – but he later added an important fourth model to his analysis – the Mediterranean model. He described this as an underdeveloped version of the corporatist model. But it was later developed further by Leibfried (1992) and Ferrera (1996), who called it **the Southern model**, stressing *inter alia* traditional conservative values, a centralised but weak state with extensive clientelism, and dependence on family and community in line with the principle of subsidiarity. While still focusing on Europe, this model would seem to have some relevance elsewhere, especially in countries with a strong religious influence, although this might now be changing.

These models are ideal types, although they tend to be associated with specific countries/regions or points in time, reflecting historical developments and associated socio-political cultures. As we acknowledged at the beginning of this chapter, the typology also reflects a predominantly OECD based view of the world. It focuses on service delivery, although we have described here and in Table 1 how it might accommodate citizenship as activism.

There has also been some debate as to whether Esping Andersen's welfare state classifications needed to include an additional dimension. Bonoli (1997), for example, suggested that Esping Andersen's welfare classifications needed to take account of the question of 'how' welfare was being provided according to different models as well as questions about 'how much' welfare was being provided. While representing a 'path-breaking work', he argued, Esping Andersen was inadequate in this respect. Other critics have taken a similar view. Langan and Ostner (1991), for example, reflected on the need to take account of differences between welfare states in terms of how they were treating women.

In addition, Mayo and Anastacio (1999) have suggested that models of welfare need to take account of the different processes involved in service planning and service delivery. How empowering – or disempowering – were these processes for service users? Statist models can be (and all too often have been) delivered in paternalistic, disempowering ways, but so too can services provided via third sector organisations. And while market-led models could be associated with choice, at least for those in a position to be able to afford to pay for them, they too could be provided in paternalistic and disempowering ways, especially for those defined as the 'undeserving poor'. There are a number of myths to be unpacked therefore about the supposedly inherent characteristics of different models of welfare, as subsequent chapters illustrate in more detail.

Be this as it may, with globalisation and associated developments such as structural adjustment policies (see Chapter Two), many commentators see a convergence across the globe around neoliberal principles and the quasi-market model. Advocates of this model see it as freeing up a third sector that has either been crowded out by the state (although research by Salamon and Sokolowski, 2004, and Boje,

2009, suggests that there is little evidence to support this), or has become too dependent on the state as a funder.

Critics of this model argue that the culture and values of the market are pervading every facet of contemporary society (Rochester, 2013). They fear for the independence of a sector that is being drawn into substituting for the state according to a global capitalist agenda, with its identity – and particularly its role as a vehicle for citizen activism – compromised. This chapter will draw on theory and evidence on the ground to ask how far these fears for the sector's independence and distinctiveness – under this or other models – have been justified. It will also ask whether that matters. It will end by discussing how third sectors in different countries are responding.

Theoretical approaches

Third sector scholars have drawn on a range of theories to describe and understand how the distinctiveness and independence of the third sector might be threatened or indeed how it might be preserved. Perhaps the most straightforward of these is resource dependency theory (Pfeffer and Salancik, 1978). This approach studies how external resources influence an organisation's behaviour and how organisations can gain control over those dependencies. While resource dependency theory focuses on the technical features of environments, new institutional theory adds to this approach by focusing on knowledge, discourse and rule systems as 'cultural frameworks' for explaining organisational behaviours (Scott, 1995, p 113). It seeks to explain how norms governing human actions and interactions come to be institutionalised, seemingly independently of individual actors. Thus DiMaggio and Powell (1983) describe how, while **coercive pressures** can be imposed by resource providers, in line with resource dependency, **mimetic pressures** lead organisations to copy practice elsewhere that seems successful, while **normative pressures** apply when certain forms of practice are seen to be the norm by those operating in any given field. Thus third sector organisations may be forced by their funders to conform to certain ways of operating or they may simply imitate others in their field who are seen to be successful, in order to gain both resources and recognition. They may, however, just take it for granted that they have to behave in certain ways because they see this as the norm.

Some argue that institutional theory neglects concepts of power and agency (Newman, 2001; Clegg, 2010). Similar accusations have been levelled at the school of governance theory that emerged during the

1990s. Governance theory challenged traditional theories of the state, suggesting that, in today's complex, fragmented and globalised society, it is no longer possible for the state to govern on its own (Stoker, 1998; Peters and Pierre, 2001; Kooiman, 2003). It needs to draw on the resources and knowledge of other actors. Governance theorists describe the emergence of new forms of interorganisational networks that do not rely on the authority and sanctions of the state and in which the boundaries between public and private sectors have become blurred (Stoker, 1998) – 'the ultimate', one proponent argues, 'in hands-off government' (Rhodes, 1997, p 10).

Governmentality theory problematises this approach. While it agrees with governance theory that, increasingly, governing takes place at a distance from the state, it is less sanguine about the freedoms that this confers. Its theorists are interested instead in exploring the domain of strategies, techniques and procedures through which a society is rendered governable and individuals come to govern themselves (Rose, 1999, p 3). This is achieved, they argue, not through coercive control but through a more complex and subtle diffusion of techniques and forms of knowledge that encourage and harness active practices of self management and identity construction, of personal ethics and collective allegiances (Rose, 1999, p 176). Thus, governmentality theorists warn that forms of power beyond the state can often sustain the state more effectively than its own institutions as citizens come to police themselves (Foucault, 1980).

Increasingly, Miller and Rose argue, these assumptions have embodied a neoliberal view of the world:

> Markets are to replace planning as regulators of economic activity. Those aspects of government that welfare construed as political responsibilities are, as far as possible, to be transformed into commodified forms and regulated according to market principles. (Miller and Rose, 2008, p 79)

The implications for citizenship are far reaching. In keeping with arguments about individualisation earlier in this book, collective responsibility and solidarity is to be replaced by active entrepreneurship and today's active citizens are to become 'entrepreneurs of the self', displaying 'free exercise of personal choice among a variety of options' and 'seeking to maximise their quality of life through the artful assembly of a "lifestyle", put together through the world of goods' (Miller and Rose, 2008, p 49).

Miller and Rose (2008, p 89) describe how, whereas community was once seen as a mediating structure between state and government channelling the obligations between state and citizen, it is now a sector 'whose vectors and forces could be mobilized, enrolled, deployed in novel programmes and techniques, which operate through the instrumentalisation of personal allegiances and active responsibilities' – it has thus become a 'site of government'. Others agree. Thus Carmel and Harlock (2008) have argued that, in the UK, by engaging civil society organisations in welfare delivery and governance, the third sector has been instituted as a 'governable terrain'. On a more global scale, Bebbington et al (2008), who see civil society and the state as mutually constitutive rather than separate entities, argue that NGOs could become 'vehicles of neoliberal governmentality (i.e. managing people and organisations in ways that reinforce rather than challenging neoliberal agendas)' (p 8).

In the UK, John Morison saw the Compact (Home Office, 1998), signed between governments in the UK and the voluntary and community sector, as a prime example of this, arguing that, in pursuit of a 'third way', the New Labour government was seeking to 'operationalise a ... managerially driven programme by influencing, allying with, and coopting the voluntary sector as a resource that they do not directly control' (Morison, 2000, p 131). He argues, therefore, that:

> what might be presented as increased autonomy, a chance to govern oneself, can also be seen as a reconfiguration of rationalities so that the self interest of the sector aligns with the interest of a state seeking to mobilise a reserve army of support effectively and on its own terms. (Morison, 2000, p 129)

As privatisation advances, critics argue that third sector organisations have thus been associated with 'shrinking state responsibilities and the progressive exemption of the state from the role of guarantor of rights', making the market a 'surrogate arena of citizenship' (Dagnino, 2008, p 5).

Cooption and institutionalisation: the evidence

How then are these arguments demonstrated in practice? In this section we consider the implications for the sector both as a service provider and as a policy actor, working in partnership with the state.

Service delivery

The last two decades of the 20th century witnessed a sea change in the relationship between the state and the third sector in many OECD countries, with the advance of neoliberal approaches to welfare. The speed and depth of the change varied from country to country, depending on the dominant model of welfare and its historical underpinning. But generally, observers commented on the growth of a 'contract culture' (6 and Kendall, 1997) across countries as part of a move to the market in welfare. This saw state funding to third sector organisations grow, but at the same time a change in the nature of that funding from grants to contracts.

As 6 and Kendall argued at the time, extensive financial relationships between the state and the third sector were not new. But in the 1990s, there was a significant change in the quality and character of these relations. A new managerialist hegemony pervaded the third sector world. 6 and Kendall identified five key elements in this change:

- a move to tighter specification;
- the increasingly legalistic nature of funding agreements;
- a perceived increase in competition for state funding within and across sectors;
- a turbulent, sometimes hostile political and fiscal climate;
- pressure to assimilate business values and techniques.

Verna Smith commented on the resulting transformation in New Zealand in similar vein:

> The resulting changes which have had an impact upon the funding of voluntary sector organisations are a heightened interest in various forms of contracting; the pervasive expectation that explicit agreements for performance of agreed objectives at specified standards of quantity, quality, and cost will underpin all funding relationships; the disaggregation of government departments into autonomous businesses, including those with explicit purchaser roles; efforts to make all businesses, including voluntary sector ones, more responsive to their consumers; and the introduction of the financial management system for government departments with its emphasis on output and outcome reporting leading to increased transparency of the effects of funding decisions.(Smith, 1996)

Business models penetrated the third sector directly through contract requirements (coercive isomorphism), but also through the spread of business management courses, the appointment of chief executives and finance officers from the private sector and the growth of consultancies promoting the improvement of management practice through the adoption of business practices. Third sector organisations were expected to behave like businesses, with brands, products and consumers (Rochester, 2013). For some, the fear was that, while third sector organisations were the acceptable face of contracting out, they were in fact a stalking horse for privatisation, with for-profit organisations the intended ultimate beneficiaries (Lawrence, 1982).

In some countries – like the US – the introduction of market principles was a gradual and long-term development. Elsewhere it was a more pronounced shift. Certainly, this was the case in the UK, where a social democratic model of the welfare state had been in place over the previous 40 years or so. Here research suggested that the move to service contracts faced third sector providers with increased administrative burdens and transaction costs, as well as often the need to top up inadequate contract fees in a competitive market. It also reported fears of goal distortion as providers responded to the demands of state purchasers. There were fears too that advocacy would be squeezed out, either by self censorship or by the burden of work involved in administering contracts (Taylor and Lewis, 1997). Research by Russell and Scott (1997) warned that formalisation, professionalisation and the demands of contracting were creating a two-tier system of volunteers, sidelining those with less 'expertise'. It also found an increased emphasis on output measurement (the 'what') at the expense of process (the 'how'). In addition, new structural forms were becoming more common – forms in which third sector organisations were setting up trading arms and commercial subsidiaries (Kramer, 2000).

These findings resonated with research elsewhere. In the US, Lipsky and Smith (1989) raised similar concerns in relation both to loss of autonomy and constraints on political activity while other US commentators noted a blurring of boundaries between all three sectors (Hammack and Young, 1993). More recently, in Germany, Bode and Evers (2004, pp 110–11) have charted a shift from the corporatist model there to a managerial state, with the contract culture forcing Germany's 'peak' welfare associations into 'task-focused and time-limited arrangements with public bodies'. They note that the public funding that these associations had enjoyed over previous decades is becoming less secure and that public contracts are eliminating 'most of the organisational slack' that had characterised previous funding arrangements. Evers and Laville (2004, p 28) thus contend that, over recent years, these large federated institutions have increasingly become 'parastate' organisations. Meanwhile, in the Netherlands, Dekker describes a blurring of the sectors as a result of cutbacks, privatisation and reregulation, with a 'strong incorporation of the ways of the market into the behaviour of [the third sector's] operations' (2004, p 149).

At the same time, the advance of the new managerialism and an obsession with performance measurement have established an operational hegemony – consistent with DiMaggio and Powell's (1983) normative isomorphism. In the new managerialism, social problems and political issues become technical problems (White, 1996; Onyx and Dovey, 1999; M. Taylor, 2011). This is not a universal phenomenon. But Uphoff (1995, p 26) has described how in many countries: 'Accountability is commonly taken to require much advance specification of objectives and means, so that evaluation can be done in terms of the achievement of those objectives and the timely utilisation of predetermined means for achieving those ends'. As such, he argues, projects are isolated from the economic, social, cultural, physical and other contexts in which they operate.

Not all the fears expressed in the first wave of contracting out were borne out in practice. The research cited above in both the UK and US at that time acknowledged that there were positive aspects to contracting in relation to transparency and a greater clarity in relation to outcomes (see also Deakin, 1996). In the early years of contracting, large national third sector providers could wield considerable influence in relationships with local authority commissioners and, in any case, local authorities across the country varied considerably in their purchasing practices. However, more recently in the UK and elsewhere (LaForest, 2013), the introduction of austerity measures, including public expenditure cuts, after the recent global economic crisis has alarmed many in the third sector. They see themselves as substituting not only for state delivery, but increasingly for state funding at a time when demand, due again to austerity, is growing. In the UK, the National Council for Voluntary Organisations estimated that third sector income from central and local government would fall by 9.4% between 2010/11 and 2015/6 (Kane and Allen, 2011) and it is now revising this prediction upwards (NCVO, 2014). Stringent cuts to funding from central to local government, which has always been the most significant source of state funding to the third sector, are likely to have a particularly harsh impact. The fact that these have been imposed disproportionately across the country (Beatty and Fothergill, 2013) means that they are likely to hit the poorest places hardest

At the same time, public service procurement practices are fiercely economistic – the UK National Coalition of Independent Action refers to them as taking place in an 'arcane technocratic environment' (Benson, 2014) – and have led to a restructuring of the market. Markets tend to go to scale. Commissioners tend to prefer a few larger contracts to multiple smaller ones. Meanwhile, payment by results and the demands of tendering can be particularly challenging for many smaller and medium-sized organisations, effectively excluding them from entering the market in the first place. In the UK, where the primary responsibility for delivering social housing was transferred to the third sector in the 1980s, Rees et al (2012) describe how the number of housing associations funded as development partners was reduced from 400 to just over 70 in the name of efficiency. This drive to consolidation and merger has continued since, with UK housing associations described as 'generally large, bureaucratized organisations with paid staff becoming the principal owners of strategy as well as operations' (Mullins and Pawson, 2010, p 213). This trend has not been confined to the UK. Mullins and Pawson found that the same applied to housing associations in the Netherlands, which had a longer history of being primary providers.

At the time of writing, the UK coalition government drives for efficiency against a background of public expenditure cuts are also affecting the UK third sector infrastructure, with pressures on them to merge as an explicit aim of government policy. In addition, a system of prime contractors and subcontractors has been introduced in some fields, which effectively outsources commissioning. This means that state funding is given to a small number of prime contractors, mostly from the private sector, who then subcontract delivery to a range of providers, with the result, as one commentator put it, that vertical supply chains have grown at the expense of the local horizontal partnerships that characterised the New Labour government (Benson, 2014). Many third sector subcontractors find themselves dependent on private sector prime contractors for work, which may or may not materialise, with third sector subcontractors often bearing a disproportionate share of the risk and costs involved (Winyard, 2011; Ryan, 2014).

Partnership working

Fears of cooption do not only apply to market models of the relationship between state and third sector. Much of the discussion of the relationships between the state and the third sector focuses on service delivery and the developments described in the previous section.

But, since the 1990s, commentators on third sector developments across the globe have also described how, through an emphasis on partnership working, new spaces have opened up for citizen voice at both national and international levels (Cornwall and Coelho, 2007). Thus John Gaventa and Rajesh Tandon describe how globalisation has brought with it:

> changing forms of power and new realms of authority, and with these, new spaces for public action. From local to global, fields of power and landscapes of authority are being reconfigured, affecting the lives and futures of citizens across the planet, while simultaneously reshaping where and how citizens engage to make their voices heard. (Gaventa and Tandon, 2010, p 3)

Third sector organisations, including international development NGOs, have been invited into a variety of new spaces as a result, whether to represent the interests of the poor, as with the World Bank's consultations on developing Poverty Reduction Strategies, to promote participation as part of development strategies more locally, or to address the 'wicked issues' of social policy in the OECD countries, that is complex problems that have proved resistant to conventional solutions.

Explanations for the popularity of policies to promote 'participation' have ranged from concerns with the democratic deficit in long established democracies to concerns to strengthen civil society and establish 'Western' democratic forms elsewhere (see Chapter Seven), whether in the wake of the Cold War, with the end of military dictatorships in a number of countries or in the aftermath of periods of violence in others. As an example of the latter, Fowler (2008) cites Afghanistan where, he argues, 'Western' democratic forms have been imposed by force, with NGOs as 'non-uniformed alternatives to the military' (Fowler, 2008, p 115). There is an extensive literature on public policies to promote participation in the new spaces that have been introduced, exploring their limitations as well as their potential in different contexts (Cooke and Kothari, 2001: Hickey and Mohan, 2004; Cornwall and Coelho, 2007; Barnes et al, 2007; M. Taylor, 2011). Despite their limitations, however, these spaces can represent a 'distinct arena at the interface of state and society', providing 'conduits for negotiation, information and exchange' (Cornwall and Coelho, 2007, p 1). As such, they can be seen as 'a project constructed around the extension of citizenship and the deepening of democracy'.

An important distinction is made by those studying citizen participation between 'popular spaces' which are set up by citizens themselves and 'invited spaces', set up by external actors including external international development actors (Cornwall, 2004; Gaventa, 2007). In 'invited spaces', the rules of the game tend to be set from outside – by policy makers, for example. It is these outsiders who determine the agenda, language used, what is acceptable behaviour and who plays (M. Taylor, 2011). Innovative participatory approaches can easily lose their power as they are adopted and adapted on a wider scale (Cooke and Kothari, 2001). This may not be intentional – well-meaning actors are often unaware of how far their practice embodies traditional assumptions and ways of operating. And community actors, too, may become coopted, declaring themselves satisfied with processes and achievements that have in no way matched up to their original aspirations.

John Gaventa – a prominent development studies scholar – thus concluded from his studies in different parts of the world:

> While [invited] spaces offer some possibilities for influence and may allow social justice groups possibilities for organising, it is questionable whether these invited spaces actually create opportunities for any long-term social change on critical issues. The danger is that they may even serve to legitimise the status quo and actually divert civil society energies from working on more fundamental policy-related problems. (Gaventa, 2007, p 7)

We will return to these issues in Chapter Eight.

Does it matter?

In the light of the previous discussion, it may be that the holy grail of third sector independence is actually a myth. Commenting on the contract culture in the 1980s, Paton and Batsleer questioned whether there ever was a golden age of 'autonomous voluntary organisations operating free from state interference or competitive pressures' (cited in 6 and Kendall, 2004, p 10). Of the models cited above, only the dual and associative models present the sector as independent of the state – and the associative model is a model that does not exist in real life. Independence may also be attributed to the Southern model, but this is often a function of a weak state rather than deliberate design and is any case often characterised by clientelism. Even in that most liberal of welfare systems – the US, with its antipathy to government welfare – Salamon demonstrated the interdependence of third sector and government, arguing that by the late 1970s, 'the private nonprofit sector had become the principal vehicle for the delivery of government-financed human service, and government had, correspondingly, become the principal source of nonprofit human service agency finance' (Salamon, 1995, p 1).

Others have argued that the whole idea of the third sector, whatever label it is given, is a recent invention (Hall, 1992; 6 and Leat, 1997; Kramer, 2000). Kramer suggests, with others, that factors such as size and field may be as significant in characterising different contributions to welfare. Thus Taylor and colleagues, studying voluntary and private organisations in social care, found that small organisations had more in common with each other than with the larger organisations in their respective sectors (Taylor et al, 1995). Research in the US in 1990s found that relatively few generalisations could be made about the consistent, comparative advantages of one type of auspice over another, except perhaps in relation to the motivations of staff, the perceptions of service users and treatment by regulatory bodies (Weisbrod, 1998).

Analysing social welfare, Evers and Laville question the degree to which 'sector' explains 'why some organisations develop distinct and different styles of action and services' (2004, p 5). On the one hand, they extend the account of voluntary action, arguing that the rationales and values that nourish civil society and the principles related to it cannot be restricted to one sector. On the other, they want to bring a wider range of organisations into the third sector field, criticising the neglect in US-dominated accounts of the sector of the cooperative and mutual tradition, based as it is in solidarity, socially and politically embedded in the political action, institutions and legal frameworks of welfare politics (Evers and Laville, 2004, p 37). More generally, they contrast the Anglo-Saxon understanding of 'clear-cut sectors' with a European view of the third sector as 'embedded in … a tripolar system of market, state and informal economies' (Evers and Laville, 2004, p 14). Thus they conceptualise the third sector as a tension field or intermediary area between state, market and community (Evers, 1990; Evers and Laville, 2004) in a wider concept of the 'welfare mix'.

Evers and Laville's concept of the third sector as a tension field focuses on service delivery but it highlights the sector's dynamic and heterogeneous nature – as a place of contradictory forces and rationales, mediating between multiple stakeholders, whose interests have to be constantly renegotiated. As such, it could be said to exemplify the networks and alliances that need to be forged across society as a whole to meet the needs of the 21st century. It thus moves our attention away from policing sector boundaries and lamenting the blurring and hybridity that occurs in practice. Instead, Evers and Laville's approach focuses on exploring the ways in which different actors and organisations within this intermediary sphere negotiate the tensions within and between these boundaries. As Evers and Laville argue, it may be more productive to consider how to heighten the potential that the hybridity of the sector embodies and how to reduce the risks rather than trying to preserve and strengthen the boundaries (see also Chapter Three; and Dekker, 2009).

The work of Billis and others on hybridity offers a complementary perspective on the question of 'sectors' and whether this matters. As Billis argues, the debate about any Faustian pact in which the [third] sector loses its distinctive characteristics in return for public and private sector resources is just one aspect of a more complex phenomenon of the changing role of the third sector (Billis, 2010, p 251). He identifies a range of responses including **erosion**, whereby third sector organisations lose their distinctive attributes, but also **emigration** whereby the third sector brings its own distinctive influence into other sectors. He and the contributors to his edited volume also highlight the importance of boundary spanners – individuals who move from one sector to another, taking their ideas and principles with them (Lewis, 2010; Howard and Taylor, 2010). And this analysis reminds us that some current third sector organisations may have originated as a collaboration between partners from different sectors, who see the third sector as the natural place for cross-sector innovation. Indeed, as Howard and Taylor comment, some partnerships that developed as the result of 'third way' policies in the UK are now formally constituting themselves as charities or community interest companies as government funding ends and they are forced to operate as self-financing entities.

These analytical approaches recognise the complexity, dynamism and diversity within the third sector terrain. We could argue that it is this diversity that safeguards the third sector's claim to act as a channel for active citizenship. While some organisations become indistinguishable from government or for-profit organisations, others may pride themselves on their ability to survive and develop autonomously, with or without state funding. And new organisations may form to challenge the new ways in which welfare is being provided by third sector as well as for-profit organisations.

How the third sector responds

The question that this leaves us with relates to the role of the third sector in expressing and mobilising active citizenship and how this is maintained and developed, especially in the light of the current neoliberal hegemony. Evers and Laville argue that 'there is a fundamental tension between the tendency to treat the third sector as an alternative to state-based services and its importance as an expression of civil society' (2004, p 22). How can the latter be preserved?

Earlier in this chapter, we discussed theories that help to explain how third sector organisations and citizens are incorporated into the agendas of more powerful actors in society. However, implicit in these theories is the concept of resistance (Taylor, 2007), which allows the articulation and implementation of alternative agendas (Atkinson, 2003, p 117). Self-steering actors outside the state can thus become 'active subjects' in the new governance spaces, not only collaborating in the exercise of government but also shaping and influencing it (Morison, 2000, p 19). Bebbington et al (2008, p 9), too, having warned of the potential for NGOs to reinforce dominant hegemonies, argue that they can also advance alternative agendas. Seeing the state and civil society as 'mutually constitutive rather than separate, autonomous entities', they see scope for civil society actors to join agents from within the state 'in forging counterhegemonic alternatives as well as dominant hegemonies'.

Hickey and Mohan cite the example of ActionAid's REFLECT programme to illustrate precisely such transformative alternatives. This international NGO programme used learner focused approaches to teaching literacy, based on the work of Paolo Freire (1976), to facilitate participation and increased community-level actions, promoting empowerment and social transformation (Hickey and Mohan, 2004). At local level, too, community associations, like international NGOs, have agency and the capacity to take the initiative, despite the well-recognised dangers of cooption (Taylor, 2007; Ostrander, 2013; see also Chapter Ten). However, the scope for promoting transformational agendas via citizens' engagement in political and policy processes may depend on their connections with broader social movements (Hickey and Mohan, 2004) as we shall see later in this chapter and in Chapter Nine.

Other theoretical perspectives also highlight the scope for resistance. Powell, one of the authors associated with the theory of institutional isomorphism, later revisited this theory to explore why, despite these pressures, there is still considerable heterogeneity of response (Powell,

1991). The factors he cites include variations in resource environments, differences in the structure of industries and how they relate to the state, contradictory pressures from different levels of the state and different jurisdictions, negotiation and compromise. Certainly, as we commented earlier in this chapter, the experience of the contract culture can vary for different third sector organisations and under different administrations.

Research by Taylor and others[1] studied the ways in which TSOs experienced 'invited' governance spaces in three different countries during the first decade of the 21st century – Bulgaria, Nicaragua, and England and Wales (Taylor et al, 2009; Howard and Lever, 2011; Miller et al, 2013). They drew on Bourdieu's concepts of habitus, cultural capital and field (Bourdieu, 1977, 1990) as developed by Crossley (2003) to consider the factors that enable or constrain the ability of civil society actors to maintain a sense of independent agency or authority. Bourdieu's concept of habitus captures patterns of thought, behaviour and taste that dispose agents to act and react in certain ways. Agents operate in a series of fields each of which has its own dominant institutions, operating logics, means of production and profit and loss accounts. And depending on their background, individuals may bring more or less cultural capital to those fields. Bourdieu demonstrates how the interplay between habitus, field and cultural capital privileges certain actors over others and reinforces dominant power structures. He argues that critique and protest are only possible at moments of crisis when there is a powerful dissonance between subjective expectations and objective outcomes. Crossley, however, describes how a history of contentious politics and the cultural capital it creates can create a 'radical habitus', sustained by support networks, social events and pedagogic agents within a field, through which knowledge, commitment and reflexivity are conveyed (Howard and Lever, 2011).

The three regions in this study corresponded broadly to the statist model (Bulgaria), the Southern model (Nicaragua) and a combination of collaborative and market models (England and Wales). The research identified a number of factors that emerged as significant in differentiating between the three countries. As well as the role of the state, these included: the influence of external actors; the degree of decentralisation; the party political system; citizen rights and

---

[1]   The research was funded by the Economic and Social Research Council in the UK as part of its Non-governmental Social Action programme, RES-155-25-0058. Other researchers in the team were: Antaoneeta Mateeva, Rumen Petrov and Luis Serra Vasquez.

Table 2: Patterns of state–third sector relations

	Bulgaria	England and Wales	Nicaragua
Welfare regime: Arrangements for meeting basic needs			
Meeting basic needs	State dominant provider. NGOs meet needs neglected by the state.	Increasingly mixed economy of welfare, coordinated by the state, with NGOs encouraged to take on service delivery roles previously performed by the state.	Needs largely met by family remittances and NGOs with external aid. A weak economy and state seeking to meet the demands of structural adjustment.
The influence of external donors/ actors	Medium: the EU now a major player; other foreign aid declining.	EU a major player in Wales. UK government a major factor in Welsh identity and policy.	High: INGOs, foreign governments and global institutions major players through structural adjustment.
Democratic processes			
The relationship between national and local government	Highly centralised state; local government has few resources or powers.	Devolution of powers combined with central regulation; citizen participation agenda driven by the national state.	Mediated by political party affiliation. New government has replaced previous citizen participation arrangements with new party-led structures.
The party political system	Multiple parties reducing in number but power remaining with the successors of the communist regime.	Three party system, increasingly focusing on the centre ground. Nationalist party also significant in Wales.	Clientelist politics with power alternating between strongly polarised parties (which nonetheless now operate under a joint pact).
Citizen participation rights	Limited to the vote; few governance spaces. Civil society and citizenship values still emergent.	Citizenship education and responsibilities strong theme in government policy; participation encouraged through a 'duty to involve' and other 'soft' measures. Not enshrined as a right. Strong cross-party commitment.	Enshrined in law. Strong sense of entitlement among NGOs, but patchy implementation. Currently under central state control.

	Bulgaria	England and Wales	Nicaragua
Political culture			
Citizen expectations of the state	Highly dependent, but mistrustful. Citizens seek advancement through the market.	High expectations as a legacy of the welfare state.	Citizens mobilise to make demands of the state, but also seek their own solutions given the low capacity of the state.
Sense of collective agency	Limited: long history of authoritarian external rule and patronage leads to high deference to authority and little sense of collective agency. History of compulsory state-led associations and corruption. Minimal sector identity: 'independent' forms of activism fragmented.	Fairly strong but fears of cooption: long history of collective action, highly professionalised voluntary sector to small solidaristic community based groups. Increasingly high profile recognition in policy accompanied by decline of traditional labour movement.	Strong: A history of struggle and strong social movements, low deference to authority and a strong sense of agency but dependent on 'mother' organisations (such as the church) and political patronage.

expectations of the state, and a cultural sense of collective agency. Table 2 summarises the situation in each region at the time of the study (2006–08) with regard to these.

In summary, the study identified three broad configurations of the governance spaces or 'fields' within which third sector actors were engaging and three corresponding responses from third sector organisations. In Bulgaria – in a statist regime – it characterised the relationship with the state as 'manipulated' and the response of third sector organisations as fatalistic; in Nicaragua – in a Southern regime – the relationship with the state was described as clientelist, but the third sector response as contentious or dissenting, while in England and Wales, the study described the relationship with the state as institutionalised and the third sector response as self disciplined. There were differences within each region – between old and new, between the more professionalised and smaller community-based organisations in England and Wales, and between party allegiances and welfare fields in Nicaragua. But the contentious response in Nicaragua contrasted strongly with the more pragmatic disciplined stance in England and

Wales, and the fatalistic stance in Bulgaria. The strong roots of the Nicaraguan third sector organisations in a social movement tradition appeared to be critical – as Crossley would suggest – in maintaining their contentious response. Bulgaria lacked any tradition of dissenting third sector activity. England and Wales, on the contrary, do have a strong dissenting tradition, but – at the time of the study – traditional routes of dissent had been disappearing at local level and partnership appeared to be the 'only game in town'.

This comparison underlined the importance of civic activists and third sector organisations having alternative anchors and networks beyond the state if they were to develop alternative agendas and nurture the belief that change is possible – 'popular spaces' from which they could enter 'invited spaces'. Indeed, in Nicaragua, local activists had spurned the invited space offered and created their own space into which they invited external actors. The research also highlighted the need to take into account external actors beyond the national context, such as international NGOs in the case of Nicaragua or the European Union in the case of Bulgaria, the nature of the party political system and the degree of centralisation/decentralisation of the state in order to understand local responses.

Since the research was completed, there has been a major change in government in both countries, and the ruling ideologies in question. It remains to be seen how this will affect the relationships between the state and the third sector in each country. In England and Wales, for example, there is an ideological move away from collaborative relationships on the part of the current government to a wholesale adoption of neoliberal principles. Coupled with the impact of austerity measures on government funding to the sector, there are signs that the 'radical habitus' of the past is being reawakened – at least in some parts of the sector (Taylor, 2012a).[2]

Discussion

This chapter has considered the context in which third sector organisations operate and how this might affect their capacity to foster active citizenship. It has explored the place of the sector in different welfare regimes and models of democracy and considered how far the sector has been coopted as the boundaries between the sectors blur and hybridise. As such, it has revisited the question of whether of

---

[2]   See, for example, the NCIA inquiry into voluntary services, www.independentaction. net/category/inquiry-voluntary-services/.

how far 'sector' is a useful concept and argued instead for a dynamic understanding of the third sector terrain as a tension field between the state, the market and communities. There are parallels here with Gramsci's approach to these relationships, as set out in Chapter Two.

It has then drawn on recent research to suggest different ways in which third sector organisations respond to the challenges of incorporation. The themes that it raises will be picked up again in future chapters, particularly Chapters Seven and Eight, which will consider further the challenges posed to activism in the sector and the role of social movements (Chapter Nine). We now move on, in Part 2, to explore different forms of active citizenship and how they manifest themselves through third sector organisations.

Part 2
Forms of active citizenship

SIX

Active citizenship as civil commitment

Introduction

Chapter Two identified one particular type of active citizenship as civil commitment. This type of active citizenship is not about political activism but rather about preserving important assets and services in the community, generating social capital and encouraging social cohesion. Citizens actively work together to preserve and protect, to enhance and improve the community in which they live. They provide services to those who would otherwise do without; they keep the wheels turning. They often avoid confrontation and 'things political'. Following the outline of the claims concerning the third sector that were identified in Chapter Four, this chapter examines further some of the claims that have been made about the role of active citizenship as civil commitment, exploring research relating to the civil commitment of volunteers: where they come from; what motivates them; how they benefit; and what they achieve. Volunteers have been seen as being at the core of social capital generation with volunteerism being oriented to fulfilling social obligations. However, volunteers are not simply passive and obedient subjects but display considerable agency, not only in maintaining existing services and organisations but on occasion in challenging existing practices.

Associationalism

This kind of citizenship as active civil commitment has been explicated through communitarian theory and the theory of associationalism, both of which have been introduced in preceding chapters. Most simply, communitarian theory is based on a commitment to community. Communitarians are concerned to redress the *anomie* engendered by neoliberalism and the erosion of identity and the lack of social solidarity in modern liberal societies. Communitarian theory rests on the argument that a cohesive and productive society requires cooperative enquiry and cooperative endeavour. To have cooperation it is necessary for members of society to accept their mutual responsibilities (Etzioni, 1996; Tam, 1998). For example, it is only when people embrace a cooperative approach to life that inclusive communities can be built. From this perspective the major task of civil society is to find ways of ensuring cooperative approaches and acceptance of mutual responsibilities. Third sector organisations offer sites for launching and reinforcing such cooperation.

From a communitarian perspective, a strong associational life is the bedrock of civil society. As Edwards (2004, p 18) argues, the most common normative understanding of civil society is based on the view that it provides the sphere, *par excellence*, where robust associational life is generated. Following de Tocqueville (1969), associationalism has come to refer to relations that are freely chosen and constructed around shared purposes or interests. It is based on a commitment of people to work together and to agree on common methods and rules. Associationalism nurtures civil society and active citizenship in many ways. It can engender cohesive communities, based not on a forced solidarity or homogeneity, but on informed acceptance of difference and respect for others. As Hirst explains, associationalism is based on the argument that 'human welfare and liberty are both best served when as many of the affairs of a society as possible are managed by voluntary and democratically self-governing associations' (1994, p 112)

Associationalism is also linked with high levels of trust and tolerance. Its advocates argue that, through involvement in associational life, citizens develop the capacities for sociability and trust (Warren, 2001, p 225). Underpinning this argument is the view that when people associate with each other in the context of mutual respect they become more tolerant and trusting. As community members become engaged in local events they come to understand their interdependence and they develop habits of mediation and representation. Importantly, they learn how to work together across differences.

Civil society and active citizenship are increasingly seen as valuable in themselves, and as a means of generating shared understandings and perspectives of the public interest. Interestingly, an NCVO study found that people are more likely to see civil society and active citizenship as civil commitment, as engaging with others, rather than as civic commitment involving engagement with political processes and institutions (Jochum et al, 2005). The focus of civil commitment for most people is contextualised in local needs and services (see Chapter Four). This theme is consistent with Walzer's civil society argument: in his view, citizenship is not necessarily about political activism, but about the pluralism of associational life in which men and women perform a great variety of useful work (Walzer, 1995, p 173).

Social capital

The theoretical concerns of communitarianism and associationalism are linked to the study of social capital. Social capital is an essential ingredient in community cohesion and wellbeing, from these perspectives. Studies have indicated, for example, that regions and groups measuring high in social capital also have a variety of positive outcomes beyond economic advantage, such as improved health and wellbeing, reduced levels of crime and better educational outcomes (Putnam, 2000; Halpern, 2005; Onyx and Bullen, 2000). As Chapter Four reported, Putnam et al (1993, p 167) defines social capital as 'those features of social organization, such as trust, norms and networks that can improve the efficiency of society by facilitating coordinated actions'. For him and others, social capital is a basic resource that is used to maintain and enhance community cohesion and collective action in promoting community–wide civic health. Bourdieu on the other hand defines social capital as 'the sum of the resources, actual or virtual, that accrue to an individual or a group by virtue of possessing a durable network of more or less institutionalised relationships of mutual acquaintance and recognition' (Bourdieu and Wacquant, 1992, p 119). For Bourdieu, social capital is a core strategy in the struggle for dominance within a social field. His focus is not on collaborative action but on the struggle for power and wealth and, in particular, the strategies adopted by elite groups to maintain their relative advantage. Other scholars have adopted a middle ground that acknowledges the capacity of social capital to be a productive resource, but also recognises it as a strategy used by marginal groups in their struggle for economic survival and human rights (Woolcock and Narayan, 2001; Halpern, 2005; Onyx et al, 2007).

Despite these different theoretical approaches, there is a growing consensus that social capital in practice must be defined in terms of networks that are durable and mutual with norms and sanctions to enforce their interactions. There is also widespread agreement that social capital is a complex multilayered concept with several components, though scholars disagree as to which elements are core and which peripheral to its definition. In particular, one point of discussion concerns the centrality of trust. For some it is critical (Putnam et al, 1993; Fukuyama, 1995; Schneider, 2009), for others simply a fortunate side effect (Portes, 1998; Schuller, 2001; Woolcock,

2001). Other scholars have emphasised different core elements of social capital, elements such as reciprocity (Putnam et al, 1993) and social agency (Leonard and Onyx, 2004).

Agency and networks

In understanding active citizenship we can draw on two fundamental points about human life. One is that we are basically social beings; experiencing life is an intersubjective activity. The second is that we are agentic, that is we are capable of deciding, choosing and initiating action (Leonard, 1997). In the context of active citizenship, intersubjective action occurs through the formation of networks. However, as recent analyses suggest, social capital is more about process than structure and includes as an essential component, that of social agency.

Evidence points to the significance of agency or a 'can do' attitude within the social network (Onyx and Bullen, 2000; Johannisson and Olaison, 2007; Williams and Guerra, 2011). Human interaction is marked by intentionality. It is not enough simply to maintain networks of mutual support. As Sampson notes, 'networks have to be activated to be ultimately meaningful' (Sampson, 2006, p 153). Hence Portes and Sensenbrenner (1998) define social capital in terms of 'expectations for action within a collectivity'. What is required is that networks mobilise into action, that is, they take the initiative in their own development. Communities that assume control over their own destiny are better able to deal with crises and natural disasters, as well as their own disadvantage. Sampson (2006) concludes that collective efficacy signifies an emphasis on shared beliefs in a collective capacity for action combined with a sense of engagement on the part of citizens. He found evidence that neighbourhoods with this combined sense of social cohesion and social control, in other words with high levels of collective efficacy, had lower levels of violence, controlling for other variables such as the effects of poverty and ethnicity.

Most discussions of social capital distinguish between 'bonding', and 'bridging' social capital (Putnam, 2000; Woolcock and Narayan, 2001). Bonding social capital is usually characterised as having dense, multifunctional ties and strong but localised trust. It is considered essential for a sense of personal identity, support and belonging. However, to the extent that it creates narrow, intolerant communities, it can be oppressive even to those who otherwise benefit.

Bridging is more complex. As the name implies, it is about reaching beyond these immediate networks of family and friends. Bridging is important for personal and community development (Woolcock and

Narayan, 2001). It can be used in at least three different ways: to cross demographic divides, notably ethnic divides; to bridge structural holes between networks; and to access information and resources outside the community in question. However, as Schneider (2009) and others (Leonard and Onyx, 2003) have argued, bridging is not simply a matter of weak or transient ties, but of more formal ties which also require the development of trust over time. Evidence is increasingly making clear that both bonding and bridging capital are essential resources for individual and collective wellbeing (Putnam, 2000; Leonard and Onyx, 2004; Edwards and Onyx, 2007; Schneider, 2009).

The individual vs the collective

Putnam (2000) sees social capital as a collective resource, located in social networks that are potentially open to all. Bourdieu similarly recognised the ways in which social capital is generated within durable social networks – although he is also concerned with the advantages individuals gain from social capital resources, which may benefit the more powerful and better networked at the expense of the less powerful and less effectively networked.

More recently, some economists have attempted to identify social capital as an individual possession, to be accumulated and used like any other form of capital, regardless of what other people may do (Glaeser et al, 2002). We argue that, by definition, and consistent with communitarian theory and associationalism as well as with Bourdieu, social capital adheres to the connections between people that are a quality of the social rather than the individual. However, as Putnam (2000) and others (including Bourdieu) have also noted, the individual may access the resources available in the collective and may do so to their personal advantage. For example, individuals in organisations are able to use their networks to gain new employment opportunities. But others have argued that, to the extent that the individual continues to draw from the collective social capital resource without contributing to it, this resource will ultimately be drained of its dynamic renewal. This raises the problem of the 'free rider'. As Ostrom explains:

> Whenever one person cannot be excluded from the benefits that others provide, each person is motivated not to contribute to the joint effort, but to free-ride on the efforts of others. If all participants choose to free-ride, the collective benefit will not be produced. (Ostrom, 1990, p 6)

If social capital resides in the social connections between people, then logically, the best measure of it also requires measures of the collective. In fact most attempts to measure social capital make use of individual survey instruments (for example, Onyx and Bullen, 2000) in which individual scores are aggregated to provide a picture of the larger collective. As a consequence of this approach, there has been little effort to apply the concept of social capital to the organisation as a whole, that is, to the organisation separate from the individuals who make it up. Several studies have sought to distinguish between individual and meso-level organisational social capital (Schneider, 2009) and to explain how associations may institutionalise social capital at the organisational level (Wollebæk and Strømsnes, 2008). Schneider (2009, p 644) defines organisational social capital as 'established, trust based networks among organisations or communities supporting a particular non-profit, that an organisation can use to further its goals'. She provides considerable evidence of the role of organisational social capital that is independent of the people involved and is contextualised by that organisation's history and reputation. So, even as key individuals move on, the organisation can continue to draw on its organisational networks as important resources. Just as with individual networks, organisational network ties are reciprocal, enforceable and durable. Schneider further makes use of Bourdieu's concept of cultural capital to explain how subcultural differences within and between organisations help to define social capital networks. Thus, organisations are likely to form social capital networks with those other organisations within the same field that have one or more core values or cultural attributes in common. Resources are more likely to be shared and collaborative action developed between organisations within this network.

The implications of these studies are that social capital occurs at both the individual and the organisational level. The two are related but not synonymous. While collective social capital, as a commons, is available for the advantage and use of the individual, it is the collective social capital itself that becomes institutionalised to shape the internal cohesion and strength of the community in question.

The interaction of the capitals

One of the most significant of Bourdieu's contributions was his broader sociological analysis of the role of capital. He argues that there are a number of different capitals, all of which are linked and under some circumstances can be converted into other forms of capital. For example, he argues:

> Capital can present itself in three fundamental guises: as economic capital, which is immediately and directly convertible into money and may be institutionalized in the form of property rights; as cultural capital, which is convertible, on certain conditions, into economic capital and may be institutionalized in the form of educational qualifications; and as social capital made up of social obligations (connections) which is convertible in certain conditions, into economic capital ... (Bourdieu, 1986, p 242)

Bourdieu later adds the concept of 'symbolic capital', which alludes to the power of prestige or reputation that accrues when economic or cultural capital is recognised and acknowledged by others. He also defines cultural capital as having several subspecies, notably embodied cultural capital, objectified cultural capital and institutionalised cultural capital. Embodied cultural capital refers to long-lasting personal dispositions such as ethnicity, religion, family background and linguistic codes. Objectified cultural capital refers to the value and power of cultural products. Institutional cultural capital refers mainly to educational qualifications as formally recognised (Bourdieu, 1986).

Bourdieu in his analysis privileges economic capital as the primary source of wealth and power; other capitals are mainly useful insofar as they may be ultimately convertible into economic capital. However, other scholars are more interested in the interdependencies between capitals for their own sake. Of particular relevance here is the link between social capital and human capital. Human capital resembles Bourdieu's institutional cultural capital and is defined by the OECD, for example, as encompassing skills, competences and qualifications (Schuller, 2007). Schuller argues that the value of social capital depends in large measure on its linkage to other capitals, especially human capital, just as human capital requires access to social capital in order to actualise its potential. Both are important ends in themselves but each is enhanced by the presence of the other capital. The generation of these capitals, as emphasised by Bourdieu and others, is seen as an ongoing process within the communities in question, one dependent on complex sets of relationships. That is, we are not examining an extant 'stock' of capital, but an ongoing process of generation.

Volunteering

Following Wilson and Musick (1997), volunteer work is defined here as time given freely for the benefit of others. It is productive activity, usually involving collective action and involving an ethical relationship between volunteer and recipient. We take volunteering to refer to the willing provision of unpaid labour. Most analyses restrict the concept to formal volunteering within the context of a formal organisation and it is usually measured as such. The provision of the unpaid work of caring and informal neighbourly support is not usually considered volunteering and is seldom measured, though it is also likely to contribute to social capital. This is referred to here as 'informal volunteering'. In all these cases, unpaid labour is conceptualised as a contribution to the wellbeing of others and the community at large

There are indeed several quite different kinds of volunteering, all of which may contribute to a healthy civil society. Rochester et al (2010) identify three different but overlapping paradigms of volunteering, the first being the dominant paradigm in the UK (and other OECD countries), which emphasises the service aspect of volunteering, based on altruism and charity. The second is termed the civil society paradigm based on mutual support, self help and activism. The third, especially dominant in Scandinavia but also widely used elsewhere, is termed serious leisure, and emphasises the serious but unpaid pursuit of various forms of sport, recreation, performance arts, music, heritage and lifelong learning. At the broader level all these forms of volunteering provide the vital role of participation within the civil life of the community. All these activities contribute to the development of social capital.

Factors that influence the decision to volunteer include both individual attributes and motives on the one hand and contextual effects that encourage or discourage volunteering on the other (Wilson, 2000). While volunteering normally involves an element of altruistic giving, a large body of literature has identified that volunteering typically benefits both volunteer and recipient (Rochester et al, 2010) and that the motivation to volunteer may best be understood in terms of benefits gained by the volunteer.

The literature on volunteer motivations is large and complex. However, one of the most overarching perspectives on volunteer motivation locates it within a set of deeper psychological needs. Self-determination theory (SDT) identifies three core psychological needs – for competence, connectedness and autonomy – all of which are oriented towards personal growth (Deci and Ryan, 2000). SDT suggests that:

> It is part of the adaptive design of the human organism to engage in interesting activities, to exercise capacities, to pursue connectedness in social groups, and to integrate intrapsychic and interpersonal experiences into a relative unity. (Deci and Ryan, 2000, p 229)

This theory can incorporate other typologies of volunteer motivation. For example, the Volunteer Functions Inventory (Clary et al, 1996) identified six motivations:

* values – the individual volunteer expresses or acts on important values like humanitarianism and altruism;
* understanding – the volunteer is seeking to learn more about the world or exercise skills that are often unused;
* enhancement – one can grow and develop psychologically through volunteer activities;
* career – the volunteer has the goal of gaining career-related experience through volunteering;
* social – volunteering allows an individual to strengthen his or her social relationships;
* protective – the individual uses volunteering to reduce negative feelings, such as guilt, or to address personal problems.

These six motivations fit well within SDT. A number of empirical studies support this approach to volunteering motivation. In a national Australian survey, the two main reasons given for volunteering are to help others or the community and to gain personal satisfaction (ABS, 2002). Narushima (2005) found volunteering to be a potentially transformative mechanism for older adults sustaining their sense of wellbeing and developing generativity. A major study in the UK (Brodie et al, 2011) tracked participation and volunteering activities of citizens in three different localities using a life story approach and found that the kind of activities and the depth of involvement varied over time according to life stage, personal motivation and available resources. This suggests that volunteering is a highly meaningful activity for volunteers, one that has the potential to contribute to their personal growth. It is also possible to argue that much of that volunteering experience involves the development of meaningful relationships within a caring environment (although the realities of different experiences of volunteering may be very different in practice, as subsequent chapters illustrate).

The relationship between volunteering and social capital

The relationship between volunteering and social capital has not been fully explored in the literature. In some cases, volunteering is seen as an equivalent concept to social capital. Some international comparative studies even use 'rate of volunteering' as a proxy for social capital (see, for example, the discussion by Dekker, 2002). However, the relationship is more complex than that would suggest. For example, Putnam (2000) questions the connection on the grounds that, while reciprocity is usually seen as an important aspect of social capital, reciprocity per se is not considered a feature of volunteering. Social capital, he argues, is about doing good *with* other people rather than doing good *for* other people. We would argue that most volunteering contains more reciprocity (that is, mutual gain) than this emphasis on altruism would suggest but also that not all volunteering is necessarily beneficial for others. Nonetheless, many forms of volunteering do generate social capital of some sort, although not all social capital is based on volunteering (Onyx and Leonard, 2000).

Volunteering and social capital are also empirically linked. A major empirical study (Onyx and Bullen, 2000) developed a measure of several aspects of social capital. Using this social capital scale, it found that formal volunteers in New South Wales (NSW) community centres scored the highest social capital scores of any group measured (such as community workers, participants, social service clients), and across all measured factors (Onyx and Bullen, 2001). Those who volunteered on a formal basis were also actively involved in informal networks of care and support in addition to their formal volunteering work. The study concluded that formal volunteers can generate considerable social capital.

While there is a growing recognition that volunteering is important and does contribute to social capital, however, there is very little understanding of the micro-processes involved. A qualitative study of volunteers and their clients examined these processes (Onyx et al, 2003). This study found that the roles of volunteers are fourfold. First, volunteers play a key role as community builders by creating new organisations and services. Second, volunteers play a key role in developing bonding, intracommunity links. Third, volunteers play a mediating role in community networks, particularly between professional and lay networks. Fourth, given their key location in community networks, volunteers also play a key role in developing bridging links with other organisations and communities of interest. Given this key locational position, volunteers may be instrumental in creating or alternately obstructing broader community networks. That is, they may play a potential bridge builder or gatekeeper role in network building, a role that may facilitate or impede inclusivity.

The data provides rich evidence of social capital and provides some insights into how this is developed. The study examined volunteering in terms of four categories of role: developing services; bonding; mediating; and bridging. The first two categories provided the type of connection that might have been expected. Volunteers as active citizens worked together to identify, create, fund and govern new services to meet identified needs in the community. The study examined volunteering in several rural and outer urban areas of NSW and found that virtually all services in all communities seemed to start like this. Frequently, the study suggests, it was the collective act of volunteers that established new services, including the establishment of branch services of existing organisations in new areas. As these services became established, then government funding would often be sought and maybe obtained. Some services in this study, such as parent support and senior citizens outings, had never received funding and continued to be provided on a volunteer basis. Some organisations continued to generate considerable fundraising for themselves and required little if any government funding. Indeed, some, particularly faith-based, organisations actually subsidised government services. Other organisations received funding for the services they provided and over time tended to become professionalised. The volunteers that established the service then took on a governance role, as members of the management committee or board. Eventually, if such a role became less attractive or necessary, the service would pass into professional hands, often within a large organisation. In this case, volunteers continued to play a token or marginalised role, but their tasks tended to become deskilled and their vision limited.

Even at this marginalised, deskilled end of the spectrum, however, the study found considerable evidence of bonding social capital generated within the community, providing support and connections to clients and members of the organisation, creating wider friendship networks among the community of volunteers and, more broadly, creating a web of caring relationships in the wider community. Almost every transcript of clients, volunteers and coordinators provided exemplars of this networking and mutual support. It is this work that created the 'glue' so often referred to in the social capital literature.

The other two role categories – mediating and bridging – were less obvious. However, the potential mediating role of volunteers may have been the most important of all in creating and maintaining a sense of community. Commentators such as Giddens (1990) have argued that our society is increasingly managed by highly qualified and specialised professionals, with citizens expected to place their trust in these expert systems. But in the shift from the traditional trust of known acquaintances to the trust in the expert, something may be lost. Indeed, there is evidence of a growing distrust of expert systems as citizens become more aware of the contested nature of much expert 'knowledge' (Beck, 1999). Onyx et al's (2003) study also suggests that there may be pressure for professionals to produce more, for more people, more quickly, at lower cost. Time is limited. Fear of litigation requires caution in not appearing too personally attached to individual clients. There is often no time or opportunity for the house visit, for the relaxed conversation, for the affectionate enquiry into people's welfare. Experts may well provide a technically excellent service, but they are less likely to provide the warmth of the human connection. Their technical knowledge also may provide a communication barrier insofar as they adopt a technical language that is beyond the easy grasp of the lay person. Intimidated, the client often fears to ask for the information they need in a readily accessible language.

This gap may be filled by volunteers. Often the volunteers in question are either former professionals themselves, or they have gained considerable training and experience such that they may play a paraprofessional role. But they are likely to have more time. They are able and willing to visit the housebound. They have time to talk. They can relate to the personal experience of the other and can provide the information requested, or at least they know where to find the required information. Above all, as both volunteers and recipients in the study noted, they can often (not always) express acceptance and respect for the person regardless of who that person is. In terms of Giddens' levels of trust, the study found that volunteers may combine the two levels of traditional and expert trust. For this reason, other members of the community may turn to them in preference to the professional, and disclose more. The volunteer then becomes a crucial node in the communication networks, connecting the client/community with the world of expert systems.

The fourth role category is the most problematic. Bridging may have several meanings. It may mean accessing external resources of expertise or finance or opportunity. It may mean bridging between different organisations within the community. It often means acceptance of difference and a bridging across demographic divides. It may mean breaking down traditional hierarchies of discourse and privilege. Communities may have high levels of bonding social capital yet remain intolerant of outsiders and of marginal groups. This is not only disadvantageous for those so marginalised, but also prevents access to new ideas and skills that may be necessary for the continued survival of the community as a whole.

What then is the role of volunteers in the generation of bridging social capital? The data provides mixed evidence. There are many examples of volunteer actions that served to build bridges across demographic divides within the community as well as important bridges to the outside world of people, ideas and skills. However, there are also a few examples of volunteer action that prevented such bridges of inclusivity, or even destroyed those that had been built. Of course professionals and ordinary citizens may equally build or destroy bridges. What remains to be identified are the conditions that maximise the likelihood of positive bridging networks emerging.

The conclusion of this discussion is that volunteers should be seen as central to the creation and maintenance of local networks of trust, reciprocity and the potential to identify and solve problems. The evidence cited here questions Putnam's (2000) separation of volunteering from the generation of social capital. To the contrary, volunteers may play crucial and quite specific roles in generating new services, creating bonding links, mediating between professionals and the wider community, and in building bridging links within and between communities. Their location as network nodes places them in a position to play a vital gatekeeping role, or as 'keeper of the culture'. Such a position bestows great power. Such power may be used destructively, to prevent the formation of bridging links. But it may also be used positively to facilitate the development of a strong and inclusive community.

A critique of volunteering and social capital

Social capital is not in itself either good or evil. It is simply the potential for collective action. How this collective action is used depends entirely on those who use it and the nature of their agendas. More powerful groups may use their social capital to reproduce their relative advantages – at the expense of the less powerful. Another example of the negative mobilisation of social capital can be seen in the operation of terrorist groups. Less obvious is the use of the norms of social capital to maintain closed and exclusive boundaries thus preventing others from gaining admission into the community in question, or even preventing members of the community from moving outside it. Migrant subcultures for instance may, in the interests of maintaining their ethnic identity, actively discourage their own young people from moving beyond the community to gain employment or other external benefits (Portes, 1998). Social capital may be seen by its community of users as virtuous and beneficial, but this may not appear so to the wider society in which it is embedded.

Similarly, volunteering is very often labelled as virtuous, an activity for the public good. But it also has a shadow underbelly. As identified in the previous section, volunteering often brings strong benefits to the volunteers themselves, which may provide the main motivation for volunteering. On occasion this personal motivation may dominate the volunteer relationship and corrupt the public good nature of it. Volunteering may provide a pathway to paid employment. It may also be used quite cynically to augment a CV or to gain considerable political power – note, for instance, the considerable vaunting of volunteer credentials among those seeking election. This is evidence of the quest for personal power through apparently charitable but actually narrowly instrumental actions.

In the past, the trade union movement and the feminist movement both regarded volunteering with deep suspicion. In this context, volunteering was seen as the exploitation of labour in order to provide services cheaply (see for instance Baldock, 1998). It is no coincidence that the vast majority of caring volunteering is done by women, who are already marginalised and their work devalued within the market and the home. As Chapter Five has already indicated, volunteering may also be used and abused, to legitimise the erosion of public services, spearheading processes of increasing marketisation.

Governments of varying persuasions provide funding at less than the market value of the cost of providing services on the assumption that the difference will be made up by volunteering. Indeed, in recent years, in Australia and elsewhere, this has led to a growth industry, or the corporatisation of volunteering, involving the training, management and monitoring of volunteers on a systematic basis and on a large scale within large, corporatised charities. Within this managerialist ideology, there is increasing pressure on organisations to manage their volunteers within strict legislative guidelines (Leonard et al, 2004). Volunteers then become part of a vertical, asymmetrical power hierarchy within the organisation, being subordinate to the paid professionals but asserting considerable power over the recipient client, who is then an object of charity (Brown et al, 2000). Volunteering so designed is likely to destroy existing social capital relations (which must be essentially horizontal) rather than to enhance social capital formation. Although even here, even the marginalised volunteer may still manage to operate in a productive manner (Onyx et al, 2003).

The cooption of volunteering by the state reaches its most negative implications when it is coerced, as in the requirements of 'work for the dole' or other forms of compulsory conscription such as is still identified in modern China but increasingly too in the US, the UK and Australia. This is 'volunteering' in name only. It is also worth noting, however, that volunteering is a largely Western concept. In this respect, it is important to understand the cultural contexts of volunteering. While in many cultures, for example. migrant cultures in Australia, people are involved in unpaid help for others in their communities, they do not recognise this as volunteering but simply see it is something one does as a member of a neighbourhood or community. While migrant groups typically record low levels of formal volunteering (ABS, 2001), in reality they engage in extremely high levels of informal volunteering, outside the boundaries of a formal organisation. This may also be the case for many community activists. This is an area that requires more investigation.

In all of this, the role of the third sector organisation requires special scrutiny. On the one hand it is the organisation that provides the structure for considerable engagement of the community, including volunteering. On the other hand we know less about what happens outside the boundaries of the organisation, in the structural voids of civil society and the informal actions of citizens, although recent research in the UK, for example, has focused on what it calls 'below the radar' organisations (McCabe and Phillimore, 2012) and on micro-volunteering (Browne et al, 2013).

The role of third sector organisations and their members: an international study

Further empirical evidence of the role of active citizens in developing and maintaining strong community links is found in a large international study (Onyx et al, 2011) involving some 1,610 respondents (approximately 30% of whom identified as formal volunteers) across eleven towns in six countries: Australia, England, Netherlands, Russia, Spain and Sweden. Within each of the six countries, the study involved third sector organisations within one major regional centre and one small village (only one town was successfully surveyed in Russia). In addition, qualitative interviews were conducted with approximately five organisations in each town. The qualitative interview data contributed to the interpretation of the questionnaire responses.

Questionnaire items covered a range of attitudes and behaviours, including attitudes to political action, at a local and national level, and the selection of preferred actions to potential scenarios that might affect their local community, as well as reasons for joining their organisation. Both the qualitative cases and the survey data provided some consistent themes and a clear though complex picture of active citizenship, as seen from the citizen's perspective.

Two major, and apparently contradictory, themes emerged from the data. On the one hand, citizens were usually actively engaged in several organisations. They were well informed about local and global issues and believed that good citizens were those who work to make the world a better place. They were concerned with issues of disadvantage and social justice and worked towards ameliorating these issues. On the other hand, citizens by and large avoided active oppositional engagement in the political process (a finding that is discussed further in Chapter Eight). They preferred to work collaboratively with government and to work at the local level to solve local problems. The first is a theme of active engagement, proactively working for a better world. The second provides a theme of social maintenance, of support for the existing structures and facilities in the community, while providing relief for the disadvantaged often within conservative charity or welfare organisations.

This suggests that many, perhaps the majority of respondents would partially fail the criteria of citizenship established by Kymlicka (2002). For Kymlicka, this kind of active citizenship requires not only that people be well informed, that is to say they listen, but also that they be prepared to publicly debate the alternatives, thus encouraging better decisions and understanding of political actions. However, our citizens did keep a watching brief to ensure that existing institutions were safeguarded and that the principles of non-discrimination were extended from government to the practical everyday concerns of civil society. And they were also clearly prepared to act when necessary, usually to defend against the loss of a local and valued service.

While the respondents avoided political activism, they were nonetheless proactive in civil society (Onyx et al, 2011). So, for example, nearly half defined a 'good citizen' as one who works to change the world for the better. There was consistent evidence of both proactivity and associationalism. That is citizens wished to be active agents of change and to act collectively, to work together to solve problems faced in the community. This was also one of the core factors in reasons for joining a specific community organisation; many joined to assist in social change. Of course, the extent to which active citizens can bring about social change is always circumscribed by contextual factors, including structural inequalities, a point that was not acknowledged by our respondents. This theme is consistent with Walzer's civil society argument cited above (Walzer, 1995, p 173)

Consistent with Walzer's argument, much of the work of citizens is at the local level. Indeed some of the survey data support the position of 'think global, act local'. Responses to the scenarios presented in the questionnaires reinforced that perspective. A dominant view was that even global problems could only be tackled through local action. An important motivation to work within the local community was to help those in need. Nearly half of all respondents placed this as equal first in defining a 'good citizen'. This understanding of a 'good citizen' might well have derived from the type of third sector activity that the respondent was involved in. Many of the case study organisations, for example, were concerned with practical assistance for people with a disability. Others were concerned with practical programmes for youth. In response to a scenario concerning refugees, where respondents were asked to identify an appropriate way of dealing with the issues arising from the scenario, the dominant response was to 'Work with local community organisations to discover how to best assist'. This work was largely positioned within a charity or residual welfare frame. However, many people interviewed also placed a strong emphasis on local self determination, self help and self advocacy, such as the Older Citizens group in Ballarat and the Breast Cancer Support Association in the UK.

This motivation – to work within the local community to help those in need – also fits within a model of active citizenship that places emphasis on the maintenance of community networks and services, on cohesion and the enactment of social capital. Such engagement by citizens has been shown to have various desirable consequences such as improved health and wellbeing, reduced crime and the potential to address a collective emergency (see for instance Halpern, 2005). Many community sports and services organisations (such as bush fire brigades in Australia) are of this sort. Such citizenship is non-oppositional, and involves support for churches and other institutions that keep the community together. It is this aspect of civil society that may be regarded as hegemonic in that it has the effect of maintaining the status quo, including existing power relations, in the interests of harmony. However, it involves the active engagement of citizens in support of the community.

Being a member of a local community-based organisation provided an ideal avenue for active citizenship. So, for example, important reasons cited by Onyx et al's (2011) respondents for joining their organisation included 'to help those in need' (44%), 'to change the world for the better' (31%) and 'as an avenue for activism' (32%). But it was also important to respondents that the organisation 'provided an opportunity to meet different people' (34%). While some people joined an organisation explicitly to effect social change, others joined for the organisation's social networks and the opportunities for positive action that these provided. These attitudes were about helping people and maintaining community, in a gentler way. Interestingly, many respondents valued the welcoming interpersonal style of the organisation (30%), even though this was not seen as a primary factor in the success of the organisation. Indeed, many people joined third sector organisations for the opportunity for personal development, including the opportunity to meet different kinds of people. This is where the interpersonal and the political meet. People wish to effect both social and personal change, a point which resonates with Touraine's perspective on living a responsible and happy life (Touraine, 2000, p 297).

The study concludes that, while there are variations in approach to active citizenship, there are very strong common themes (Onyx et al, 2011). Active citizens wish to work collectively and collaboratively to solve the immediate social and environmental problems faced by their community. Community maintenance and social change were not necessarily seen as mutually exclusive. Making the world a better place could be seen as social change, but in the eyes of these respondents, this social change could be incremental. Acts of citizenship were by and large pragmatic and practical, assisting those in need, enriching their culture and preserving what was valued in the community. Activism may be in defence of preserving local heritage that is threatened. Active citizens may prefer a collaborative to a confrontational political style. Few were visionary in the sense of working for a radically different new world or of challenging existing power structures. They were working towards the maintenance of what was seen as being good in their community, while rectifying what they saw as obstacles to this. They wished to ameliorate the distress of disadvantaged people without radically calling the status quo into question. But they were prepared to fight if necessary, if what they saw as the good was severely threatened, and/or to resist the unjust or negative effects of action by the state or the market. Their citizenship was embodied in the form of the third sector organisations to which they devoted their energy. Importantly, people emerged as being involved in organisations because they cared about the particular issue to be remedied. The specific issue emerged as the driving force of involvement, not a desire to be an active citizen in the general or abstract sense.

This view of active citizenship, which avoids political activism, resonates with Turner's analysis (2001) and with Touraine's analysis in particular. As Touraine notes, new practices centre on 'concrete issues involving or relating to direct interpersonal relations' (2000, p 57). What the studies cited here demonstrate then is the extent to which active citizenship in third sector organisations is driven at the grassroots level, rather than through the mechanisms of the political machinery. They reveal the ways in which active citizenship can seek to create the conditions for the rights of all to live a responsible and happy life. Sometimes that appears as a conservative form of maintenance, but equally it can appear as a creative new form of association and mutual support. The active citizen is one who seeks the freedom of the personal subject, in solidarity and cooperation with others through third sector organisation.

SEVEN

Active citizenship as civil commitment: cultural considerations

Introduction

This chapter further investigates manifestations of active citizenship as civil commitment in the third sector. It draws on empirical studies in non-OECD countries with different historical and cultural backgrounds. However, before exploring these empirical studies, it is important to consider a concern that arises periodically in discussions of the global ramifications of the romance with civil society and its affiliated concepts. This concern, which Chapter Three touched on, revolves around the question of the applicability of civil society concepts to non-Western settings. The 'Westernisation thesis', as it is often called in these discussions, holds that economic, political and social development are dominated, both intellectually and in practice, by Western assumptions (see Latouche, 1993; Escobar, 1995; Schuurman, 2000; Ziai, 2004; Rist, 2008). Westernisation can be seen as positive or negative for a country, depending on the perspective and values of the perceiver. For example, where democratic processes are held in high regard and 'the West' is equated with democratic values, then Westernisation is perceived to be a good thing. However, over the past decade, Western ideas of democracy have received a bad press from some quarters, based on revelations of corruption in Western democracies as well as the perceived hypocritical legitimation of interventions in other countries which have been championed as 'bringing democracy' to the people (by force and/or to facilitate neoliberal forms of economic development; Hanieh, 2013). Commentators have also pointed to the apparently failed experiments of democracy in the MENA (Middle East and North Africa) region.

Criticisms of attempts to 'democratise the world', of course, go back decades. By the 1990s there was a chorus of voices arguing that Western concepts of democracy and civil society were part of a crusade to 'Westernise' the whole world (Latouche, 1993; Escobar, 1995). From this perspective, civil society concepts are seen as part of the hegemonic armoury of the West. Other commentaries, such as on the global reach of civil society today, simply assume the universality of civil society concepts, without any explicit judgement of their value, although often implicitly accepting the positive contribution of civil society to all societies.

The ascendancy of commitment to human rights over the past 20 years has been of particular relevance to the study of citizenship internationally. One response to this ascendancy has been rejection of the principles of human rights on the basis of the argument that individual rights, democracy and a free and open public sphere are Western values and do not fit with the values of all cultures. Sen (1999) discusses this argument in relation to what is sometimes understood as the 'Asian values' or 'Asian particularism' argument. He considers the viewpoint that Asian cultures are intrinsically authoritarian and therefore not amenable to the application of human rights (Sen, 1999, p 231–2). His view is that in Asia, as in all regions of the world, there are many cultural traditions that are heterodox. Asia is a very vast area and involves a myriad of diverse cultures, which, as with all cultures, have fluid boundaries and are never static. In the 'Asian values' argument, he argues, Asia is reduced to a simplistic essentialised concept. The same applies to Africa (Sowa, 2014).

A similar problem occurs with the concept 'Western'. As Wieviorka (2012, p 227) points out, English terms, like those in all languages, are not static. The 'Westernisation thesis' fails to grasp the complex character of all cultures, including the ways in which they interpenetrate. Similarly, as Chapter Three argued, the idea of civil society is multidimensional and fluid. It can be politically and ideologically loaded, but it can provide strategic advantages to both crusading Western policy makers and anti-Western political movements alike. For example, in any setting, NGOs seeking support and aid might adopt the discourse of civil society for opportunistic purposes rather than as a discursive framework within which to construct practical relations of mutuality and collective endeavour.

Empirical study of the assumed or possible universality of specific concepts and practices would involve the investigation of equivalences in language and equivalences of phenomena across the globe, which would be a massive task. It is possible, however, to sketch out what might be involved in such an investigation and demonstrate this with examples. Take the issue of equivalences in language, for example. In regard to the term civil society, it is naïve to assume that this term civil society always has linguistic equivalents globally. The study of linguistics reveals the deeply circumscribed nature of equivalence between languages, including the many languages spoken in 'Western' societies. But this is not to argue that there are no cognate terms or that, when an English term is adopted in a non-English setting, it loses its original meaning entirely. Meanings change and they are modified, but not necessarily lost. The issue of equivalence of a phenomenon is a more difficult one. As discussed in Chapter Three, even Western understandings of the concept and practices of civil society vary.

Yet the idea of civil society embodies certain moral precepts about the equality of all humans, social imperatives concerning the importance of agency and freedom of expression, and association and political imperatives constructed around commitment to engagement with social, political, economic and cultural processes. While these precepts are deeply embedded in the histories of Western societies, they are also evident in non-Western societies, albeit often in different forms (Sen, 1999). There is a growing body of comparative knowledge about citizens' experiences of expressing their voices, participating in decisions that affect their lives and sharing solidarities (Gaventa, 2010). Regardless of whether there are terms in the various societies which describe participation as active citizenship, or indeed terms that describe civil commitment or social activism, *acts of citizenship* do exist, and are now being studied in new contexts, as indicated by Gaventa and Tandon (2010, p 3). All societies have processes through which people engage, politically, socially and culturally. Whether these engagements are always freely chosen or public, and can be understood through the idea of civil society, depends on a number of contextual factors. It is incumbent on researchers of civil society and active citizenship to explore the possible equivalence of forms of engagement.

As indicated earlier, one important way of investigating the veracity of the Westernisation thesis and *inter alia*, the universality of the concepts of civil society, is to start by undertaking empirical studies and describing acts of engagement in different settings, all the time probing their meanings. These are challenging tasks. One recent approach draws on the idea of interculturalism, which attempts to provide a way of understanding how we relate to each other in the context of the diversity of cultural encounters that are an increasing global reality in people's lives. Interculturalism emphasises recognition of both diversity and globalisation as permanent features of society, while at the same time understanding that human relations are based on concepts of interdependency and interconnectedness (Cantle, 2012). It involves curiosity and dialogue to find the areas of mutuality. At the same time, as Lewis (2001, p 5) argues in his discussion of the relevance of the idea of civil society in Africa, local context matters and the historic Western idea of civil society should not be applied too rigidly. For

Lewis, while the concept of civil society cannot be easily dismissed as having little meaning outside its Western origins, it should not be simply exported opportunistically for such purposes as government policy or academic analysis (Lewis, 2001, p 11).

The two empirical studies that follow describe active citizenship in different settings, focusing on manifestations of civil commitment. The first study is concerned with active citizenship in one context in Indonesia, focusing on the role of third sector organisations in response to the devastating earthquake and tsunami that hit the northern tip of Sumatra on 26 December 2004. The second study considers forms of active citizenship in a study of Russian NGOs.

The third sector and active citizenship in Indonesia

As previously indicated, one starting point for investigating the applicability of English concepts and terms of civil society is to probe for language equivalences. One of the difficulties in Indonesia is that there are more than 700 spoken languages. However, there is one language that is officially spoken by all Indonesians. This is Bahasa Indonesia, which is a version of the trading language of Malay. As a new official language, Bahasa Indonesia contains a number of words that are quite similar to English. For example, the English term third sector is simply translated into Bahasa Indonesia as *sektor* (sector) *ketiga* (third) and the term third sector organisation is translated as *organisasi sektor ketiga*. There are also terms in Bahasa Indonesia that broadly correspond to similar English terms. For example, the term civil society can be translated as *masyarakat madani* with *masyarakat* referring to a society, community or people. In government, academic and civil society circles the English acronym NGO is used quite widely and can be translated as *organisasi non-pemerintah* in Bahasa Indonesia. Similarly the English term 'civil society organisation' (CSO), which translates as *organisasi masyarakat madani*, accords with common English usages. In the study discussed below we use the term NGO to describe a third sector organisation, because this was the term most commonly used and understood in the interviews.

It is important to note that, during the repressive years of the Suharto's New Order regime (1965–98), the term NGO tended to be avoided because of its connotation as an 'anti-government organisation' (Nugroho, 2013). There are two terms which, unlike the terms CSO and NGO, have a solid Indonesian lineage. These are *lembaga swadaya masyarakat* (LSM), which was commonly used during the New Order regime and is often understood as *perkumpulan* or association; and *yayasan*, which can be understood as a foundation. These organisations are different legal entities, with *yayasan* being the older of these two, its history dating back to the Dutch colonial era. *Yayasan* are commonly connected with social, religious and educational functions, although they have also been used for profit and money-laundering activities (Antlov et al, 2005). There is also a term for citizenship in Indonesia. This is *kewarganegaraan*, which is linked to ideas of nationality and civics. As is the case in the English term active citizenship, the word *aktif*, derived from English, is added as a descriptor. Thus *kewarganegaraan aktif* translates to the English term active citizenship.

Post-tsunami reconstruction in Aceh

On Sunday 26 December 2004, an earthquake measuring 9.0 on the Richter scale occurred in the Indian Ocean where the Eurasian and Indo-Australian plates meet. The resulting tsunami directly affected 11 countries, killing up to 300,000 people. The closest land mass was the province of Aceh, or Negara Aceh Darussalam, the northern part of the Indonesian island of Sumatra. Over 800 kilometres of the coastal area of Aceh was flattened. No warning systems were in place and local populations were caught completely unprepared. While there was no final body count, over 130,000 people were said to have been killed and another 500,000 people displaced (UNDP, 2006). In addition, the geography of the coastal areas was changed, with much of the land being dragged into the sea, shorelines shifted hundreds of metres inland and previously rich agricultural land rendered unusable. The scale of the devastation and ensuing human suffering prompted an unparalleled outpouring of global sympathy, leading to unprecedented donor commitments of over US$13 billion to assist the reconstruction effort (Telford et al. 2006). Within days an international relief effort was in operation with over 60 international NGOs providing assistance (growing to more than 200 within weeks) alongside many other Indonesian NGOs who were also providing assistance (Kenny et al, 2010, p 3–4).

Many of the media reports of the reconstruction process focused on the role of international nongovernment organisations (INGOs) and emphasised the role of civically minded 'global' citizens arriving as 'knights in shining armour' to save the victims of the tsunami. The reality was much more complex. There were many active citizens, who came from many different places and operated through a range of diverse third sector organisations. Engagement in the reconstruction process also took different forms. Indeed, the story of the reconstruction of Aceh is one of many approaches, players and intentions, resulting in different experiences, perceptions and tensions.

The research reported in this chapter is based on fieldwork and interviews with 96 respondents in the period from February 2005 until February 2009. Respondents included: individuals involved in a range of international, Indonesian and Acehnese agencies and NGOs; local village and religious leaders; local activists; and political commentators.[1] To illustrate the complexity of the contexts of active citizenship we begin by describing the types of third sector organisations involved and the tasks they performed. In the complex mix of organisations involved (estimated to be over 2,000 overall) were *yayasan* and LSMs as well as small and large international NGOs. All those interviewed in the study reported here were familiar with the English lexicon of civil society and NGOs. As noted earlier, the most commonly used term to describe their organisation was NGO, although several organisations linked to the UN described themselves as CSOs.

In the immediate aftermath of the tsunami the first responders were the Acehnese themselves. With all the Western hype about the extensive donor money and the number of INGOs flooding into Aceh, it was easy to miss the extent to which local village organisations, existing NGOs and religious organisations stepped up to the task of both immediate relief and longer term rehabilitation and reconstruction. Immediately after the tsunami it was these groups that began to collect bodies, draw up lists of the survivors, set up communications hubs, and organise food and clean water (here they had help from the Indonesian and Australian military). It was also these groups that identified the need to begin the rebuilding of livelihoods and began to organise projects that provided 'Cash for Work', for the aim of providing survivors with both much needed cash to support their family's livelihood and a purposeful activity. The type of civil commitment demonstrated in their actions involved horizontal relations organised around principles of mutuality and solidarity. Many of the participants had already developed strong

[1] The research described in this chapter was part of a six-year project, funded by Deakin University and the Australian Research Council, which began in 2003 and was undertaken with co-researchers Dr Ismet Fanany and Professor Greg Barton. The senior researcher in Indonesia was Mr Achmad Suaedy. The project set out to study the perceptions of capacity building among members of Islamic NGOs in Indonesia and to track the ways in which NGOs have interpreted and responded to change. During the process of research, the northern coastal region of Sumatra was devastated by an earthquake and the subsequent tsunami. After the tsunami a new area of focus was added to the study. This was capacity building and NGOs in Aceh.

capacities for mutuality through established *yayasan* and LSMs. Indeed, an added impetus for solidarity had been the bitter and often violent struggles for Acehnese independence from Indonesia that had been taking place over more than three decades. To these existing Acehnese organisations were added newly established NGOs that were led by returning Acehnese diaspora. The motivations of the diasporic NGOs were also to provide assistance in the spirit of solidarity. Interviews with those involved in both existing and newly formed NGOs revealed a well-articulated understanding of the term NGO, and NGO practices and constraints.

What was particularly interesting about these newly formed NGOs was their disregard for formal organisational structures and protocols, a disregard which, it would seem, enabled them to respond very quickly to local needs. Other Indonesian NGOs soon followed. According to interviewees, their agendas varied between providing resources such as food and transport, re-establishing schools, rescuing children who had lost parents, staving off perceived attempts at Christian proselytisation on the part of some Western NGOs and staving off opportunistic attempts to access the swelling aid funds. Of course, opportunistic attempts to access donor money were not limited to Western NGOs. Examples could be found throughout the aid effort. That is, while genuine acts and expressions of civil commitment dominated the practices of active citizenship, for some NGOs the appeal of accessing hitherto unseen amounts of donor aid was the driving force behind their activities.

As stated earlier, it was the Western international NGOs, both large and small, that received the most international media coverage. Interviews with members of these organisations revealed their strong commitment to working in solidarity with Acehnese people and, for some, a cosmopolitan outlook. A few of the smaller Western organisations involved volunteers but most were staffed by paid professional workers operating through established aid protocols. Many set about the task of building urgently required accommodation for survivors. Some NGOs assisted in livelihood programmes, which provided microcredit, small grants and loans to families to restart or start a small business. Thus for many aid workers this was their professional job, requiring them to distance themselves from the heartache and losses of the 'victims' and to apply technical procedures during both the relief and reconstruction phases. Their status as professional workers suggests that their active citizenship has been circumscribed by the fact that they were usually paid for their involvement. Nevertheless, part of the basis of their recruitment was their commitment to helping others and on this basis they can be described as active citizens. At the same time their civil commitment was vertical, rather than horizontal, as they set out plans for 'what would be best' for the victims and emphasised the importance of 'building back better'.

The 'build back better' approach was a source of tensions between those active citizens who were survivors and those who were outsiders wanting to help. It involved a struggle between local people, who predominantly wanted to reclaim their own land and occupations, and those who argued for reconstructing settlement and skilling up survivors to make Aceh 'better'. In the event, it was the desire to return to 'how things were' that prevailed, although in many cases this was actually not possible (for example where land was lost to the sea and/ or the breadwinners in a family had disappeared).

There were attempts to consult with local people, but these were often desultory in nature and the local viewpoints that were being heard were often not representative of majority views. Some locals complained of being 'overconsulted', while also commenting that in any case, when they were consulted, their wishes were ignored (Kenny, 2010). Interestingly, interviews with local people revealed a clear preference for 'getting back to normal', whatever this was, rather than 'building back better'. Many of these interviewees also expressed a desire to be identified as 'survivors' rather than 'victims' indicating a desire to be accepted as people with agency who could take control of their own destinies. They were critical of anybody who used the label 'victim' as a way of gaining favourable support from aid agencies.

The citizenship *bona fides* of some Western NGOs indicated ambiguous or narrowly instrumental intents, including the proselytising functions of Christian NGOs already mentioned. Seizing opportunities opened up through the marketisation of aid (Klein, 2007), some NGOs, having no apparent interest in civil society functions, entered into lucrative contracts to manage and deliver expert reconstruction. The marketisation of aid is one indication of the extent to which neoliberalism has permeated aid and development.

Having said this, the vast majority of Acehnese interviewees perceived the intents of Western NGOs to be well-meaning, rather than opportunistic. Yet, while we can argue that the form of active citizenship practised by most Western international NGOs was one based on civil commitment to assist survivors, this was sometimes derailed by the primary imperative of fiscal accountability to donors, as in cases where formal audits and evaluations were prioritised over needs perceived by the Acehnese people themselves. Civil commitment was also circumscribed by the many complexities on the ground, many of which demonstrated the asymmetrical power relations between the aid workers and local people. While most Acehnese interviewees indicated that they understood NGO activities within the context of civil society, the term active citizenship as a descriptor of the actions of those involved in relief and reconstruction had no resonance. However, when it was explained that the concept referred to the ways in which people engage in society and attempt to control their own futures, there was an immediate and positive response.

There was, in addition, another group of international NGOs, which were largely overlooked by the Western media. These were the NGOs coming from other Muslim countries, many operating under the banner of the Red Crescent. Notable among these NGOs were those from the Muslim countries of Turkey and Malaysia and also two of Saudi Arabia's largest charity organisations, the International Islamic Relief Organisation (IIRO) and its affiliated World Assembly of Muslim Youth, which we discuss below. Fanany (2010) describes the interactions between Turkish Red Crescent, as donors and the survivors in a small coastal village south of Banda Aceh, called Lampuuk. Unlike in many of the Aceh reconstruction projects, the villagers of Lampuuk demanded a collective and active role in the construction and reconstruction of infrastructure and homes of the village. The establishment of a small operational team representing the villagers was central to the high quality of the eventual reconstruction of the settlement. Lampuuk residents served as field supervisors. They were able to influence the design and choice of materials for their houses and present any concerns during the building process. The good working relationships between the donors and recipients resulted in a high degree of satisfaction on both sides, which was not commonly found in the reconstruction processes elsewhere. What is interesting in this example is the nature of the civil commitment of Turkish Red Crescent, which was interested in understanding the real needs of the villagers and balancing power relationships through facilitating the active citizenship of the Lampuuk villagers. In the context of this particular reconstruction project, active citizenship involved people working together for a common goal, and to this extent involved mutuality, mutual respect and genuine engagement.

The Lampuuk reconstruction can be contrasted with a number of projects undertaken in other parts of Aceh by organisations with a clear Islamist agenda.[2] Miller (2010) discusses how aid workers were concerned that some foreign Islamic NGOs were using the opportunities presented by the tsunami for their own religious or political gain. Indeed, as suggested earlier in relation to Christian NGOs, post-tsunami Aceh promised fertile ground for proselytizing. Among the radical Islamist groups that assembled in Aceh after the tsunami were religious militias. Some had been recruited, armed and trained by Indonesia's armed forces in an effort not only to continue to repress those supporting independence for Aceh but also to combat the potential secularising impact of civil society activities and the putative immoral influences of Western aid workers.

Yet even if some Islamist groups and NGOs were using the situation in post-tsunami Aceh as a recruiting ground for political Islam, does this mean that their activities cannot be described as active citizenship based on civil commitment? This is a difficult question to answer. It certainly draws attention to the vexed issue of the universality of notions of civil society. Chapter Three argued for a broad working definition of civil society, as a sphere in which people come together freely and independently to discuss, debate and negotiate issues and work collectively to influence and shape their society. Members of Islamist groups do join voluntarily. The Islamist groups in our study acted independently and they did discuss issues and plan their activities collectively. Their aim was for a better society, based on the principles of their understanding of the good person, who, by definition, was a good Muslim. Relationships between members were largely horizontal, in the sense that they saw each other as equals, although members were deferential to those with greater religious knowledge. However, the secular concepts of civil society and active citizenship were foreign ideas. Obligations were constructed as religious obligations. Civil commitment was extended only to fellow Muslims and in some cases only to certain Muslims. For example, some Islamist groups in Indonesia argued that the beliefs of the Muslim sect Ahmadiyya constituted apostasy. Given the deeply conservative Islam that was being practised in Aceh, there is a clear argument that Islamic groups from both inside and outside Indonesia were acting in the spirit of religious

[2]   There is some slippage in the terminology and meaning of Islamism. Among our interviewees it was also referred to as radical Islam, political Islam or neofundamental Islam. In its simplest sense Islamism involves commitment to building an Islamic state based on Islamic or Sharia law (Roy, 2002, p 2). It can involve neofundamentalist views, which are closed, scripturalist and conservative, as well as commitment to a universal community of all Muslims (*ummah*).

solidarity and mutuality, a spirit that differs from the way in which this has been commonly understood in Western contexts. At the same time Muslim militias also had a political agenda antagonistic to civil society and thus to opportunities for establishing or deepening a civil culture based on a strong public sphere, with freedom of speech and association. Their active citizenship was of a kind that was dedicated to weakening more commonly understood notions of civil society.

In concluding this part of the chapter, in regard to the role of NGOs in post-tsunami Aceh there is evidence that the primary role of the vast majority of NGOs was to practise civil commitment and to nurture and facilitate a robust active citizenship based on the desire to assist the wellbeing of survivors. Rights discourse was largely absent in discussions and interviews undertaken for our study, although there was a general undercurrent of thought that survivors had the right to be supported by both their government and international aid organisations. For local NGOs the principles of mutuality and solidarity were dominant. For international NGOs, while there was commitment to assisting fellow humans, professional imperatives often formed a wedge between the providers of aid and the recipients, resulting in more vertical, sometimes proselytising and often quite tenuous relationships. For example, different levels of pay and the knowledge that international workers would return to other lives circumscribed the meanings of solidarity. In regard to the discourse of civil society, while most of the interviewees understood the term civil society and some groups even described themselves as CSOs, the terms civil society and civil sphere were not used. NGOs were more likely to be conceived as instruments through which active citizenship could be practised than as originators or nurturers of active citizenship.

The third sector and active citizenship in Russia

While the research undertaken into the third sector in Indonesia was clearly set within non-Western cultural traditions, Russia offered a more ambiguous setting. Contemporary Russia stretches from the Baltic sea to the Pacific Ocean and comprises cultural traditions in the western part of the country that are comparable to those in Western Europe, but also the many diverse ethnicities, particularly in central and eastern Russia with roots in a wide range of different traditions. The period of the Soviet Union from 1922 to 1991 saw a highly centralised state covering what is now known as the Russian Federation and included, in 1991, 15 Soviet Socialist Republics (SSRs). With the breakup of the Soviet Union most of the SSRs became sovereign states, ending seven decades of control from Moscow. Yet this has not stopped interventions from Moscow in some of the previous SSRs, which have led to conflicts with Georgia and Ukraine. Regardless of how the political alliances or conflicts with Moscow have been played out, the powerful centralisation processes of the 70 years of the Soviet Union, including the promotion of the Russian language, arts and literature, have left many common cultural elements which have affected the development of civil society. These cultural elements, of course, are still changing and are full of contradictions. What is of interest here is what research into the third sector can tell us about ideas of civil society in Russia and the forms of active citizenship nurtured in third sector organisations. Chapter Six discussed some aspects of the Russian research, which was part of a broader comparative study. This chapter probes the data with the question of the applicability of the Western constructions of civil society in mind, focusing on qualitative material.

The qualitative part of the international comparative study of the third sector involved interviews with members of 18 third sector organisations in Moscow and two of its outlying areas, Mytichi and Karaslova, which took place between 1996 and 2005.[3] As already stated, the dominant form of active citizenship in the study can be described as civil commitment. The term 'civil' had clear resonance in the interviews and, similar to the English usage, meanings varied between the idea of a sphere of action, a way of relating to other people (politely and urbanely) and civilised or accomplished. The term third sector (*tretiy sector*) was not used by respondents in interviews, while the term citizenship tended to be equated with national citizenship constructed around national identification papers. Respondents pointed out that during the Soviet period the formal address 'citizen' carried a negative connotation, while the more common and preferred address was 'comrade'. The term and concept of active citizenship had little resonance per se. The preferred terminology used in interviews was civil society and NGO and so the term NGO is used in the discussion which follows.

Approximately half of the organisations in the database had been established during the Soviet period, in which time they had little autonomy from the local branches of the communist party. With the collapse of Soviet communism it became increasingly important for

[3]   This research was funded by the Australian Government, Deakin University and the Australian Research Council. The research team consisted of Professor Sue Kenny, Professor Jenny Onyx, Dr Kevin Brown and Professor Terry Burke. The senior researcher in Russia was Mr Leonid Reznichenko.

them to demonstrate that they were no longer 'transmission belts' for state policy (Sperling, 1999; Zdravomyslova, 2002) or functioning according to a Soviet style structure, although attempts to break with the state had always been a challenge (Frohlich, 2012). The largest groups were concerned with welfare issues. Established through the local communist party, the major purpose of these groups was to care for the wellbeing of their constituents, such as the inhabitants of a group of apartment blocks, Second World War veterans or disabled people. 'Care' involved moral support and specific programmes, such as organising handicrafts activities and cultural events. In discussions for the study, ideas of a civil society and the notion of operating in a public sphere were of no interest to them. The major concerns of interviewees were the continuation of their programs and lobbying local government for support and welfare provision. A smaller group of organisations, also predominantly established or expanded during the Soviet era, were concerned with supporting and promoting local artists. For example a local artists' association, which dated back to the 19th century and had been a member of the USSR League of Creative Workers, was a member-serving association. It promoted the work of local painters and since perestroika had expanded to be part of a network of national and international artists. While registering as an NGO in the mid 1990s, this organisation, like many others with Soviet origins, had recently struggled to maintain members and hold exhibitions.

The organisations in the study that had been established since the early 1990s were a multifarious group. They were generally prepared to identify as NGOs and often had contacts with, or even funding from, Western agencies. Locally sponsored and funded NGOs included the Environmental Foundation and Museum, which was founded for the purpose of educating local people about environmental issues, a Cat Owners' Club and a children's charity, Maria's Children, that was providing an art studio and social contacts that had been unavailable for such children during the Soviet period.

Given their commitment to raising awareness of pollution and protecting natural flora and fauna, the interviewees at the Environmental Foundation were strong supporters of a robust public sphere. In addition to funds provided by Moscow City Council, Maria's Children has been supported internationally and has publicised its activities widely. It has had a strong presence on the internet, has organised tours for its children and received visitors from many places internationally. Thus this organisation, too, was committed to a strong public sphere

Another group of NGOs was based on a concept of active citizenship that had elements of both civil commitment and activism. These were the organisations constructed around human rights issues. At the time of the interviews there were considerable ethnic tensions, particularly over independence movements, in parts of the Russian Federation and several organisations were devoting their energy to supporting the members of such ethnic groups, often exciting the hostility of both government and the public at large. Discussions with such organisations were framed by their commitment to supporting the wellbeing and human rights of all fellow citizens through publicity, protest and lobbying. One organisation in particular, called Memorial, has received international attention for its work to commemorate the experiences of those who suffered persecution during the period of the Soviet Union, as well as publicising contemporary attempts to limit the freedoms and dignity of citizens of Russia and the Commonwealth of Independent States. Since perestroika it has collected KGB documents and produced radio programmes, books and magazines which record the fate of tens of thousands of victims of political repression. The organisation has also provided aid and support to former political prisoners and members of their families. Its charter emphasised mutual respect describing relations between all those involved as based on the importance of friendship. Thus members of the human rights organisations in this study described their work within the context of recognition, mutuality, solidarity and respect for others.

Most local organisations in the Russian study were driven by a small number of active and dedicated volunteers. There appeared to be an unquestioning acceptance of provision 'by those who could to those who were in need', understood in terms of solidarity. There was also a strong sense of mutuality in conversations with respondents, which translated into a commitment to the collective good rather than individual service.

In some interviews respondents reminisced about the 'heady' days of the early 1990s in which there had been an explosion of civil society activity (Leitch 1997; McFaul, 2000; White, 2002). By the late 1990s, they argued, the scope and influence of the NGO sector was already waning and the state was increasing its oversight of the sector through increasing regulations. By 2006 new national laws required NGOs to reregister with the government in order to continue their operations (Sakwa, 2002, p 343–4). Several interviewees expressed concern about the increasingly heavy-handed actions of the state, in particular the way in which some local government departments had introduced new taxes and invoked obscure laws to threaten or even close an organisation that was deemed to be an 'activist threat', regardless of its benign welfare work. Many organisations used their own members' apartments as their offices and these failed to adhere to health and safety regulations, providing an excuse for state coercion. These concerns foreshadowed the alarm with which the deepening forms of state surveillance were greeted in 2012.

During the early years of the 21st century, some international funding organisations, such as the Ford Foundation and the Soros Foundation, began to retreat from Russia. While this retreat led to some discomfort on the part of organisations that had received Western funds, it perhaps foreshadowed further rifts between international agencies and Russian NGOs. By the end of the first decade of the 21st century it was evident that the Kremlin maintained support for NGOs that were loyal to the state, while harassing those which were critical, particularly NGOs still in receipt of international funds. Robertson (2011, p 214) argues that we are witnessing a new configuration of civil society which he calls 'licensed civil society'.

By 2012 the licensing of civil society was clearly evident in the passing of new legislation which required NGOs that were involved in any political activity and received any foreign funding to formally register their connections with 'foreign agents'. The official rationale for the legislation was to protect Russia from interference from unwanted 'outside elements' and increase transparency and accountability. However, NGO leaders saw it as way of crushing criticism and dissent and as reminiscent of the Soviet era discourse that equated the term 'foreign agent' with spy. Indeed, this law has ushered in a new period of coercion in which, during 2013, several thousand NGOs, including Memorial, were inspected and threatened with large fines. The coercive effects of this law, along with an increasingly repressive regulatory environment for all NGOs (including the majority that have been concerned with civil obligations and mutual support), suggests a problematic future for the third sector in Russia. We are probably only seeing the beginning of this new politics of intimidation but the signs at the time of writing this book are ominous. From one perspective, this apparent return to a culture of suspicion of civil society should be no surprise. This is because of the impoverished civil society legacy that had been bequeathed to the new non-Soviet Russian state in 1992. As Sakwa (2002) points out, the Soviet system had been built on a society that was essentially hierarchical and patterns of social authoritarianism were deeply embedded in Russian culture. Even during the apparent blossoming of third sector organisations post-1992, our Russian interviewees commented on undercurrents of criticism and scepticism that they believed fed into hostility towards their organisation. In retrospect, the civil society scenarios that were set out for post-Soviet development were too optimistic and underestimated the power both of the legacies of Russian and Soviet history and culture and of the 'cowboy capitalism' that was established in the post-Soviet period.

Conclusion

By investigating different settings of active citizenship, empirical studies can indicate the complexities of the relationship between active citizenship and the third sector. The studies above were chosen because of the common thread of an active citizenship that expresses civil commitment. However, there were differences in the ways in which this form of active citizenship was practised. First, unlike the Acehnese NGOs, which were generally seen by informants as providing an organisational framework or vehicle for active citizenship that already existed, many of the interviewees in the Russian third sector saw their organisations as the primary progenitors and nurturers of active citizenship. In part this can be explained by their earlier experiences of people's organisation in the Soviet Union, where individual initiative and agency were suppressed and the generation of active citizenship was the function of the formal institutions of the communist party as well as being tightly controlled by the state.

Second, processes of decision making in the organisations differed. Ironically, a legacy of the Soviet system was a commitment to a form of local democracy that supported participation in local committees. When questioned about how decisions were made, respondents in Russian NGOs appeared blasé about local democracy, commenting that democratic processes were a 'taken for granted and natural' part of the activities in Russian third sector organisations. They pointed out that this was a reflection of the importance given to acting for the collective good. Being able to participate in decision-making within an organisation encourages people to become engaged in local activities and to act in the interests of the collective and thus is a path to civil commitment.

There was a variety of views and practices concerning democratic processes in the Aceh reconstruction study. Some local organisations, especially at the village level, emphasised the importance of local participation in decisions, but this did not extend to all members of the village, and often excluded women. International NGOs varied in the extent to which they involved local people in decision making. One persistent argument from aid workers was that during the emergency relief phase, a sense of urgency made it difficult to consult with survivors in deciding actions. Yet during this phase local communities often took charge, not on the basis of democratic processes as might be understood in the West, but through complex networks of informal exchange, based on horizontal person to person relationships. As the full reconstruction process began, most international agencies attempted at least some kind of consultation with local people although, as commented earlier, this was often desultory and, of course, consultation is not democracy, or even participation (Arnstein, 1969; Cornwall, 2008). Yet international agencies did organise workshops, albeit with different levels of success, where survivors, local Acehnese and Indonesian and international NGOs came together to discuss planning options.

Third, in investigating differences in active citizenship practices, an argument of this book is that, given the Western roots of civil society concepts, it is important to probe the meanings of these concepts in non-Western settings. As discussed in Chapter Three, the idea of civil society is framed normatively. The third sector organisations that are considered in this chapter provide examples of how civil commitment, as a discourse and a set of processes, can be practised in countries outside the OECD. With some important exceptions, the third sector organisations discussed here were seen positively. This was certainly the case for local NGOs in Aceh, particularly the women's groups, as well as the human rights organisations in Russia. Yet even in the studies reported in this chapter acceptance of Western NGOs was not universal. In particular, in discussions with conservative and radical Islamic NGOs, several Western researchers reported discomforting interviews and some experienced animosity to the whole Western aid presence. This chapter has already noted the ambiguities in locating radical Islamist groups in civil society. But local Acehnese respondents reported other concerns about Western projects. They were especially critical in regard to the 'red tape' of auditing and reporting that was required in the name of accountability to funding donors. This meant that local NGOs were required to operate according to Western management methods, which they saw as quite inappropriate to Acehnese social and cultural traditions. This view of Acehnese disquiet accords with the findings of a study of Western funded NGOs in post-communist states, where Western assistance meant that local customs were often ignored (Mendelson, 2002).

On the other hand, the Russian study reported here did not find that Western assistance necessarily required operating according to Western organisational protocols. This may have been due to the limited nature of the assistance. As indicated in earlier discussion, since the collapse of Soviet communism there has been continuing ambivalence towards Western influence on the part of ordinary people in Russia, the seeds of which were cultivated during the Soviet period, particularly during the Cold War. While Russian NGOs concerned with documenting human rights abuses drew succour from the West during the eventful days following the collapse of the Soviet system, their optimism for a sustainable public sphere had dissipated by the first decade of the new century. Indeed, the concept of global citizenship is often seen as providing a false Western overlay that undermines the development of an authentic Russian civil society. From this perspective, the triumphalism of Western and pro-Western NGOs operating in the heady days of the early 1990s has blinded them to a different citizenship heritage in Russia, based on compliance and conformity. However, while the ambiguities in civil society processes in both the Acehnese and the Russian studies indicate the necessity of caution in assuming the universal applicability of civil society, they do not render the concept and its practices redundant. What we are left with in these two studies is a picture of different and sometimes shifting perspectives with regard to the how third sector organisations nurture active citizenship.

EIGHT

Active citizenship as activism: political engagement through the third sector

Introduction

Chapter Four introduced the claims made for the contribution that third sector organisations can make to democratic life, acting as 'schools for democracy', giving citizens voice, and providing space for deliberation and debate. The work of Robert Putnam, for example, has linked engagement in voluntary associations with the development of social capital and hence to the development of the civil norms and trust that, he argues, form the basis of effective local governance (Putnam et al, 1993; Putnam, 2000). Others have argued that associationalism, as the primary means of both democratic governance and organising social life, should be at the root of democracy (Hirst, 1994, p 26). As indicated in previous chapters, this model resonates with a communitarian ideal of self-governing communities, which would enable all their members to participate in collective processes affecting their lives (see also Taylor, 2011).

Chapter Five then discussed the various ways in which both globalisation and the advance of a neoliberal ideology have affected the relationship between the state, market and the third sector in different parts of the world, opening up new opportunities but also posing new challenges. It described the risks to third sector independence posed by the move to market models of welfare and the way in which nongovernmental agencies (NGOs) have been socialised into the establishment and thus 'have made a contribution, albeit minor in comparison to other actors, to the rolling back of the state' (Hulme and Edwards, 1997, p 9). It also reported that, over recent decades, new spaces have been opening up for citizen voice at local, national and international levels (Cornwall and Coelho, 2007) and considered the risks of cooption but also the potential for resistance. This has clear implications for the promotion of active citizenship via political engagement. This chapter therefore explores further the third sector's role in promoting democratic engagement through civic engagement and citizen activism, the latter in the sense of challenging or changing dominant power relations and structures. In doing so, it draws on case studies for illustration.

The changing role of the third sector in democracy

The roots of modern democracy are usually traced back to ancient Athens, where citizens had a direct vote in decision making in the city state (Foley and Hodgkinson, 2003). Though sometimes seen as an ideal, in reality only free men were enfranchised and, as society has become more complex, representative forms of democracy have developed based on popular elections and individual rights as well as gradually extending the franchise across the population. These models have spread throughout the world but, as more and more citizens have access to the ballot box, their limitations, too, have become more apparent. A form of democracy which allows citizens little more than the chance to vote at periodic intervals still leaves power in the hands of an elite, and critics have over the years urged more pluralist models that allow the diversity of overlapping interests in society to be expressed and heard (Dahl, 1989; Barber, 1992; Hirst, 1994; Saward, 2005). To some extent this has been recognised in the adoption of corporatist models in some countries (examples include Germany and the Netherlands), whereby major interests in society are institutionalised along religious or economic lines through 'peak organisations' that are incorporated into the policy making process (Schmitter, 1974). But these still privilege certain interests over others and offer no guarantee against elitism. The same might be said to apply to the lobbying industry that has grown up alongside representative forms of democracy over the centuries, but which has mushroomed over the past 50 years or so, privileging those (including some third sector organisations) with money and connections. Concerns about growing apathy and disenchantment with the formal representative system have therefore triggered growing interest in participatory forms of democracy, offering new channels for engagement, seeking to engage a broader swathe of citizens and often focusing on the need to engage the most marginalised or 'hard to reach'.

As Chapter Four reported, advocates of associational democracy argue that voluntary associations are essential for ensuring that the range of citizens' voices are heard in the democratic process (see, for example, Hirst, 1994; Putnam et al, 1993). Voluntary associations have also been seen as significant in the process of opening up totalitarian forms of government to democratic ideas and practices, sometimes managing to survive in some shape or form even in situations where their very existence is discouraged. For instance, in 1980s Latin America, women's mobilisations were crucial in providing mutual support and in maintaining forms of resistance to the authoritarian regimes of the time. In the first case, for example, they provided food collectively in communal kitchens in Chile (Johnson and Bernstein, 1982); an example of the second is the mobilisation of the mothers of the disappeared in Argentina. In many societies, as earlier chapters have also argued, third sector organisations mediate between the citizen and the state, building democratic awareness and skills, mobilising citizens, acting as a channel for the range of different voices, framing public debate, and organising citizens to engage with political processes, to put issues onto the political agenda and to help to formulate policy. They have thus been a way for groups excluded from political and economic power to gain a stake in society, develop networks, discuss and formulate strategies and gain an organisational base from which to make their voices heard. They provide public spaces where people can come together and sites for resisting power. The roles they can play are developed below.

Building democratic awareness and skills

Engaging in third sector activity, even at the simplest level, can give people the skills, confidence and knowledge to engage in the democratic process. Engaging with others can allow them to see that their experiences, views and concerns are shared; it has the potential to teach them the basic skills of expression, listening, deliberation, negotiation and compromise. It also has the potential to turn resignation into the hope that change is possible. At a time when public spaces are being privatised and the public sphere is under attack, third sector organisations can also, as Chapter Four reported, provide public spaces for people to come together and engage in deliberative processes – although this is by no means always the case.

Much of this is implicit – a group's main aim may be social or service oriented but members will need to learn to work collectively and to interact with external power holders in order to achieve this aim. For example, a respondent in a study of UK organisations in the early

21st century – *Willing partners?*[1] (Craig et al, 2004; Parkes et al, 2004, p 313) – explained how:

> 'Voluntary and community organisations have a role in the education of the individual or person in a broad setting because your ideas are best formed when you are meeting with and talking to other people, that helps to channel ideas … They will say things based on their self-knowledge and on their knowledge of what is going on.'

However, there are also organisations that have been set up explicitly to build political skills and to raise awareness amongst their members, in order to organise around shared issues and/or to establish solidarity around identity. For example, in his book on *The Making of the Working Class*, the UK writer, E.P. Thompson describes the important role of organisations such as the friendly societies, trades unions, workers education associations and mechanics institutes, as well as the nonconformist churches of the 18th and 19th centuries, in establishing working class identity and in political education (Thompson, 1963). More recently, Chapter Four reminds us that, as attention has turned from class inequalities to increasing focus upon other forms of discrimination and disadvantage, third sector organisations have provided sites where dispossessed and marginalised groups, such as disabled or unemployed people and asylum seekers, who find themselves excluded from the public sphere, can find support and claim their identities (Young, 1990; Honneth, 1992).

People can and do learn positive lessons from their experiences of third sector engagement, as Foley's (1999) study of learning in social action in Australia, Brazil and Zimbabwe has illustrated. But people can also learn negative lessons from their involvement, concluding, for example, that they have been wasting their time 'beating their heads against brick walls'. These potentially negative experiences highlight the importance of the contributions of adult educators and community development professionals, skilled at drawing out the lessons for active citizenship (Merrifield, 2010).

---

[1]   This research – *Willing partners? Voluntary and community organisations in the democratic process* (award number L215252001 – was funded by the UK's Economic and Social Research Council as part of its 'Democracy and Participation Programme'. Quotations in the text which do not have a citation are taken from unpublished working papers by the researchers: Gary Craig, Tessa Parkes, Marilyn Taylor, Diane Warburton, Mick Williamson.

The work of Paolo Freire and other liberation theologists, initially in South America but increasingly across the globe, has provided the basis for more explicit approaches to consciousness raising (Freire, 1976; Ledwith, 2005). An example can be found in the Active Learning for Active Citizenship Programme in England, which was a government initiative but delivered through third sector organisations. When the first New Labour government was elected in the UK in 1997, one of its aims was to address the democratic deficit, strengthening civil society by promoting active citizenship, starting with citizenship education in schools and colleges. The next stage was a two-year programme to extend learning for active citizenship to adults in communities. Active Learning for Active Citizenship (ALAC) was launched in 2004, to be delivered via third sector organisations, building on best practice, rooted in Freirean approaches to enable people 'to support each other in identifying the issues that concern us, and develop the confidence and skills to make a difference to the world around us' (Woodward, 2004, p 1). Equalities were to be centre stage, together with the principles of valuing diversity, strengthening cooperation, social cohesion and social solidarity, in the pursuit of participation for social justice. And the methods were to be participatory, starting from learners' own priorities, developing interactive workshops and group visits as well as providing more formal learning opportunities. Significantly too, in relation to the international focus of this book, ALAC learning programmes included study visits for women, both to the national parliament in Westminster, London and to the institutions of the European Union in Brussels (Bedford et al, 2010). As other learning programmes also recognised, citizens needed to know how the external world operates and learn about structures at supranational as well as at national levels, knowing 'where to go to get what you want' (Bedford et al, 2010, p 197) through taking part in a European learning programme.

The experiences of the ALAC programme demonstrated the value of opportunities to engage in ways that were playful and imaginative. Citizens appreciated spaces 'to take part in, and feel part of, something that was both collective and local', whether or not this involved taking part in more overtly political spaces (Rooke, 2013, p 166). This is a common finding (Meade and Shaw, 2007). Kabeer's study of a third sector organisation's contributions to social mobilisation in Bangladesh, for example, reiterates the importance of cultural dimensions when providing training for active citizenship – songs, theatre, stories and role play (Kabeer, 2005). Community arts and music also featured prominently in Hoi Ok Jeong's (2013) study of citizen initiatives in

South Korea, while folk music and dance societies were sometimes one of the few ways in which citizens could engage with each other during the Communist era in Central and Eastern Europe.

Mobilising and organising

It has been through third sector organisations that many citizens have been able to contribute to public life. As a respondent in the *Willing partners?* study cited in the previous section commented:

> 'People are so disenfranchised, except through the informal and formal groups that they belong to (sometimes even the family). That's the nearest they get to participating in a democracy.' (Parkes et al, 2004, p 313)

In some societies and at some points in time, the third sector has been one of the few arenas through which women or religious minorities could enter the public sphere. Certainly this was the case in pre-20th century Britain, where women were disenfranchised and nonconformists and Catholics excluded from public office, establishing traditions on which to build even when they were no longer formally excluded. What was particularly important for the organisations in the *Willing partners?* study was that the third sector engaged people through collective action:

> 'If you can carry other people with you than that should carry more weight – that is democracy and to make democracy effective you have got to get people together in groups working for what they want.' (Parkes et al, 2004, p 313)

Third sector organisations by their nature bring people together to address common issues – potentially turning private troubles into public issues, as Zygmunt Bauman (1999) put it. In the US, Smith and Pekkanen (2012, p 38) argue that many third sector organisations 'begin as an informal group devoted entirely to advocacy or a specific case, such as the prevention of drug abuse', only then evolving into a mix of service and advocacy as they acquire resources. Sometimes, the order will be reversed – a group that is rooted in a desire to help others or in mutual aid may find they need to engage in advocacy as part of their mission, running campaigns on issues that affect their members and service users – or indeed their own survival (see Chapter Ten).

The extent to which participants identify this as political activism will vary according to issue and context. While research in democratic countries suggests that relatively few people see their participation in third sector organisations as 'political' activity per se (see Chapter Six; also Brodie et al, 2011), there are countries where governments construct any form of organising as political, as Chapter Seven illustrates in relation to contemporary Russia, and many others – like Nicaragua in Chapter Five – where third sector organisations have emerged from a history of political contestation (Howard and Lever, 2011), forming strong political identities through resistance. Here, as in many countries with weak or dysfunctional states, the state's inability to provide for basic needs means that third sector organisations with a strong critical and political voice can combine activism with service delivery in order to fill gaps in service provision.

Third sector organisations not only act as a channel for political engagement: mobilisation may be central to their mission. Many NGOs engage in community development, bringing people together to identify their needs and address them, by drawing on their own resources and/or through engaging with external power holders. This sometimes goes hand in hand with the type of educational approach described earlier in this chapter. The Bangladeshi study cited there is just one of many that illustrates this approach. It focused on Nijera Kori (NK), an organisation that aimed to build the capabilities of poor people, to enable them to understand and so to be able to demand their rights. The aim was to nurture values of solidarity, self reliance and collective action, as part of wider strategies for social change, 'growing citizenship from the grassroots' (Kabeer, 2005, p 184). Reflecting on their learning, NK members felt that, even if the organisation were not to be there in the future, 'its ideals and objectives will remain with us. (T)he basis of our existence will be what the members have learned about the difference between what is just and what is unjust' (p 197).

Community development is an approach that has come under fire in different parts of the world for its past colonial connotations and, more recently, for its alleged collusion with neoliberal policies to reduce the role of the state (Hulme and Edwards, 1997; Bebbington et al, 2008). To a number of critics, community organising offers a more radical alternative (Beck and Purcell, 2013) – although some would see this more as a particular model of community development than as an alternative (Rothman and Tropman, 1993; Smock, 2003; Gilchrist and Taylor, 2011). It is an approach that has attracted considerable attention in some parts of the globe in recent years. In part, this is because of the background of the current US president – Barack Obama – in community organising, much publicised when he applied community organising principles to his election campaign. Beck and Purcell (2013, pp 1–2) cite Obama's description of community organising:

> Organizing begins with the premise that (1) the problems facing inner-city communities do not result from a lack of effective solutions, but from a lack of power to implement these solutions; (2) that the only way for communities to build long-term power is by organising people and money around a common vision; and (3) that a viable organization can only be built if a broadly based indigenous leadership – and not one or two charismatic leaders – can knit together the diverse interests of their local organisations. (Obama, 1988)

This approach – which has also attracted controversy – was developed by Saul Alinsky in the United States in the mid 20th century (Alinsky, 1969, 1971) and has spread through the Industrial Areas Foundation across the US as well as to affiliates in a number of countries. It is based on building power through organisations of organisations – typically, associations, tenants' groups and block clubs, churches and labour unions – in order to change policy and practice within government and other institutions which have an impact on the community, through negotiation or, where this is ineffective, through more confrontational tactics.

Alinsky's model has been criticised as focusing too much on those who are already organised, with not enough attention paid to the need to organise at grassroots level (Delgado, 1986), for neglecting issues of race and gender, and for being focused on immediate and short-term gains at the expense of the deeper long-term analysis that underpins a Freirean approach (Mayo et al, 2013). As a result, a range of alternative models have since been developed which seek to address these issues (see Beck and Purcell, 2013). And while Alinsky's mission – and that of his followers in different countries – has been to tackle poverty and oppression, his methods are not always applied in the interests of social justice, as the use of similar methods by the deeply conservative Tea Party movement in the US demonstrates.

So far, we have described how third sector organisations can act as a route into public engagement, how they may combine service and advocacy and how they may engage in mobilising citizens as part of their development mission. In addition, of course, there are many third sector organisations that are set up explicitly to campaign on specific issues.

Some are strongly member-based; others employ a small, dedicated staff, although they may then mobilise a broad constituency. Amnesty is a long-established example of the latter, organising international support for its campaign against torture through postcard campaigns. More recently, we have seen the rise of internet based campaigning organisations such as Avaaz, 38 Degrees, change.org and GetUp, who have mobilised a new form of activism to attract signatories to petitions aimed at raising the profile of a range of issues. Whether clicking on a petition – dubbed as 'clicktivism' – can be called active citizenship is currently a subject for debate. But as this form of action develops it will be interesting to see how 'clicktivism' can be enhanced and mobilise support for other forms of activity. These developments are discussed further in Chapter Ten.

Third sector organisations can also support social movements or indeed generate a social movement themselves. Summarising the literature on social movements, Caniglia and Carmin (2005, pp 202–4) underline the importance of their links to formal structures, not only in mobilising people but also in providing stability, developing talent and ensuring maturation. Thus, Sidney Tarrow (1994) describes how third sector organisations can act as containers for change over the longer term, as the energy of movements waxes and wanes. The formality of clear roles and structures that third sector organisations offer can also help to reduce conflict and ambiguity. Tarrow argues further that a blend of formality and informality is needed in social movements if movement actors are to channel the energy of their component networks both to take action and to be accountable to the wider community. The risk is, however, that formal social movement organisations (SMOs) can become detached from the wider movement. The challenges and dilemmas that this poses are explored more fully in Chapter Nine, including the specific challenges and dilemmas that apply to organisations and social movements operating on an international scale.

A channel for citizen voice

Another claim identified in Chapter Four relates to 'giving voice'. Commentators from de Tocqueville onwards have seen third sector organisations as the expression of pluralism and diversity in society. As a third sector respondent in the *Willing partners?* study cited earlier argued:

> 'The voluntary and community sector adds variety to the whole picture, and more choice generally. It provides

> different ways of working, different values and philosophies
> – it is more democratic than if things were only set up
> by the government rather than lots of others groups that
> provide choice.'

And, as Chapter Four also argued, it is through third sector organisations that marginalised voices can be heard. This does not of course mean that individual third sector organisations are necessarily tolerant and diverse or indeed inclusive. Indeed, left to itself the sector might easily fall prey to its own differences and divisions, while the voices of those with the most economic, social and cultural capital would crowd out those of the most disadvantaged. We will return to this. But there are potentially positive ways of working and outcomes here, despite these inherent risks.

A study of 'moderate' Islamic organisations in Indonesia provides a good example of the way in which third sector organisations express this pluralism and diversity. This research involved extensive interviews with participants in 36 organisations and took place over a seven-year period, in 20 locations and in different provinces in Indonesia. The 36 organisations in the study explicitly articulated a commitment to a liberal or civil pluralist form of Islam (Hefner, 2000, pp 12–13) that values some degree of theological flexibility and a balance of the powers of state and society. It also supports freedom of speech, openness, tolerance, equality and justice. This 'civil Islam' approach contrasts with the much publicised contemporary revival of a political Islam, which, in various ways, condemns theological flexibility and the separation of state and religion, calling instead for a religious orthodoxy based on Islamic law.Interviewees in these moderate or liberal Islamic organisations saw their role, as active citizens, in giving voice to those committed to civil Islam in Indonesia, supporting this commitment in practical ways. A leader in one of these groups explained how, following the principles expressed by the late Abdurrahman Wahid, or Gus Dur as he was affectionately known, her group was "committed to promoting progressive Muslim thought and promoting tolerance and understanding in the world, by working at the grassroots level" (www.wahidinstitute.org/wi-id/).

The activities of these groups included projects and campaigns to assist those in need of help, such as finding alternative accommodation for survivors of domestic violence, producing brochures supporting highlighting the effects of deforestation and lobbying politicians to help farmers stay on their land; and organising interreligious meetings between Muslims and Christians. They also self identified as human rights organisations. While both obligations and rights discourses were evident in these organisations, the dominant discourse has been constructed around human rights and the dominant practice can be identified as activism. For example, in Jakarta a Muslim human rights organisation has been campaigning to support the rights of gay and lesbian groups. The majority of interviewees identified themselves as advocates for those who had little voice, particularly where the marginalised groups had been physically attacked, such as in the case of the persecuted members of the Islamic sect, Ahmadiyya.

Framing and debate

It has often been through third sector organisations that citizens have put issues on the political agenda. There is a long history of campaigning groups that have brought neglected issues to public attention, framed policy debates and carried out research to inform the policy process. Many of the issues first raised by third sector organisations in previous centuries have found their way onto the statute books in established democracies – in the UK, examples include clean air, divorce, civil liberties, capital punishment, and equal rights for women, ethnic minorities, disabled people and LGTB communities. Across the world, third sector organisations have focused attention on homelessness, AIDS, the plight of refugees and asylum seekers, and so on. They challenge the way that the democratic process itself works. They carry out research that informs or challenges policy decisions; they keep issues in the public eye and stimulate debate. In the *Willing parnters?* research cited earlier, one organisation described how it had "done some very good research about a scheme in Australia that seemed to work well. Within a matter of months there was a pilot scheme operated by the [government]". Indeed some government respondents in this study reported that they found the third sector invaluable for providing feedback into the system – they were, one local councillor said, "our eyes and ears" (Parkes et al, 2004, p 315). This links to another of the roles that respondents identified in that study, the role of holding policy makers and service providers to account (although, of course, there is no guarantee that these will respond as positively as the government respondents quoted above).

Linking citizens into formal political processes

Chapter Four cites Almond and Verba's landmark cross-national study from the 1960s, which covered Germany, Italy, Mexico, the UK and the US. This presented evidence that membership in associations was correlated with support for democracy, trust in others and in government and a greater willingness to participate in civic life (Almond and Verba, 1963). There have been a number of critiques of this view in subsequent years, although later scholars have reinforced it, notably Robert Putnam, for whom, as we have seen in earlier chapters, the associations in civil society build the trust that 'makes democracy work' (Putnam et al, 1993).

We have already seen that active citizens do not necessarily see what they are doing as 'political' in terms of engaging in with formal party politics or the electoral process (Brodie et al., 2011; see also Chapter Six). The Take Part programme, which was the successor to the ALAC initiative described earlier, found that those who were taking part did not necessarily want to progress in the sense of moving on from making their voices heard to becoming more directly involved in formal political processes (Mayo and Annette, 2010). There was strong evidence of appreciation for courses that enabled learners to understand civic roles, such as the role of school governor or local councillor. However, this was typically because the courses enabled them to understand these roles better in order to engage with them from the outside, rather than because they wanted to take on these roles for themselves on the inside (Recknagel and Holland, 2013).

A recent South Korean study found that civil society participation was linked to some forms of political participation – including attending demonstrations and signing petitions. But this was not the case when it came to taking part in voting, for example. Citizens were making their own choices about how and where to participate in political processes. This does not necessarily imply that they had limited concepts of active citizenship; they may simply have preferred to engage in the ways that they considered to be most likely to make an impact (Hoi Ok Jeong, 2013).

Kabeer's Bangladeshi study similarly found that 'Whilst much of what NK does is political in nature, actual participation in the formal political domain was not a priority in its early years' (Kabeer, 2005, p 193). Over time, though, there were observable impacts on political participation more generally. For example, the women who had been involved via NK were less likely to vote as instructed by their husbands, and they were less likely to have 'sold' their votes (Kabeer, 2005, p 194). Nonetheless, some third sector organisations work actively to engage citizens in formal political processes – encouraging them to register for the vote, or to use it. They have also supported citizen participation in the formal structures that have opened up over recent years.

So far in this chapter, we have discussed the way in which citizens are organising for themselves – in their own 'popular' spaces. But earlier chapters have remarked on the increasing interest in citizen participation from institutions across the world (Hickey and Mohan, 2004; Cornwall and Coelho, 2007; Gaventa and Tandon, 2010). As a result, citizens are increasingly being 'invited' into spaces that have been opened up by governments and international organisations. Although the owners of these spaces sometimes select individual citizens to participate – or invite individuals to volunteer – it is often through third sector organisations that citizens engage or are invited to participate. Third sector organisations may elect representatives, hold them accountable and give them support. Thus, Castello and her colleagues argue, 'We are not witnessing simply an increase in opportunity for citizen participation, but a broader process of *reconfiguration* of political representation 'in which civil organizations play a central role' (Castello et al, 2007, pp 114–15). But being invited into these spaces is not enough on its own. Third sector organisations often work on both sides of the equation to build 'a more active and engaged civil society and a more responsive and effective state that can deliver needed public services' (Gaventa, 2004, p 27), working with external power holders to open them up to citizen influence, building 'linking social capital', and setting up opportunities for marginalised groups to engage with power holders.

Challenges

Third sector organisations face many challenges in carrying out the roles we have described. To what extent can service delivery and activism be combined, especially as third sector organisations are increasingly drawn into providing services that were previously seen as the responsibility of the state? Can they maintain a critical edge if they are drawn into state agendas? And who do third sector organisations represent? Do they speak for or with the disenfranchised and disadvantaged? In the former case, they can become part of the problem when it comes to tackling the 'democratic deficit' rather than being part of the solution. In representing diversity, how far do they succumb to the 'mischief of factions', and how far are they able to find a common voice?

Maintaining a critical edge

Independence has long been the mantra of the third sector and many commentators have lamented the extent to which, over the decades, third sector organisations have been drawn into partnership with the state, as agents of service delivery or as partners in policy making. Ralf Dahrendorf, for example, was a strong critic of the English Compact, warning against 'the embrace of the state' (Dahrendorf, 2001), a concern echoed by a number of other commentators over the years (Morison, 2000; Haugh and Kitson, 2007; Carmel and Harlock, 2008; Rochester, 2013). Indeed, in the UK case, a number of flagrant breaches of government's commitments along with the increasingly instrumental approach taken to the Compact with successive 'refreshes' lends some support to this argument (Zimmeck, 2010; Taylor, 2012b)

In the Bangladeshi study referred to earlier, Kabeer argues that one factor in NK's success was the fact that the organisation was not caught up with the challenges of service delivery. She suggests that there is an inevitable tension between 'NGO service delivery (whether government-funded or not) and NGO capacity to demand accountability and responsiveness from public services' (Kabeer, 2005, p 196). Certainly, in countries such as the UK, commentators warn that, as the focus of government funding to third sector organisations shifts decisively away from grants and towards contracts for services, there is a high risk that advocacy will be crowded out either by the demands of service delivery or by fears of losing government funding (Minkoff, 2002; Milbourne, 2013; Rochester, 2013). For example, Purkis (2012) describes how housing associations, who over the last 30 years have become the major providers of social housing, do not campaign because they do not want to prejudice their government funding (although they have an umbrella body that does campaign). In the US, Beck and Purcell (2013, p 56) describe how the Back of the Yards Neighbourhood Council (BYNC), which was the fruit of Alinsky's early community organising efforts in Chicago, eventually lost its campaigning edge as it became involved in service delivery – the poacher turned gamekeeper. They remind us that NGOs may themselves be the 'enemy', to the extent that they indulge in 'welfare colonialism' (Beck and Percell, 2013, p 62). Indeed, as the disability movement grew in the UK, big national care charities were often as much the target of its critique as public and private organisations

However, the research evidence to date is mixed. A number of studies have found that the risks have been overstated (Craig et al, 2004; Suarez and Hwang, 2008; Cairns et al, 2010; Smith and Pekkanen, 2012). Indeed Smith and Pekkanen cite evidence that government funding can be associated with greater advocacy (Chaves et al, 2004; Child and Gronbjerg, 2007; Mosley, 2011). Beck and Purcell (2013, p 81) also describe how working in coalition – or forming alliances – can help to avoid the risks. They describe how member organisations of the Sydney Alliance, which is an affiliate of the Industrial Areas Foundation, 'are perceived as being one step away from the action' and are thus 'to some extent protected from backlash, thereby making their funding more secure'.

The English Compact did recognise the right of third sector organisations to campaign if they were in receipt of government funding. But the pressures on campaigning in this country have been growing, with increasing demands on the Charity Commission to be tougher in enforcing the rules and regulations as well as challenges to the rights of those in receipt of public funding to campaign on matters of public interest (Baring Foundation, 2014; Snowdon, 2014). Indeed, the government's Work Programme has introduced a 'gagging clause', prohibiting subcontractors from 'making public announcements that may bring the department into disrepute' (Baring Foundation, 2014). The UK government has also introduced legislation to curb the right of charities and others to campaign in advance of national elections – a move which was fiercely contested by an alliance which brought together a broad third sector constituency: the major third sector umbrella bodies and traditional service providing charities as well as campaigning bodies and the new internet based organisations, such as 38 Degrees. This legislation has drawn fierce criticism from the UN's special rapporteur on peaceful assembly and association international organisations, who describes it as a 'stain on British democracy' (Kiai, 2014).

Cairns and his colleagues (Cairns et al, 2010), arguing from a British perspective, argue that dual roles in providing services and campaigning for change stretch back to the 19th century at least in this country, long before the advent of the 'contract culture'. And these roles have not proved incompatible. Citing Young (2001) and Vanderwoerd (2004) in the US, they argue that 'organisations with a high level of organisational self-consciousness …and deep sense of their own identity and traditions' are likely to be able to manage the conflicts between these dual roles (Cairns et al, p 204). The same might be said in other cultural contexts, as this chapter argued earlier, where third sector organisations have long combined a contentious tradition with the need to provide services the state fails to provide (Taylor et al, 2010; Howard and Lever, 2011), although in these cases third sector organisations are not so likely to be providing services under contract to government. Indeed, in this wider context, Edwards and Hulme argue that there are strong arguments for NGOs and grassroots organisations combining service delivery and advocacy functions (1995, p 225).

But what about partnerships? By entering partnerships with the state, do third sector organisations compromise their independence? Any number of studies from different parts of the world have warned against the risk of cooption, as third sector organisations get drawn into the policy making process (Atkinson and Carmichael, 2007; Cornwall and Coelho, 2007; Barnes et al, 2007; Taylor, 2011). As Chapter Five explained, an important distinction is made by those studying citizen participation between 'popular spaces', which are set up by citizens themselves, and 'invited spaces', set up by external actors including external international development actors (Cornwall, 2004; Gaventa, 2007). Studies of partnership working across the globe demonstrate how the new spaces for citizen voice are characterised by unequal power relationships, with cultures and practice dictated by state and other powerful partners and third sector players marginalised (Larner and Butler, 2005; Atkinson and Carmichael, 2007; Barnes et al, 2007; Cornwall and Coelho, 2007; Cooke and Kothari, 2011; Taylor 2007, 2011). Studying regeneration partnerships in the UK, Atkinson (1999) thus describes how new technologies of governing operate to secure the 'willing compliance' of participants, ensuring that policy communities operate according to common norms and assumptions, framing and addressing problems in similar ways.

'Invited spaces' often come with a consensus orientation which sweeps difference and dissent under the carpet (Cleaver, 2004) and several commentators have observed a diminishing of critical political perspectives (de Filippis et al, 2009; Barnes et al, 2007; Cornwall, 2008; Bunyan, 2010), suggesting that invited spaces can crowd out popular, citizen-created spaces. For example, one recent study in Wales reported how a community group left a partnership because it felt that it was being sidelined – in fact other members agreed that it was being patronised by professional staff – but it found it had nowhere else to go. The working class institutions of the region's industrial past – the local union branches, local political party branches, working men's clubs, workers education institutes that constituted 'popular spaces' – no longer existed. Eventually it felt forced to rejoin the 'invited space' of the partnership if it was to have access to the networks and information it needed to serve its members (Taylor et al, 2010). What this suggests, as Chapter Five argued, is that effective working in invited spaces needs to be underpinned by the presence of 'popular spaces' in which citizens can find their voice and from which they can draw strength.

In or against the state

This leaves third sector organisations with the decision of whether to operate 'in' or 'against' the state in the context of wider processes of change. The ALAC was extended after its first two years and renamed Take Part. But the focus narrowed, with increased emphasis on encouraging citizens to take on formal roles within existing structures – as school governors, local councillors or magistrates, for example – that is practising active citizenship as civic commitment, rather than focusing on active citizenship in its more activist sense, that is involving actions aimed at social change more generally. And there was mounting pressure to meet targets defined by government. Recknagel and Holland (2013, p 23) studied this and other UK government initiatives and found increasing government emphasis on encouraging citizens to be active in filling the gaps left by a 'reduced and reconfigured Welfare State' rather than enabling citizens to influence – and where necessary challenge – public institutions and public policy processes. But she also highlighted the remaining spaces and the continuing scope for human agency. Both Craig and his colleagues in the UK (Craig et al, 2004) and Cornwall and Coelho internationally (2007) emphasise the importance of working on the inside and outside. The actors on different 'sides' may reject each other's approaches but mobilisations from the outside place issues on government agendas and keeping the pressure on while champions on the inside can work with government to negotiate policy change.

Nonetheless, even when actors on different 'sides' do find ways of working in collaborative ways, with the 'hard cop' pressuring from outside while the insider plays 'soft cop', as the 'reasonable' negotiator, this does not necessarily produce the desired results. Situations can and do change and spaces can shrink. A third sector organisation that is coopted by the state under one administration may find itself on the outside if there is a change in government – this is a particular risk in countries where clientelism is rife. In Nicaragua, for example, spaces that opened up under the administration in power between 2001 and 2006 became coopted when Ortega was returned to power (Taylor et al, 2010) and third sector organisations that had been active in them found themselves squeezed out in favour of those faithful to the Ortega regime. Nonetheless, in the right circumstances insider–outsider alliances can result in pincer movements that work very effectively

In addressing this challenge, we should perhaps also unpack what we mean by the 'state', recognising that states are rarely monolithic. There may be discontinuities and differences within and between different levels of government. Third sector organisations may find allies in local government against national government for instance. Public sector professionals may be potential allies, working alongside service users' organisations to protect their services from marketisation and/or the effects of neoliberal austerity cuts. And there may be opportunities for creatively exploiting differences between different levels of the state – local, regional, national and international. There have been times, for example, when third sector organisations in Europe have appealed human rights issues over the heads of their national government, taking these issues on to the European Court. Conversely, interventions by international actors can rebalance the power relationship between the state and third sector organisations at national level, as Chapter Five suggested (Taylor et al, 2010). The relationship between national government, indigenous NGOs and international NGOs can therefore be complex, with varying opportunities and challenges – issues that are explored further in Chapter Nine.

Leadership and representation

The first part of this chapter argued that third sector organisations can act as a channel for enabling the diversity of citizen voices to be expressed and heard. And Chapter Four rehearsed the claim that third sector organisations model democratic forms of organisation. But this is a claim that needs further scrutiny. Whose voices do they enable? And how far are they accountable to those whose interests they claim to represent?

The first challenge to this claim relates to Ernest Schattschneider's famous claim that the 'heavenly choir' in the 'pluralist heaven .... sings with a strong upper class accent' (1960, p 35). A respondent to the *Willing partners?* study (Craig et al, 2004, www.wahidinstitute.org/wi-id/?) suggested that:

> 'The more resources you have, the more you can do ... and the resources tend to be the more middle class or upper class. Certain groups in society might have the ear of a policy maker, or a particular organisation might have the money for a worker. There are very few people at the bottom or black groups who have the money for a worker. So it can be the opposite of democracy.'

Indeed, back in the 1960s, in the years of the US War on Poverty, Marris and Rein (1967) commented on the difficulty of organising a constituency around poverty – a challenge that we will return to in Chapter Nine.

Some critics differentiate between larger organisations – the not-for-profits – and smaller community-based organisations in this respect. The associational claims reported in Chapter Four would hold that smaller community-based organisations are likely to be closer to those whose interests they represent than larger organisations and to have more opportunities for frequent and informal feedback (see, for example, Chanan, 1991; Knight, 1993; Rochester, 2013). Putnam (2000) argues that professionalisation has eroded the connections many third sector organisations have with local citizens, for example (see also Chapter Six). And large organisations, as reported earlier in this chapter, may even find themselves the target of campaigning by their users and smaller organisations.

Certainly, as organisations grow and become more professionalised, there is a danger that they will lose touch with their members and/ or constituency. Against this, Smith and Pekkanan argue that many smaller organisations do not have the resources to engage in advocacy (2012, p 45) or indeed may not have this as part of their mission. They find that the more resources an organisation has in terms of funds and paid staff, the more likely it is to be involved in advocacy. Being able to fund a staff member to focus on this part of the organisation's work can clearly be an asset. But this does not necessarily mean that smaller organisations lose out. Craig and his colleagues (Craig et al, 2004) found that some of the larger organisations they studied were providing resources and support to their service users to enable them to find their own voice and speak for themselves. Or they were acting as 'docking points' for smaller organisations by inviting them into meetings with policy makers – indeed, being able to link a policy maker with a 'real person' often lent the larger organisations considerable credibility with those they were trying to influence.

Smith and Pekkanen go on to underline the importance of accountability and engaging users and members, suggesting a range of ways in which this can be done. But they point out that 'many non-profits are not well situated for this type of community engagement and participation because of small boards, a lack of membership and insufficient resources' (Smith and Pekkanen, 2012, p 43). And, ironically, being recognised by power holders and invited into spaces of power can prejudice the very links that give organisations their legitimacy. A number of studies of government–community sector partnerships, for example, have found that such engagement risks absorbing the time and energies of community leaders at the expense of their day-to-day contacts with their constituency. If they are also absorbed into the cultures of the power holders, as this chapter has suggested, they risk losing their critical edge.

It is unwise, therefore, to assume that small is beautiful when it comes to advocacy. Clearly, it has its advantages. However, community-based groups can be exclusive and their leaders unaccountable. Sometimes this is because of personalities who find it difficult to share power and act as 'gatekeepers'. Purdue et al (2000) point out that community leaders may self select in ways that do not make them the best person for the role. But the much criticised 'usual suspects' can also be much maligned. There is an inevitable tension between leadership and widespread participation. Citizens may be happy to let their representatives get on with the job as long as they are going in roughly the right direction – participation in formal structures is, after all, very much a minority sport and can involve high costs in terms of the time and energy required (Taylor, 2011).

Smith and Pekkanen point out that many advocacy groups have a small, middle class staff. Some will have members, some will not. Either way, for these organisations, demonstrating their legitimacy is at a premium. Many household name campaigning groups, as well as the prominent newcomers like Avaaz, 38 Degrees and GetUp mentioned earlier, are using the internet to demonstrate public support, particularly through petitions. How far this will in the long term address the issues raised in this section and give voice to the diversity of citizens, however, has yet to be seen. In the meantime it seems clear that size per se is not the determining factor. More important are the perspectives and the politics of those concerned and their commitment to genuinely democratic forms of accountability downwards (using the term 'politics' in the broader sense of being concerned with issues involving politics and power, rather than in the narrower sense of 'politics' in terms of formal party political structures).

Finally, in this section, it is important to recognise that third sector organisations do not always advocate in order to defend the interests and concerns of others. They can also engage in advocacy in order to defend their own self interests or promote their market share, just as a business might do.

Factionalism

To say that the third sector as a whole can advance democracy and diversity does not, of course, mean that every individual third sector organisation actually does so. Third sector organisations can oppose each other and compete with each other for attention and funds – a tendency which is exacerbated in a climate of austerity and cuts. A further temptation, as the market becomes the dominating principle in public service delivery, is for third sector organisations to become protective of their knowledge in the name of commercial confidentiality. The sector contains organisations with widely divergent and conflicting beliefs and missions and there are difficult decisions to be made about when it is important to maintain a cohesive voice and when to acknowledge difference. The very commitment that binds a third sector organisation together and makes it strong can militate against cooperation and solidarity with outsiders. Its organisations are also prey to what Cohen and Rogers (1992) called 'the mischief of factions', as groups fall apart because of conflicts between members. Owen (1964, pp 94–5) describes the proliferation of sects in the Victorian era in the UK, describing how poor households might find themselves subjected to visits from three or four societies on a Sunday, all wishing to peddle their own brand of salvation. In campaigning, different messages from groups who appear to have the same aims can fatally undermine the legitimacy of campaigns with both decision makers and the wider public. In conflict situations in particular, alignments between third sector organisations can break down over strategic issues, with the ensuing hostility between organisations becoming especially bitter, as groups struggle against more powerful opponents in quests for independence (see Longland, 1994).

Conclusions

This chapter has described a number of ways in which third sector organisations can contribute to the political activism of citizens, acting as schools for democracy, mobilising and organising citizens, acting as channels for the diversity of voices in society, linking citizens with formal policy making structures and providing a route into public life. But organisations engaged in this kind of activity face a number of challenges and do not always enhance democracy. It is sometimes hard for them to maintain an advocacy role in the face of the demands of service delivery – instead, critics of government funding to third sector organisations claim that service delivery compromises their advocacy role. And while third sector organisations can indeed provide a channel for the diversity of voices in society, they are not necessarily democratic in themselves. Those with more resources are likely to have a greater voice than those without, organisations of all sizes can be exclusive and unaccountable and there is certainly no guarantee that they will be concerned with social justice. And there are tensions inherent in carrying out these roles: between the leadership that is required to lead a successful campaign and the opportunities they provide for widespread participation; between operating outside the state in order to place contentious issues on the agenda and operating within in order to negotiate change; between the need to provide a cohesive voice for change and the need to recognise diversity and difference.

The extent to which third sector organisations take up their potential roles and address these challenges will depend on the fields in which they operate, and the political and historical context. In some states, third sector organisations engaging in advocacy are under threat, except maybe those sponsored by or controlled by the state, as is happening in contemporary Russia (see Chapter Seven); in others their advocacy role is accepted, although there may be regulations barring those with tax-exempt status from engaging in party politics or election campaigns (as in the UK or US, for example). In some countries with a strong contentious or dissenting tradition, many third sector organisations retain their radical edge. Elsewhere many involved in third sector activities do not identify their engagement as in any way political, even in the sense of being political with a small 'p', engaging in issues of political concern without necessarily being involved in formal party politics with a capital 'P'. However, it is important to recognise that they too can contribute to democratic life. As Beck has argued, 'even "subpolitical action" can contribute to political life – forms of action and social participation that have no explicit democratic and policy purpose can in fact produce democratic and civic externalities' (Beck, 1993 cited in Evers, 2013, pp 152–3).

NINE

Active citizens, social movements and social transformation

Introduction

This chapter builds on the previous chapter's analysis of active citizenship via third sector engagements in public policy processes and politics. The discussion moves on here to explore active citizenship and social movements, with a particular focus on social movements committed to mobilising for social change. As previous chapters have already suggested, the distinction between third sector organisations and social movements is not totally clear cut and active citizenship may be nurtured in both. Moreover, social movements have been presented as being potentially transformational, their relative freedoms and flexibilities standing in contrast with the typically more restrictive pressures on third sector organisations, especially if third sector organisations are involved in competing to provide public services – in increasingly market-driven contexts (Milbourne, 2013). Without the pressures towards professionalisation, bureaucratisation and mission drift that have been associated with contracting processes themselves, social movements have been able to pursue more independent, creative – and inherently more radical – agendas for social justice and social change, pushing previously accepted limits, breaking the rules where necessary in ways that question the legitimacy of existing power structures and demonstrate the potential for alternatives. As the slogan accompanying World Social Forums proclaimed, 'another world is possible', another world that was being brought into being and exemplified within the lived practice of social movements on a global scale (Gitlin, 2012). Or so it has been suggested.

This chapter therefore sets out to explore a number of varying ways in which social movements have been forming part of more complex scenarios and illustrates a number of the tensions that have already been emerging from previous chapters. Are social movements or social movement organisations inherently more transformational than other parts of the third sector more generally? Or do they encompass a similar range of aims and objectives, underpinned by a comparable range of political perspectives from different parts of the globe, including varying perspectives on the changing relationships between the third sector, the state and the market? The chapter asks whether social movements actually face similar challenges to other parts of the third sector in terms of building flexible but sustainable alliances between organisations and individuals with varying experiences and differing approaches to strategies and tactics. These include questions about whether and how far to work inside and/or outside formal decision making processes and structures (or both) and the challenges of ensuring that social movements are both inclusive and genuinely representative of the range of interests involved. And it asks how far these challenges might become magnified in the context of transnational social movements promoting active citizenship at the global level as well as at local and national levels.

The chapter opens with some discussion of the varying definitions of 'social movements', and 'social movement organisations', rooted in differing approaches to the whys as well as to the hows of their developing histories. It explores the competing theoretical explanations of the reasons why, and the ways in which, active citizens come together to promote varying social change agendas, at different levels, locally, nationally and/or internationally. This leads into a brief consideration of the (supposed) distinctions between the 'older' social movements and the 'newer' social movements and networks, challenging stereotypes such as that 'older' and/or more organised social movements are inherently less relevant, or less effective, let alone inherently less progressive or transformational, than 'newer' social movements. Most importantly, this chapter moves on to clarify that, here too as in other chapters, there are fundamental differences of purpose, goals and value orientations involved, from social justice and equalities movements through to more socially conservative agendas such as the agendas of the Tea Party in the US, for example.

As previous histories of active citizenship via social movement campaigning have also illustrated, social movements can include – and often have included – different approaches and varying types of organisations and networks, with varying goals, some more limited and specific than others, with differing levels of commitment to particular types of strategies and tactics. One example here might be the civil rights movement in the US. This brought together both formally organised sections of civil society such as black churches and the National Association for the Advancement of Coloured People (NAACP) and looser networks of black activists, white students, trade unionists and other activists. It thus faced the challenge of accommodating elements with widely varying goals, from the relatively limited aim of obtaining the right to vote (in practice as well as in principle) through to broader, more transformational goals of racial equality and social justice (Tarrow, 2011). As this chapter argues, then, social movements face many of the challenges that confront the third sector more generally – although this is in no way to devalue social movements' potential for contributing to active citizenship and social justice agendas, both locally and more widely.

The final section of this chapter focuses on some of the implications for building broad and sustainable alliances between active citizens, committed in their varying ways to work for social change. How can NGOs and other third sector organisations (including international NGOs, faith-based organisations and trade union organisations) provide support without undermining the active engagement of less organised activists, including 'horizontal' networks of community activists, young people outside formal employment, homeless people and squatters among others, taking account of differing organisational strategies, tactics and styles (including the use of new media) (Mason, 2013)? This section explores how social movements might be supported in sharing their learning about the most effective ways of building such alliances, including via the provision of learning for active citizenship, globally as well as more locally, using the example of community/ university partnerships.

Definitions and approaches in different contexts

So what do we mean by the term 'social movement'? And how far do definitions and theoretical approaches to the study of social movements that have been developed in Europe and North America apply, in very different contexts, elsewhere?

A range of perspectives needs to be addressed. Tarrow has provided a very useful starting point here, setting social movements within the context of what he has described as 'contentious politics', meaning the mobilisations that take place when ordinary people 'try to exert power by contentious means against national states or opponents' (Tarrow, 2011, p 6). As he goes on to explain, 'in the last fifty years alone, the American Civil Rights movement, the peace, environmental and feminist movements, revolts against authoritarianism in both Europe and the Third World, and the rise of new Islamist movements have brought masses of people into the streets demanding change'. While they often succeeded, he adds, 'even when they failed, their actions set in motion important political, cultural, and international changes'

As Tarrow recognises, people have been engaging in contentious politics since the dawn of history. However, in his view, in more recent times, it has taken social movements composed of active citizens to ensure impact, mounting, coordinating and sustaining contentious mobilisations even in the face of powerful opponents, including both powerful opponents in the state, at whatever level, and powerful opponents representing private sector interests. Social movements are to be distinguished from contentious politics more generally, by their roots in 'underlying social network(s)' together with 'resonant collective action frames, and (on) their capacity to maintain sustained challenges against powerful opponents' according to Tarrow (2011, p 7). In other words, social movements can be characterised by their capacities to build on existing networks together with their capacity to frame grievances and/or demands effectively, presenting these in ways that will resonate with their supporters and inspire them to collective action. And finally social movements are to be characterised by their capacity to sustain themselves over time – over decades in some cases and/or in waves, over successive decades, as in the case of first, second and now third and fourth wave feminism.

There are parallels between Tarrow's analysis and Diani's definition of social movements as 'informal networks of individuals and/or organisations, sharing a collective identity and the same side in political and/or cultural conflicts' (Diani, 1997). But this is not to suggest that this definition has been unanimously agreed. On the contrary, for Eyerman and Jamison, for example, social movements have been characterised in more transitory ways as 'temporary spaces, as moments of collective creation that can provide societies with ideas, identities, and even ideals' (Eyerman and Jamison, 1991, p 4). For Escobar and Alvarez, meanwhile, 'the whole idea of a "social movement" as a description of collective action should be abandoned because it traps our language in conceptual traditions that have to be discarded' (1992, p 7).

Definitions of social movements have been contested, then, based on varying theoretical perspectives. Social movements have also pursued contentious politics for varying aims and objectives. Some of the best known examples, such as the civil rights movement, could be classified in terms of the pursuit of human rights and social justice agendas. Others cover a potentially wider range of the political spectrum. For instance, environmental movements have varied in their overall orientations and ultimate impacts, pursuing environmentally friendly goals that can, however, on occasion rebound, to the detriment of the livelihoods of local communities in the poorest places (Simpson and

Waldman, 2010). And social movements can pursue aims and objectives that privilege some while excluding others, whether intentionally (as in the case of anti-immigrant mobilisations for example) or unintentionally by default (as with the exclusion of the homeless from some of the mobilisations of the Occupy movement in the US for example). These various differences will be discussed further in subsequent sections of this chapter.

There is not the space here for detailed discussion of the varying theoretical traditions that have underpinned the study of social movements. In brief, however, these may be summarised as follows. First, in the US, functionalist sociologists' preoccupations with the study of social order led them to focus on the ways in which social structures held together and reproduced themselves, rather than focusing on processes of social change. From such perspectives, groups or communities engaged in collective action to address grievances were seen as behaving exceptionally in an otherwise well-functioning social order. Outbreaks of contentious politics were associated, even, with the behaviours of irrational mobs, according to such functionalist approaches.

In contrast, social movement theorists (particularly theorists in the US) started from the assumption that social movements arose as rational responses to social problems, including problems such as social deprivation and social inequality (Fox Piven, 2011). These theorists explored the ways in which activists identified opportunities and mobilised for collective action, developing a variety of strategies and tactics to precipitate social disorder, interrupting, obstructing and rendering uncertain previously accepted norms and structures. Scholars emphasised the importance of political opportunity structures, here, together with the capacity to mobilise resources to maximise such opportunities, in order to promote the desired social changes. And they explored the ways in which social movements 'framed' the issues in question, focusing on the options and targets for change in ways that would maximise the resonance for existing supporters and potential supporters (Snow and Benford, 1998).

Meanwhile, in Europe, as Melucci and Lyyra (1998) argue, scholars were more concerned with questions as to 'why' rather than 'how' 'new social movements' were emerging, focusing on the challenges posed by student mobilisations in 1968, for example, together with the challenges posed by feminism and the environmental movement. These movements included concerns with identity, ideology and culture, rather than concerns with the more immediately material problems that had been the bread and butter of class conflict in capitalist societies. These new conflicts, according to Habermas (one of the thinkers who particularly emphasised new social movement theories), were 'not ignited by distribution problems (such as wages struggles)', 'but by questions having to do with the grammar of forms of life' (Habermas, 1987, p 392, cited in Crossley, 2002, p 160). Politics was being broadened to include issues of identity, culture and lifestyle – the slogan of 'the personal is political', taking on relationships of power at every dimension.

The extent of the supposed differences between the so-called new social movements (such as feminism and the environmental movement) and older social movements (such as the trade union and labour movement and tenants movements) has been challenged. This will be discussed further in the following section. But this question does indicate that more nuanced approaches are needed. The slogan 'Bread and Roses' seems suggestive here – highlighting the importance of addressing immediate material needs such as wages and conditions at work and rents without neglecting issues of culture, identity and emotion, including the politics of everyday life.

Meanwhile, social movement theorists from North America and Western Europe have been developing what have been described as 'attempts to meld different theoretical perspectives into a new synthesis' (Della Porta and Diani, 1999, p 4). They have been exploring ways of encompassing the 'why' as well as the 'how' questions via political process approaches (Della Porta and Tarrow, 2005), focusing on the interrelationships between human agency and socioeconomic structures.

What might be the relevance of such theoretical approaches, though, for very different contexts in other parts of the globe? As Thompson and Tapscott (2010), among others, have pointed out, historical contexts differ widely. For example, social movements that developed in the struggle for freedom from colonial rule and/or racial domination (as with the African National Congress in apartheid South Africa) have become parties of government, posing new challenges in terms of the changing relationships between civil society and the state (Piper and Nadvi, 2010). Political opportunity structures may be widely different in one party states in any case, just as they may be widely different in contexts of more extreme material deprivation, where collective action may be driven by the immediate necessities of survival rather than by any conscious framing of options. 'Thus for example, the immediacy of the threat posed by forced eviction is such', Thompson and Tapscott suggest 'that there is little need to persuade slum dwellers of the need for collective action' (Thompson and Tapscott, 2010. p 14).

Overall, Thompson and Tapscott conclude that, while social movement theories developed in North America and Western Europe have significant contributions to make, they have analytical limitations when applied to very different contexts elsewhere. The issue of the applicability of third sector institutions originating in North America and Western Europe has been noted in earlier chapters. For the purpose of this chapter it is important to acknowledge concerns about the universality of social movement theories and keep this caveat in mind, when it comes to considering transnational social movements – social movements that aim to span very different global contexts. Before coming onto the discussion of transnational social movements though, the differing aims, objectives, strategies and tactics of social movements need to be considered at more local and/or national levels, together with their varying approaches to questions of organisation, inclusivity, representation and accountability.

Aims and objectives, strategies and tactics

As signalled in the discussion so far, social movement theorists have been moving away from earlier debates on the similarities and dissimilarities, strengths and limitations of the so-called new social movements as against those of the older movements, contrasting older forms of solidarity with newer forms of fluidity. As Holst among others has argued, whether 'these new social movements actually exhibit "new" characteristics' has been the subject of debate (Holst, 2002, p 36), while the demise of older social movements has similarly been called into question. Although deindustrialisation has been impacting only too clearly in parts of the older industrialised countries, this has not led to the death of the trade union and labour movement, as some social movement theorists predicted, despite the scale of the challenges faced. Recent mobilisations – from those associated with Occupy to those associated with the 'Arab Spring' – have included trade unionists and students as well as the unemployed, for example, according to Paul Mason's study of 'The New Global Revolutions' (Mason, 2013). But this is in no way to suggest that there have not been genuine differences between movements, just as there have been and continue to be genuine differences within social movements, whether at local, national or transnational levels. These have included: differences in terms of overall aims and objectives; differences over questions of strategy and tactics; and differences with implications for organisational forms and practices.

The US welfare rights movement, launched in the US in the 1960s, provides an example in point, illustrating differences concerning aims and objectives, strategies and tactics. Reflecting on her experiences as a key activist as well as a theoretician, Frances Fox Piven returned to her earlier work on the welfare rights movement, highlighting the ways in which this had challenged welfare policies in the US. In the process, she concluded, it had enabled participants to solve the problem of 'a desperate need for a measure of dignity' (Fox Piven, 2011, p 104). The welfare rights movement was a nationwide movement, she explained, if not a huge one, bringing together welfare recipients and supporters to organise around the welfare system, challenging its degradations as well as its material inadequacies in response to unemployment and poverty.

The National Welfare Rights Organization began in the wake of the civil rights movement as a broadly based movement of some black – and a few white – people dedicated to attacking the relief system. One impact of the US War on Poverty in the 1960s had been to provide community action programmes that activated new leadership in the black ghetto, and 'they also activated masses of black poor' (Fox Piven, 2011, p 111). This illustrated the relevance of addressing the underlying structural problems of poverty and unemployment as well as taking account of the political opportunities provided by these community action programmes. Community activists, including antipoverty lawyers, supported poor people to challenge policies, rules and regulations that were keeping them off the welfare rolls, leading to test cases that established welfare rights more widely. Applications doubled between 1960 and 1968 (a significant year, as Fox Piven pointed out, as this was also the year that rioting reached a crescendo of contentious politics, adding pressure for positive responses from the state).

While there were common aims and objectives there were also differences within what was a broad coalition. For some the aim was to enable the poor to claim the welfare relief to which they were entitled – alleviating their lack of income without undergoing humiliating treatment in the process. For others it was about extending welfare provision, taking test cases, for example, to expand the coverage of rights to welfare. And for others, including Frances Fox Piven herself, the aim was to promote more far-reaching change, demonstrating the fundamental inadequacies of the system that was then in place and thereby pressurising the powerful to develop alternatives. As she explained, there was a belief that 'a disruption in welfare could be expected to activate lobbying by other and far more powerful groups for a goal which the poor could not possibly hope to achieve were they simply to lobby themselves' (Fox Piven, 2011, p 122). This approach did produce results, in her view, as by the late 1960s 'political leaders in the major northern states became articulate spokesmen for federal action in the welfare area' (p 123). The point to emphasise here then is that there were varying aims and objectives, just as there were varying results, including the impact of participation as active citizens on the poor themselves.

What the National Welfare Rights Organization's experience also demonstrates is that social movements can and often do represent coalitions with differing views on strategies and tactics. Frances Fox Piven herself argued that 'political influence by the poor is mobilized, not organized' (2011, p 125). By this she meant that it would have been extremely difficult, if not impossible, to organise the poor in a formal organisation, on an effective and sustainable basis, given their situation and given the lack of available incentives to maintain commitment over time. As we saw in Chapter Eight, similar arguments have been put forward by others, including Marris and Rein in their seminal study of the War on Poverty (Marris and Rein, 1967). But the poor could be mobilised to disrupt in their masses, Fox Piven argued, whether simply by claiming benefits and/or by engaging in other forms of protest. Although she was not referring to Alinsky's style of organising here, there are perhaps echoes of his 'Rules for Radicals' (Alinsky, 1971), pointing out that even if they lack resources in general, the poor do tend to have numbers on their side, together with the ability to cause disruption and embarrassment for the powerful.

The implications for such a mobilising approach would, in principle, be to develop a national network of cadre organisations rather than a national federation of welfare recipient groups. Rather than building organisational membership, the aim would thus be to build the welfare rolls as part of this strategy, backed by marches and one-off demonstrations. As Frances Fox Piven recognised, however, this type of approach struck organisers as being manipulative rather than democratic. The poor had a right to run their own organisations, the critics argued, and to determine their own policies and strategies. So the national organisation was formed, focused on benefits for existing recipients as the incentives for continuing participation.

As subsequent events demonstrated, she argued, this turned out to have had negative consequences, however. The focus on organising on this basis contributed to the fragmentation of the welfare rights movement, in her view. By the early 1970s, in the face of more regressive policies at federal government level and diminishing militancy more generally organisers and recipients were drifting away. Fox Piven concluded that 'an era of protest had inexorably come to a close' (2011, p 135). The National Welfare Rights Organization continued to lobby against regressive welfare 'reforms' but local organising was petering out. The membership base was dropping off – a decline that was followed by bankruptcy and the closure of the national office

Whether or not alternative strategies and tactics would have been more successful in achieving the National Welfare Rights Organization's goal of 'Bread and Justice' – or whether alternative approaches would have been more sustainable for longer – is beyond the scope of this chapter. The point to emphasise here is simply that social movements have been characterised by differing approaches, as well as by differing aims and objectives. And these differences – whether to mobilise or to organise – have continuing resonance in debates on social movements and the ways in which they operate within civil society today. This brings the discussion to more current debates about different organisational forms, framed in terms of whether to organise horizontally or vertically.

Horizontals versus verticals

World Social Forum debates have included vigorous discussions on the merits of horizontal versus vertical approaches to social movement organisational forms. There are resonances here with earlier theoretical debates, within and between social movements, old and new. In summary, traditional organisational approaches had been the subject of criticism, including the criticism that movements such as the trade union and labour movement tended to operate in overly bureaucratic ways, lacking flexibility in their decision making mechanisms. While trade unions were strong on formal mechanisms for ensuring accountability to their members, critics argued that these were rooted in representative rather than participative forms of democracy, mechanisms which tended to empower the leaders, rather than actively engaging the members at the grass roots.

Such criticisms have often been associated with feminist arguments about the ways in which formal procedures have tended to result in the predominance of men rather than women in positions of authority and influence. Indeed feminist critics have argued further that these have tended to be white men, rather than men from black and minority ethnic (BME) communities, let alone women from BME communities (for a critical discussion of these debates, see Phillips, 2004; Fraser, 2008). Such criticisms have also been associated with libertarian socialist perspectives as well as the perspectives of those concerned with more direct, including more deliberative, forms of democracy (Della Porta, 2013). Without going into further detail here, the point to emphasise is simply that social movements have been associated with such criticisms over time.

Critics of vertical approaches have argued the case for developing more fluid ways of engaging in contentious politics, ensuring flexibility though non-hierarchical networks, building consensus via deliberative dialogue. However, horizontal forms of organisation have themselves been the subject of criticism – and from a variety of positions. In brief, these may be summarised in terms of debates on different forms and approaches to democratic decision making, transparency and genuine accountability, and debates on the extent to which horizontal forms of organisation can be effective, let alone sustainable over time (Della Porta, 2013). Do open forums and the use of electronic media actually lead to more genuine forms of accountability? Or do the more formal structures that have characterised trade unions and political parties on the left of the political spectrum provide sounder mechanisms for ensuring that, when the votes are finally counted, the result does actually reflect the views of the wider membership? The horizontal argument fails to understand the ways in which more vertical structures operate to safeguard the rights of their members, including the rights of minorities. Thus Della Porta and Rucht (2013), amongst others, have been aware that looser organisational forms can actually mask informal structures of leadership – the 'tyranny of structurelessness'. Do less formal organisational forms genuinely promote participation and inclusivity? Or can they be as exclusive as more formal organisations in their turn? And finally, do deliberative forms of decision making simply take too long to be effective, whatever the horizontals' claims to the contrary? There are echoes here of some of the concerns that have already been identified in previous chapters, exploring potential challenges for third sector organisations and civil society more widely.

There is not the space in this chapter to develop the theoretical debates that underpin these questions in more detail. Rather than attempting to take these further here, it may be more helpful to provide examples to illustrate some of these debates and their associated dilemmas, as these have been manifesting themselves in practice. A first set of questions – about accountability/lack of accountability and inclusivity/exclusivity – may be explored via examples from the Occupy movement (Gitlin, 2012; Schein, 2012). Meanwhile a second set of questions – about effectiveness/lack of effectiveness – may be illustrated by examples from a study of the Global Justice Movement (Della Porta and Rucht, 2013).

Occupy? 'We are the 99%' – or are we?

As the title to Paul Mason's book on the new global revolutions suggests, 'it's kicking off everywhere' (Mason, 2013). Among the civil society mobilisations that he covered internationally, from the 'Arab Spring' to student occupations from Moscow to Quebec, Mason included the Occupy movement, starting with the calls to occupy Wall Street, New York's financial centre, in the summer of 2011. Drawing on international experiences of occupations in public squares, activists set up camp in Zuccotti Park, New York, expressing their feelings of outrage about the impact of the financial crisis of 2008 and the ways in which austerity policies were increasing inequalities. 'Banks got bailed out' it was argued 'but we got sold out' (Gitlin, 2012, p 24).

As the slogans illustrated, there were shared sources of anger and frustration. The financial systems that had led to the crisis were benefitting the 1% of bankers and their associates, it was argued, while the remaining 99% of the population were bearing the brunt of the bankers' reckless self aggrandisement. But there were also wide-ranging differences of view as to what should be done in response. Some argued for very specific reforms, such as taxing Wall Street financial transactions, while others argued that 'we are the beginning of the beginning' (Gitlin, p 76) of far more radical processes of change. Meanwhile, the movement spread to other cities in the US, just as it spread to other countries, including the UK.

The first occupiers included unemployed graduates, frustrated by the lack of employment opportunities but with large loans to repay. They were joined by a wide range of activists, with supporters from a variety of organisations and movements, including the trade union movement. This breadth of support was a source of strength but also a source of potential tensions – a point to which this chapter will return. Occupy set out to be inclusive but this was potentially problematic, according to Gitlin, despite his overall sympathy with the movement and its youthful energy.

In some ways Occupy aimed to prefigure alternative, participative and more directly deliberative forms of democracy – 'the process is the message' (Gitlin, p 68) with horizontal approaches to decision making via general assemblies. But this did not mean that there was total spontaneity. At one point some 3,000 meals were being served a day. There were working groups set up to get things done, with facilitators, even if not leaders. And there was energy and creativity. Despite the commitment to non-violence however, there were problems too, including problems with drugs and the harassment of women. There were, in addition, expressions of frustration at the length of time that decision making processes were taking, described as 'driving some participants crazy' (Gitlin, p 94). While movements are energy, Gitlin reflected, they can also attract the unruly and the manipulative. There may even have been some sense of relief, in some quarters, when the occupation was finally dispersed.

Others too have reflected on some of the challenges involved in Occupy's approaches. They have recognised important achievements in addressing these without abandoning commitments to deliberative decision making as part of wider commitments to participative forms of democracy. But they have also highlighted the dilemmas involved. As Schein argued, for instance, the slogan that 'This is what democracy looks like' was all very well and good but what would happen when there were conflicts with the homeless people who were occupying these spaces themselves, simply looking for spaces to sleep? It was not going to be so easy to meet their needs for food and clothing let alone their needs in terms of issues such as mental health and addiction (Schein, 2012). For Schein these experiences also raised concerns about the impoverished and imperfect nature of public institutions, prompting questions as to who should actually be providing services to meet such needs and what, indeed, should be the role of the state.

Smith and others (Smith et al, 2012) raised similar issues about the challenges of aiming to be inclusive, drawing on experiences in El Paso, Texas. In fact, Occupy had initially excluded homeless people, leading to objections that the homeless were also part of the 99%. As a result of these objections though, homeless people were eventually involved as occupiers themselves. For Smith et al, this demonstrated the movement's ability to cope with such challenges democratically: 'The acceptance of homeless people as Occupiers gave coherence and strengthened the movement while simultaneously providing dignity and solidarity for homeless people' (Smith et al, 2012, p 356).

How sustainable such mobilisations can be over time remains to be seen, however, whether in terms of their survival as mobilisations and/ or in terms of their impacts on the individuals and networks involved, let alone in terms of their impacts on the structures of power.

Meeting democracy: power and deliberation in global justice movements

This leads into the second question, the extent to which decision making processes can actually be conducted in very different ways while still being effective. Della Porta and Rucht's comparative study of global justice movements in different European countries provides illustrations here (Della Porta and Rucht, 2013). Like Occupy, the Global Justice Movement has been characterised by widespread commitment to deliberative forms of democracy, with preferences for prefigurative approaches to politics, as exemplified in this particular case by taking decisions on the basis of having reached consensus (Della Porta, 2013). In their study of global justice movements in different European countries Della Porta and Rucht explored the ways in which power and decision making processes were actually operating within social movements. They started by recognising the dangers of the tyranny of structurelessness, 'the implementation of informal power structures' which serve 'to maintain the subtle but firm leadership of one or several individuals in a group, to domesticate dissenters, to ignore unwanted remarks and so on' (Della Porta and Rucht, 2013, p 5). And they recognised the potential conflicts that could arise between democratic values in principle and organisational efficacy in practice. How far, then, could the Global Justice Movement groups that they set out to study succeed in balancing these tensions? How were they managing the challenges and how might their approaches develop over time?

In summary, this research identified strong commitments to deliberative forms of decision making. The groups that were studied demonstrated awareness of the challenges involved and so had tended to establish rules and procedures 'to reduce the use of unwanted and illegitimate forms of power' (Della Porta and Rucht, 2013, p 229). Despite this, the researchers concluded, 'Still (mostly informal) hierarchies tend to persist, though probably to a lesser extent when compared to right-wing movements and to more established and non-movement-related voluntary associations' (p 229). Leadership per se was not being denounced, despite the egalitarian values being held more generally. On the contrary leadership was accepted and respected when it evolved more or less organically, based on 'outstanding capabilities, personal traits, a credible and time-consuming investment for the common cause and respect for the other group members' (p 229). And leadership could be effectively shared between different group members, each bringing particular qualities, whether instrumental or expressive.

The groups that were being studied were mostly fairly small. The largest group, the French ATTAC board, had 42 elected members, and the Italian Water Campaign had up to 85 participants at national meetings but most groups were far smaller. There would seem to be parallels here with Gilchrist's findings on networks, concluding that the optimal size was no more than 40 (Gilchrist, 2009). In addition, the groups in Della Porta and Rucht's study tended to include a large proportion of women. These characteristics emerged as potentially significant factors, contributing to the ways in which the groups operated, which was described as being generally cooperative and friendly. Even serious discussions were accompanied by jokes and laughter, the researchers noted, and this was particularly marked in Italy and Spain, 'possibly reflecting a more general trait of Southern European culture' (Della Porta and Rucht, 2013, p 217). There was evidence of friendship and trust in general then – although the researchers also noted the exceptional situation in the French ATTAC board, which was then 'shaken by a deep crisis of the overall French organization (culminating in a complaint of electoral fraud)' (p 217).

By and large, the researchers concluded, despite problems, tensions and challenges, the groups were mostly friendly and respectful of differences. Deliberation, they argued, 'is not just a utopian ideal'. This could be put into practice, at least under particular conditions. But 'contrary to common assumptions', they pointed out 'horizontality does not necessarily go hand in hand with "structurelessness". In fact', they went on to argue, 'we have noted that deliberation is facilitated by the spread (linked with the culture of direct action) of rules and roles that are anchored in informal institutions' (p 231). The groups that they studied were generally able to communicate effectively with others too, including those who were part of the machinery of representative democracy. By implication then, there is room for horizontalism within social movements, whether others organise in similar or very different ways, provided that there is mutual understanding and respect.

How far does this all apply globally?

Della Porta and Rucht's research has provided evidence to demonstrate that social movements could operate in participative ways, reaching decisions democratically and inclusively via processes of deliberation. But the groups that they studied tended to be small and relatively cohesive – with significant proportions of women activists involved. While these groups were concerned with issues of global justice, they were also more locally, or at least nationally, rooted. How far might these research findings apply in wider contexts?

As the discussion earlier has already suggested, social movement theories have been questioned in terms of their relevance beyond Europe and North America. Thompson and Tapscott (2010) pointed to differences in material circumstances, including the resources available for mobilisation, for instance, just as they pointed to differing historical experiences in countries that had been colonised – where civil society organisations developed as part of struggles for national liberation. As Piper and Nadvi (2010) have argued, in the context of post-apartheid South Africa, organisations that played key roles in civil society struggles could subsequently take on leading roles in the structures of governance. This posed new challenges for the movements in question (the African National Congress and its allies), just as it posed new challenges for civil society more generally. Piper and Nadvi concluded that civil society had become relatively weaker in post-apartheid South Africa. What would be needed to revitalise state–society relations, they argued, would be 'the rebirth of oppositional movements strong enough to make ruling parties pay attention and take communities seriously' (Piper and Navdi, 2010, p 234). Without going into further detail here, the point to emphasise is simply that social movement theories that have been developed in Europe and North America may need to be adapted or rethought to take account of such different histories and circumstances of civil societies elsewhere.

Transnational social movements, including the Global Justice Movement, face particular challenges here, highlighting challenges that been identified in civil society and the third sector more generally. How can social movements effectively represent and address the different interests involved? Who speaks for whom, when organisations and individuals have very different access to power and resources, including the resources to communicate at international levels? And how can social movements operate effectively and inclusively, enabling mobilisations at the local level to both strengthen *and be strengthened by* mobilisations at the global level?

Transnational social movements need to recognise and respect the differences of interest that can and do exist. There are numerous examples for illustration. For instance, Simpson and Waldman's study of mobilisations to claim health rights on asbestos issues in South Africa provides a case in point. Despite the fact that transnational litigation was deemed successful in its own terms, a view shared by many claimants, other claimants interpreted the case as a bitter defeat, raising questions about the extent to which transnational mobilisations had actually led to citizen empowerment (Simpson and Waldman, 2010). Although compensation was achieved, the court case was not seen as a means of enforcing corporate social responsibility, nor did the legal framings resonate with more local cultural assumptions and framings of justice, leaving one community feeling marginalised and deeply dissatisfied. 'International values, interpretations of processes, and determinations of successful mobilizations do not, ultimately, always hold true in

Southern contexts', Simpson and Waldman concluded (p 105). There are potential differences of interest involved here as well as potentially different priorities, even within the same campaign.

Earlier chapters have already referred to the extensive literature exploring the significance of globalisation, with new spaces for citizen engagement at international levels (Held and McGrew, 2002; Gaventa and Tandon, 2010). The key questions here concern the engagement of citizens and social movements at different levels. Can civil society mobilisations at different levels actually reinforce each other, interacting in mutually beneficial ways (Scholte, 2005)? Or do 'Southern' activists feel like 'second class citizens among their Northern partners', 'welcomed as sources of information and legitimation but not as equals' (Clark, 2003, p 24). 'Northern' partners tend to have far more resources and far greater opportunities to contribute to international consultations in Washington and New York, for example, which raises the question of who speaks for whom at this level – although, as Batliwala (2002) has also pointed out, this resonates with the question of who legitimately speaks for whom within social movements *within the 'South'* which have their own internal hierarchies of voice and representation.

The Global Campaign for Education (GCE) provides illustrations of the types of issue that need to be addressed (Gaventa and Mayo, 2010). Yet despite such challenges the GCE also illustrates the possibilities for building transnational coalitions, enabling local actions to be strengthened as a result. So what exactly were the challenges in question and how did the GCE manage to address these? Why did parents concerned about their children's education in rural India or rural Nigeria choose to become part of an international campaign, keeping up the pressure on donors to meet the Millennium Development Goal of Education for All?

The new spaces that have emerged from this campaign, enabling citizens to claim their rights (Della Porta and Tarrow, 2005) have included new spaces to claim the right to education, at international as well as at national and local levels. For example, key decisions about funding for education in poorer countries were agreed in 2002, to be overseen by the World Bank via a mechanism known as the Fast Track Initiative. Pressure to deliver on this funding agreement was then maintained in various ways including via Global Monitoring Reports, annual reports produced through UNESCO and backed by an international advisory board including several international NGOs, such as the Global March Against Child Labour and ActionAid. This space for GCE to be involved with the Fast Track Initiative was potentially significant, opening up opportunities to pressurise international agencies as well as providing ways of keeping up the pressure on nation states (who could be embarrassed by a poor showing in Global Monitoring Reports). Whatever the conclusions of theoretical debates on the notion of 'global citizenship', the reality was that there were opportunities as well as challenges for the development of active citizenship at the transnational level. Building on previous campaigning on the right to Education for All, the GCE was established in 1999 to take up these opportunities and challenges.

So how did the GCE manage to build and sustain a transnational coalition with firm roots at the local level (Florini, 2000), maintaining accountability downwards while operating effectively at a global level? The nature of the GCE was precisely to link across all levels of action simultaneously, avoiding hierarchical international divisions of labour characterised by concentrations of power among elite campaigners jetting between global capitals – with the global defined as being actions "in Washington, New York, the cosmopolitan media hubs of the North" as an NGO leader from the 'South' reflected (Gaventa and Mayo, 2010, p 149). As a veteran GCE campaigner reflected,

> 'now anything which is just local is not going to solve the problem (of the lack of resources and commitment to Education for All). The sites of authority and power have changed, and when sites of authority and power have changed, the sites of struggle will have to be changed ... The struggle for a just and democratic governance is not a linear struggle, it means being local, it also means being global.' (Gaventa and Mayo, 2010, p 146)

Citizen engagement at the local level remained key though – not only to give legitimacy but also to ensure that resources would actually be directed as needed to provide quality education for all. This included action at the most local levels to ensure that parents sent their children – including their daughters – to school on a regular basis (a major challenge in far too many places). These local initiatives would then be reinforced, in their turn, as a result of the activities of the global campaign, including the Global Weeks of Action that were being organised across continents each year, activities that directly involved the children themselves.

Several factors were identified as central to the GCE's resilience over time (Gaventa and Mayo, 2010). The first was the level of trust that was developed, building on the GCE's strong roots from the 1990s.

This was supported by carefully built governance structures, to ensure democratic accountability and involvement at all levels, rather than allowing the campaign to be run by the international NGOs.

The campaign messages were then framed through inclusive processes of consultation. The themes for the annual Global Weeks of Action were carefully chosen after widespread consultation, for instance, which ensured that activists from different countries bought into these themes at every level. The contributions at each level were recognised and valued. And there were resources (provided via the Commonwealth Education Fund) to support the campaign – essential given the costs of international travel, for example.

This is not, of course, to suggest that there were no tensions or issues to be resolved within the GCE. There were. Although the goal of Education for All commands very widespread support, in principle, there have been differences of interest to be addressed – for instance between teachers' trade unions and international NGOs with a history of providing informal education (provision that teachers tended to view as undermining the case for public resources to provide formal education for all). There were also differences of perspective on how to address the problem of child labour: whether to oppose it on principle, and/or whether to recognise that poor families may have depended on their children's labour in order to survive at all. The question was not whether there were differences therefore but rather how such differences were negotiated, building on relationships of trust at different levels.

In summary, the GCE illustrates the potential for building alliances transnationally in ways that can actually reinforce, rather than undermine, citizen activism at the local level. But this was achieved as a result of the long-term commitments of key activists, working in democratically accountable ways, building relationships of trust between key international NGOs, international trade union organisations (teachers' unions), national coalitions, and more local voluntary and community organisations and groups. This was a broadly based coalition committed to working in mutually respectful ways, putting the collective interests before the concerns of particular organisations and individuals. Without claiming to have achieved the goal of Education for All, the GCE can realistically claim to have made a difference – at every level, internationally, nationally and more locally. The GCE experience provides an example of how, regardless of the state-based theories of citizenship (see Chapter Two), active citizens are now thinking and acting their rights and obligations transnationally, and in so doing are prefiguring cosmopolitan forms of active citizenship (see Chapter Four). As Schattle has commented, 'like it or not, individuals all over the world are choosing to think of themselves as global citizens and to shape their lives as members and participants in communities reaching out to all humanity' (Schattle, 2008, p 24). It can be an iterative process, with active engagement in transnational campaigning strengthening participants' senses of themselves as global citizens. This would be consistent with the experiences of many of those involved with the GCE. As a GCE activist reflected,

> 'the very fact of being involved in GCE joint endeavours does change perceptions and increases members' sense of involvement. You do get a sense that you are actually part of something. This activity helps produce the "glue" that builds the representation and accountability structures. This builds solidarity – giving the role of agency and active engagement to activists.' (Gaventa and Mayo, 2010, p 155)

As an international campaigner added, these campaigns were "genuine educational experiences which have changed people's understanding of power and of themselves as actors. It will also change their understandings of North and South" (Gaventa and Mayo, 2010).

Towards conclusions

The opportunities for the development of civil society globally would seem greater than ever. Among other factors, the spread of access to new information technologies has been centrally important. The internet has enabled global activists to communicate in ways that would have seemed literally incredible for previous generations. And as recent accounts have demonstrated, new communication tools have facilitated extremely rapid and effective mobilisations, from the 'Arab Spring' to the Occupy movement (Gitlin, 2012; Mason, 2013).

But the challenges of building effective and sustainable social movements – movements that are genuinely inclusive, participative and democratically accountable – would seem formidable too. Whether at local, national or international levels, social movements tend to be composed of a range of interests, organisational forms and approaches. This calls for understanding, taking account of such differences on the basis of mutual respect. Formal organisations and less formal networks can and do find ways of working together on the basis of recognising that both have key contributions to make and that neither has a monopoly on democratic decision making processes. There are issues here that resonate with those that have been explored in previous chapters, including questions about the most effective ways of sharing the learning – how do we build alliances and how do we strengthen civil society as part of wider strategies for equalities and social justice?

Part 3
New forms of active citizenship: emerging forms and challenges

TEN

Active citizenship and the emergence of networks

Introduction

As we have argued throughout this book, active citizenship involves agency. Turner (1992), among others, emphasises the importance of people shaping rights and obligations through their participation in society, as active rather than passive citizens. Humans are viewed as autonomous self-determining beings, as agents who shape and change society (Touraine, 2000). This approach places agency at the centre of societal development. Crucially, the focus on agency has opened up citizenship research to questions about different ways in which subjects enact themselves as citizens. To explore some of these questions, it is necessary to adopt a micro analysis, one that examines the formation of active citizenship from below. Such an analysis may complement the more usual sociopolitical analysis, which examines the macro factors that also shape and at times limit the formation of particular kinds of citizenship.

We are here dealing with the question of how change happens. How do new organisational forms emerge? How do new products, new systems of production and new ideas of any sort materialise? Organisational theory tends to assume that new organisational forms are created by good managers, perhaps entrepreneurs, within an organisational context and drawing on organisational resources. In other words, citizens assume power *from above*. Someone with power and resources makes something happen. However, by focusing on collective agency, this chapter turns this assumption on its head, and focuses instead on the ways that creative new forms may emerge *from below*.

As Chapter Four discussed, there is now a substantial body of literature that identifies the importance of the third sector in the development and support of active citizenship (for example, Onyx et al, 2011) and the creation of social capital (Putnam, 2000; Onyx and Bullen, 2000). But there is another story to be told about the formation of third sector organisations. What kinds of actions lie behind the formation of these organisations or indeed of larger social movements? And what of the ordinary, everyday lived reality of active citizenship? What are the actual processes and structures that underpin social capital, community capacity and active citizenship?

This chapter argues that, while third sector organisations are crucial in the maintenance of civil society, in order to understand active citizenship and the formation of third sector organisations, it is necessary to look beneath the surface manifestations of these organisations and understand their emergent nature. The vast majority of civil society networks and organisations are formed from below, emerging from the dynamic and creative turmoil that is driven by social disequilibrium and the search for new responses to contemporary issues and problems. Current global concern about climate change is generating just such a creative turmoil, for example, and is generating many grassroots climate action groups.

Not all networks become fully fledged and recognised associational forms. All emergent networks go through a period of formation, though, much of which will be invisible to the outsider and lack any coherent shape. Some online activist sites for instance may well remain as loose and mutually supportive networks of individual agents. Other embryonic networks may remain as informal friendship networks or loose connections between residents of a given area. Such loose networks may remain dormant for most of the time but have the potential to be activated into more formal networks in the event of an emergency, such as bush fires or the need for political action in defence of a threatened amenity. Others will gradually form into stable ongoing third sector organisations to meet a continuing community need.

Complexity theory

Complexity theory can help us understand the emergence of social capital networks in the community and the way in which these networks then become the crucial ingredients in the creative development of new community projects and new organisational forms. Chia (1999) argues for a 'rhizomic model' of organisations, in which change and transformation is the norm. He argues that we need to shift our thinking from assumptions of institutionalised structure and stability to ones of flux, in which 'all things flow' in a continuous process of becoming, in which what *is* now contains the traces of what was, and the seeds of what is yet to be – that is the principle of immanence.

Complexity theory offers an insight into the fundamental issue of *emergence* (Chiles et al, 2004). It offers an explanation for 'how system-level order spontaneously arises from the action and repeated interaction of lower level system components without intervention by a central controller' (Chiles et al, 2004, p 501). This theoretical approach can be applied to emergent self-organising networks within civil society. So complexity theory suggests a number of crucial dynamics that may explain the process of the self-organising emergence of networks.

Goldstein (2011) summarises the emergent process in organisations as follows:

- A period of disequilibrium in which spontaneous fluctuations emerge forming the seeds of new emergent order;
- Positive feedbacks which amplify the fluctuations of #1;
- Recombinations and new correlations of existing resources, capabilities, symbols, language, and work patterns;
- Coordinating mechanisms that stabilise the new emergent order.

Goldstein was still here focused on the organisation. However, this dynamic of emergence occurs throughout civil society, often within what may be termed the 'institutional void', that is outside any particular organisation and indeed crossing the boundaries of organisational sectors (Baker et al, 2011). The process emerges first out of states of disequilibrium or a tension between disequilibrium and equilibrium in the wider context (Plowman et al, 2007). The early stages of emergence may be marked by conflict, not only between the member agents and some wider social or political issue or event, but also between the member agents themselves. The state of disequilibrium may be deliberately created or amplified; it is only through such turmoil that a new, creative milieu can emerge, though, one that seeks innovative solutions to perceived problems.

Taking the implications of complexity theory further, it is possible to argue that this state of disequilibrium draws agents together. These agents may be individuals or organisations or both, interacting, discussing, and exploring options for action. These consequent actions may be small and localised, involving the active initiative of concerned agents. Some of these actions may lead nowhere, but others may appear promising and so are communicated to others in the embryonic network, which, at this stage, may be little more than a fertile milieu for action. Others hear about the actions and discussions, through word of mouth and/or electronic technologies, and/or published papers and media reports. Someone, usually a group, calls a meeting, and a network begins to take shape as various agents share information and agree to further action.

Positive feedback loops are crucial in establishing new modes of operating (Goldstein, 2011). That is, it is essential that some actions lead to some sort of positive outcome, perhaps partial and temporary, but enough to motivate others. Such results must be communicated to others in the network.

It is likely that the discussion and forms of actions will be volatile and full of uncertainty and potential conflict. However, while disequilibrium may be welcomed and further encouraged, there may also be counter forces towards some sort of new equilibrium. Stability within the embryonic network may be dependent on 'deep structures' involving shared intrinsic values, and operating principles of the participants. Normally these will be articulated in terms of a common set of principles or objectives signed off by all participating agents. Thus creative turbulence may be contained within a broad set of objectives that are shared.

Within the context of civil society, complexity theory focuses attention on the coalescing of relationships between individuals who may be operating as individuals or as members of organisations. This coalescing of relationships can create a fertile milieu out of which may emerge new ideas, formations and intentions for collaborative action. An emergency or perceived crisis of some sort may then be enough to trigger the rapid formation of a new organisational form, or collective action of some sort. Complexity theory would suggest that there is here an ongoing process from individual agency to creative milieu to emergent network structures and ultimately to formal adaptive organisational forms.

The role of leadership

Complexity theory gives leadership a central place, but a different kind of leadership where adaptive leadership is dynamic and 'is the product of interaction, tension, and exchange rules governing changes in perceptions and understanding' (Lichtenstein et al, 2006). This approach to leadership is in marked contrast to the classical organisational model of leadership, which emphasises hierarchy and control (Avery, 2004; Chiles et al, 2004). Such classical views of leadership rest on the assumption 'of organisations as equilibrium seeking systems whose futures are knowable and arrived at by leaders who plan interventions and control behaviors' (Plowman et al, 2007, p 341). By contrast, within complexity theory, leadership should not be viewed as individuals operating in isolation as they influence their followers or in terms of individual traits. Leadership is seen as an emergent phenomenon that arises from interactions and events (Lichtenstein et al, 2006). A similar approach (Surie and Hazy, 2006) argues that, with respect to innovation, generative leaders create conditions that nurture it rather than direct or control it. In a similar manner, some forms of collective entrepreneurship, involve emergent and/or dispersed leadership in a social context. Johannisson and Olaison (2007) argue for a concept of 'enactive entrepreneurship' associated with social creativity and made particularly visible in the case of a natural disaster or emergency situation facing a community. Research by Onyx and Leonard (2010) suggests that leaders are embedded within the social networks, and are more likely to be part of a group rather than operating as a single individual.

Implications of complexity theory for the study of active citizenship

Table 3 provides the basic principles of complexity, which must be acknowledged in any attempt to analyse emergent forms of active citizenship, as a phenomenon which defies linear causality, a phenomenon which may appear chaotic as observed within the lenses of 'normal science'.

Thus, from this perspective, it is neither possible nor desirable to try to predict the shape or effect of emergent actions. However, studying locally situated interactions may provide insight into how the micro

Table 3: Principles for complexity

Multiplicity of legitimate perspectives: Need to take into account multiple stakeholder viewpoints.
Non-linearity: Relationships are non-linear resulting in a magnitude of effects not being proportional to the magnitude of the causes.
Emergence: The 'whole is more than the sum of its parts... True novelty can emerge from the interaction between the elements of the system'.
Self-organisation: The phenomenon by which interacting components compete to produce large scale coordinated structures and behaviour.
Multiplicity of scales: Hierarchic nature in that each element of the system is a sub-system of a smaller order system, and the system itself is part of a larger 'supra-system'. There may be strong interactions between levels and different rates of change within levels. Implying plurality and uncertainty.
Irreducible uncertainty: Reflexive social systems are capable of their own observation and analysis becoming part of the activity of the system, but also capable to influence it in certain ways. This may be through purposive, deterministic behaviour, or less predictable chaotic forms.

Source: Adapted from Gallopín et al (2001, p 225)

level builds meaningful interactions between individuals and groups within communities. According to Griffin and Stacey:

> it is not possible for committed groups of individuals to intentionally change the widespread patterning of their interaction. All they can change is their own interactions, and from this the widespread patterning will emerge in ways that they cannot intend or fully understand … The aim of the method is, therefore, not one of changing the social 'wholes' but of making sense of the 'live' experience of interaction. As people make sense differently they act differently, and it is this action, in continuing interaction with others, that macro patterns change in emergent ways which cannot be predicted or controlled. (2005, p 33)

Through examining multiple situated communities of action and the interactions occurring every day we may begin to view some temporary patterns of emergence or identify some common factors that ignite more purposive action. To capture some of the richness of this process, the ideal methodology is the case study.

The case studies[1]

As a heuristic device, some of the key processes of this proposed theory of emergence are illustrated with reference to four community case studies, one drawn from Australia, one from Peru, one from Uruguay and one from Sweden. The case studies were selected because they had demonstrated community development. They all relate to definable small communities (<5,000 people) that had created a clear project for the social or economic benefit of the local community. The case studies were conducted between 2000 and 2010. A thematic analysis identified the major issues for each case, roughly approximating a grounded theory approach. It is from this analysis that insights concerning the emergence of community formations is possible.

Maleny, Australia

Maleny is a small town in the hinterland of Southeast Queensland. A major disequilibrium occurred when the struggling dairy farming area experienced an influx in the 1970s of new residents, who held a

---

[1]   The material for the case studies is drawn from Onyx and Leonard (2010).

commitment to an environmentally sustainable lifestyle. These new residents identified the need for more services and four of them, led by one woman in particular, held meetings of residents to explore the possibility for community development – that is the possibility for creating new networks and processes and new organisations to better serve the community as a whole. The main leader was one of the first of the new residents, living in an organic farming housing settlement on the outskirts of Maleny.

The idea emerged of developing cooperative organisations to serve the community, starting with a credit union and an organic farm produce outlet. The active initiative of the group was particularly evident in their study tours of other centres and in their obtaining an expert to assist in setting up the first cooperatives. Since these were moderately successful, a positive feedback loop was formed and other cooperatives followed the first, including a community café and various commercial enterprises. Some local residents, especially the dairy farmers, were initially resistant to the new developments but increasingly they became more fully included in community plans and a local newspaper was formed to keep the wider community informed. The main leader appeared to work with great skill and dedication, involving many other people in the gradual evolution of the town. Although she was central to the formation of each new venture, she seldom took a management position.

Maleny became a prosperous community with a population of approximately 4,000 and a large number of community organisations spanning diverse functions. According to the database created through the local Maleny Working Together (MWT) project, conducted in 2003, and involving a survey of 411 households as part of a community audit (and initiated by the same woman leader), there were 136 community groups within the Maleny local area. Many people (40%) volunteered their time in some capacity and there were strong interconnections between these community organisations: over 90% of local community groups dialogued with others locally indicating a tightly interwoven collection of community organisations.

These interconnections were partly due to individuals belonging to many different organisations simultaneously. Informally, this provided a flow of information between these different organisations and sharing of resources. The majority (88%) of the sample felt that it was easy to be involved in the community.

As Maleny reached a new equilibrium there was evidence of the formation of deep structures based on shared values. An important shared value has been to create as near as possible self-sufficient sustainable communities based upon local cooperation and place-bound networks. A related value was its commitment to the environment: Maleny received an award for Environmental Citizen of the Year. The openness of the local community was another related value that made the town special. According to one interviewee:

> 'It's an energy thing you just seem to tune in to. It's vibrant, it's interesting, it's very diverse and to a large extent it's the people. It is very accepting. It doesn't matter what your background is, age, sexual preference whatever, it makes no difference.' (Female informant)

As evidence of the strength of the shared values, survey data revealed that Maleny recorded the highest social capital factor across all those communities surveyed in Australia (Edwards and Onyx, 2007). Maleny scores were high across all the social capital factors including *community connections, trust, neighbourhood connections, tolerance of diversity* and *social agency*.

The strength of these deep structures was tested by a recent experience of disequilibrium – caused by the approval by the local council of a large new supermarket for a national retailer, sited on the bank of a river with endangered platypus. The Obi Obi campaign signalled a general community resistance to the development involving most groups in town, including the cooperative movement and local business owners, as well as environmental and social groups. At the time of the Obi Obi campaign, the woman who had been the early leader was active, but no longer central to the organisational resistance. Although the complex was built, local residents continued to boycott the stores.

Anapia, Peru

Anapia, population 2,000, is the most remote of the islands in Lake Titicaca in the Andean part of Peru. At the time of the fieldwork, reaching Anapia required a 2.5 hour car trip from Puno, the regional capital, followed by a 1.5 hour boat trip. The people identified as Aymaran and the main economic activities were agriculture and fishing. It was basically a subsistence economy, with little money exchange. Most people owned land and/or a fishing boat. However, there were a few landless families who worked on other people's land in exchange for a share of the produce.

A major disequilibrium occurred in the mid 1990s, when a local entrepreneur, who had completed some tertiary education in Puno, explored the possibility of developing eco-tourism on the island as a means of economic development, but without losing the island's cultural heritage and ways of life as had happened in other islands where tourism had already been developed.

Anapia had a unique process of decision making. On the first Saturday of each month, the entire community met in the central plaza. Under the management of the Mayor, issues of community-wide concern were discussed. It was through this process that the social entrepreneur was able to present his case for the tourist project and to have the project thoroughly discussed and debated. There was some conflict as some community members were concerned that outsiders would bring new diseases and that the proposed developments would change their way of life. Others feared that they could not provide adequate services to these strangers. They reported that they had to overcome fear and shame in interacting with the tourists, and they were very anxious about their ability to please. It took two years of intense discussion within the community before they were ready to undertake the project. Although not all the dissenters were convinced, an association called Adeturs was formed.

Unfortunately there was no immediate positive feedback as only a few tourists arrived the first season and none the next. The entrepreneur persisted, however, and sought a partnership with a travel agent, in which the community would maintain the initiative and control. All Ways Travel agreed to promote the island as an ecotourist destination, and to assist the islanders to develop a quality product. Communication with Puno was difficult (and still is) with unreliable telephone services. So the leader went to Puno to find the tourists and bring them back to Anapia.

With several thousand years of shared culture and lifestyle there were very deep structures and shared values. These principles were used to organise the new venture. The organisational system they chose was consistent with the traditional *Iynu* system of organisation in agriculture where work was collectively organised but each family had their individual plot from which they obtained the produce. Translating this into tourism meant that, in strict rotation, each family would host tourists and benefit from the financial return. A strict limit was applied to the number of tourists to be hosted by each family (one couple per week). Other families were involved in related activities such as transport and meal preparation. This system ensured an equitable distribution of income, whereby no one person could get rich at the expense of others.

All those involved in one of the four tourist activities were members of the relevant sub-committee (maximum of two activities per family) and all decisions were made by consensus. Each committee, as well as Adeturs itself, had a president elected every two years, as well as a treasurer. Adeturs provided overall coordination of the four committees. Within Anapian society and Adeturs, the women played a major role. Although most of the senior offices were held by men, women took an active role in public meetings and on committees and in developing their homes for tourists. And all families involved in Adeturs were required to work collectively to improve the village, keep streets clean of rubbish, and so on.

The new venture required creative thinking, so as members of Adeturs realised they needed to increase their skills and knowledge they also created the necessary solutions. Some training and advice was provided by All Ways Travel but residents needed to travel beyond the island. So groups of women travelled, sometimes for the first time in their lives, to gain the skills they needed and to promote their programme.

However, the residents had also been gradually recognising the value of their traditional knowledge, taking pride in it and sharing it with the tourists. And the programme had been providing fertile ground for other ventures. One woman gave a presentation on their programme in a community development competition in the national capital, for example. With the prize money the residents built a community centre with a small library. And a volunteer tourist programme helped to paint the school.

The entrepreneurial leader who started the tourist project, and who was president of Adeturs for many years, then became Mayor of the municipality and a new leader was elected for Adeturs. The community was by then confident that they could maintain control of the development process, and were ready to expand further.

Juanico, Uruguay

Juanico is a small village of 1,300 people in the department (district) of Canelones, located 80 kilometres from the capital of Uruguay. The population has been entirely European, comprising early migrants mainly from Spain and Italy. While most villages in the area experienced population decline, Juanico experienced an increase in population of 90% from 1996 to 2004.

Juanico is located on rich agricultural land that has mainly been producing fruit and wine. The largest employer in Juanico has been the vineyard. Most villagers did not own land to farm and were dependent on employment at the vineyard, or commute to Montevideo. Wages were very low. Although within Juanico there has been a handful of middle class families, professionals and small business owners, the economy has been dominated by one major employer, the owner of the vineyard, who was living in Montevideo.

Juanico appeared to the visitor to be a comfortable village. It had 16–20 active local, civil society organisations (CSOs), including various neighbourhood committees, children's organisations and sports clubs. Of particular importance has been the 'CAIF'. The CAIF is a state institution in charge of childhood and family care centers across the country in cooperation with CSOs, set up originally as a United Nations (UNICEF) initiative. In Juanico, the CAIF was formed during the 1990s by a small group of local residents, mainly women at the suggestion of the bishop. It ran a preschool programme for 1–5 year olds, including the provision of a hot meal for each child (the food was provided by the Ministry of Food). The CAIF was also providing a range of other programmes, including a' father and son' programme, supported by a range of professionals. The local staff were also working closely with the mothers to deal with a range of other issues that were affecting children and families, including domestic violence.

At the local level CAIFs have been governed by a committee of volunteers from the community. As an extension of this, the Juanico CAIF committee formed a 'Club de Ninos', which provided daily meals, supervision and professional care for school children. As a result of these food programmes, malnutrition in Juanico was virtually eradicated.

Other organisations have also been very active. The polyclinic was formed following lobbying from the CAIF and other local groups, thus providing medical help on a regular basis (several days a week on average). There was a grandparents club, also run by a local, elected management team, with 200 members attending various functions organised by the club. There was an active football club with eight categories of teams for children aged 5–13, plus adult teams. The club was working to create a community park with barbeques and play equipment. There were also several (at least four) neighbourhood committees working to improve conditions in the district, such as via improved sanitation, street lighting and paved roads.

Of particular importance has been the Coordinating Organisation, with representatives from each existing CSO to deal with community-wide issues. This coordinating committee was formed at the beginning of 2007, following the initiative of the CAIF and one municipal representative. It met twice a month, and became the primary voice of the community in discussions with the municipality and other organisations. At the first meeting of each year, all organisations would bring ideas for improvement for the whole community. These were discussed and where possible a consensus reached as to the top priority project. At the time of the fieldwork, that project involved the restoration of a large building that was destroyed in the storm of 2002 into a community health centre. All member organisations were committed to this project, and to contributing to its completion.

Many of the existing projects and CSOs originated from the initiative of the women on the CAIF committee and the work of one woman in particular. She was the founder and current leader of the Coordinating Organisation at the time of the study. The achievements of this group of women are best illustrated with the story of Mevir, which was the community housing scheme.

In the 1990s a small group of local women became concerned with the relatively large number of single parents who had no access to housing. At that time the major rural employers provided housing to their employers. Many of the vineyard workers were women, working increasingly long hours for little pay. While the practice of provision of housing (although substandard) applied to male employees, it did not apply to women. So these single mothers were placed in an untenable situation.

A group of four local women (with one man) who were active in the CAIF became aware of the need for housing and support for struggling families, especially for the single mothers working at the vineyard. Over a period of several years from 1996 they successfully lobbied Mevir, a branch of the Ministry of Housing, to obtain the development of a housing plan. Mevir was providing basic funding to build houses under a plan in which people receiving a house helped build it. Each family had to contribute 96 hours per month for 18 months (depending on the speed of construction). Each family then paid 350 pesos a month for 20 years, after which time they owned their home outright. At first it was hard to convince families in Juanico that they could own a house by paying a contribution and helping to build it. But finally this was achieved.

A second stage of the plan was then greeted with enthusiasm. At the time of the study a total of 170 simple but attractive houses were occupied. A committee continued to manage the estate, collecting rent and dealing with any problems. The community, including the original committee of women, learned the skills of building, such as bricklaying, and physically built the houses. They also went on to successfully lobby the Ministry of Housing for money to build a more suitable house for the CAIF childcare and children's club, which the women also built themselves.

Lovik, Northwest Sweden

Lovik is a tiny village of fewer than 100 people, located in the remote region of northwest Sweden. Many towns had been left to die following the mechanisation of the timber industry and the loss of subsidised support for farming. However, despite this severe crisis, the village was determined to revitalise itself.

This process began in 1989 with a public meeting called in neighbouring Hoting. One of the women went "just for entertainment". But as a workshop exercise participants were asked to write their thoughts on the future. Her vision and that of another woman were of Lovik as a well-developed centre. A female economist challenged her to "go away and do it".

She could not sleep at night and was worried that the men would laugh at her. But nonetheless she called a public meeting at Lovik and much to her surprise 25 of the residents came. Some men were sceptical but one older man was encouraging. The Community Development Advisor (CDA), also a woman, attended and gave helpful examples of what had been done elsewhere. So they agreed to a second meeting at which they formed a voluntary association: 'Ideal Village of Lovik and surrounds'. Its mission was the economic, social and cultural development of the area. The first activity was a cabaret to raise money using local musical talent. With the profits they repaired the community hall and put on a series of social fundraising events, especially in the hunting season (ongoing). They also created an annual accordion festival with up to 1,000 visitors, many from other countries, for which the local residents provided accommodation in their own homes.

From 1989 the older people in the village talked about the need for a retirement centre and asked the organisation to speak about this to the municipality. They were helped by the CDA, who was employed by the municipality but funded by the national government. There were many obstacles: first, the municipality said the village was too small; second, they knew nothing about setting up a cooperative. Little happened for a year. Then four women (a teacher, a teacher's aid, a post office worker and a bank worker) and the CDA formed the task force. They worked on a tight schedule and achieved their goal in 17 months (which included the building of the home).

They experienced jealousy and resistance from the municipality, however, and the CDA resigned as a result. The prevailing attitude of the municipality was: 'Don't think you are better than anyone else'. They did, however, get good support at the national level from one Minister in particular, a woman herself, and so obtained a low interest loan. Our informant said that it was because she was acting in a voluntary capacity that she was able to speak out and therefore achieve this level of support.

The eldercare cooperative had 18 members – those who lived there, those who worked there and those from the village. The membership required 1,000 Kronor ($200) and 40 hours of work per year. Husbands of the four women mowed the grass, delivered materials and food and carried out maintenance. There were six apartments each with ensuite facilities and kitchenette. It had an attractive modern design with ecological awareness (for example, heating from under the earth). And the service cost less than similar municipal services because of all the voluntary labour involved.

Voluntary labour was seen as part of helping to develop community. Day-to-day decisions were made around the kitchen table (such as the decision to keep hens). A recreational account was built up from miscellaneous sources of income. The municipality funded 3.5 personal care positions (shared by five women), so this brought employment to the village. A qualified nurse came once a fortnight. At night there was an emergency call button and a night patrol. And there was a room for relatives to stay. All in all then, this was an exemplary project. Other villages subsequently developed similar eldercare cooperatives. The Lovik eldercare centre became a model for Sweden and received thousands of visitors from all over Sweden and other countries.

The latest project was an initiative for the five children in the village. At the time of the fieldwork the association was building a playground next to the eldercare accommodation. It was also planning a 'revivalist' meeting of ex-residents with the Minister of Agriculture in Stockholm. The aim was to encourage people to return to the village, particularly those nearing retirement.

Discussion

These four rural case studies from different parts of the world each have unique conditions and problems but they were selected because they demonstrated a capacity to develop or to reinvent their community. In all cases some kind of project was developed and managed by the community. That is, each case clearly demonstrates the rhizomic phenomena identified by Chia (1999), in which change and transformation is the norm. The study did not find institutionalised structures and stability but rather ongoing situations of flux, in which 'all things flow' in a continuous process of becoming. Each case also demonstrates the fundamental issue of *emergence* (Chiles et al, 2004). That is, system level order spontaneously arose from the action and repeated interaction of lower level system components and were not directed by a higher authority or a central controller (Chiles et al, 2004)

The concepts of complexity theory were also useful in describing the sometimes difficult and haphazard paths to developing a new project. Each case evidenced disequilibrium, sometimes in terms of a crisis as in Lovik, sometimes in terms of changing economic conditions and the desire to create alternative sources of income, as in Anapia. Conflict was evident and sometimes encouraged as new ideas were introduced and debated, and sometimes resisted. In all cases there was a series of meetings and a variety of discussions leading to the creation of new organisations and a search for the necessary resources or knowledge to achieve a desired outcome.

In each case there were serious obstacles to the development of the project. These included obstacles of resistance from within the community (Anapia, for example), obstacles imposed from outside (as in the case of Lovik in particular) and the difficulty of obtaining the necessary human and financial capital. In most cases these obstacles created an initial period of inaction or discouragement. It took a year or more before there were clear signs of successful achievement. During this interim period it was usually the (informal) leader(s) who maintained optimism and persisted in the search for solutions to the obstacles. As Johannisson and Olaison note (2007, p 58), these entrepreneurial practices are 'driven by passion and joy'. It was probably this perseverance that earned leaders the lasting respect and trust of their community.

In each of the communities reported here, the wider community networks mobilised themselves in a self-governing and self-regulating manner. In each case this process within the project appeared to mirror established decision making processes within the community at large. That is, there was, in each case, a culture of grassroots participation and decision making for all the issues affecting the community at large. Anapia was the strongest example of this. Action occurred at several quite different points within the community, with many people taking some initiative at different times. Some of these actions led nowhere, while other actions coalesced into a larger community campaign, as in Maleny.

What was also evident in each community was a deeper set of shared values and a common commitment to sustainable development. These shared values highlighted the deeper levels of trust within the community and strong bonding social capital. They did not override or eliminate conflict but, on the contrary, made it possible for differences to be openly debated and compromises negotiated. Within the specific community projects, deeper structures of shared objectives emerged. Much of the early work of the project required extensive negotiations with a variety of key stakeholders both inside and outside the community. It was out of this negotiated consensus of often quite different positions and interests that the project was able to proceed. Hahn et al (2006) also refer to the importance of resolving trade offs in creating a collective vision. In every case the project was then supported by a management committee with representation across the community and with decision making responsibility.

Despite vast geographical and social differences there were also some important similarities in the nature of the leadership. In each case the identified leader or leadership group was strongly embedded within the formal and informal networks of the community. In most cases leaders took a strong initiating role in establishing the project. But while they may have had a temporary governance role in the new project, they were not at that time in any other position of formal authority. One – the leader in Anapia – was subsequently elected as Mayor but he obtained that position after having demonstrated his capacity in the earlier mobilisation of the community project. In the other three cases, the mobilising leader was one of a small group of active women who gave her the support she needed and shared some of the leadership responsibilities. The leader was regarded always as 'one of the people', not as an outsider. Although she or he may have had slightly better qualifications or status, the difference was not marked. Above all, each leader was trusted by the community, as a person of integrity who held the public interest foremost.

In all cases the leaders appreciated that they were working with open systems and that they needed to engage with other places and structures. So they developed good links outside the village. This was especially important where most links were bonding links within the village and few people ventured outside and also where there was a culture of self sufficiency. The leaders may have had some bridging links to begin with but, in each case, they formed new ones in the course of the project in order to fill identified gaps in knowledge, skills and material resources. For example, the leader in Maleny began the cooperative movement through an initial study tour and then invited external experts to come and assist. Similarly the leader of Anapia sought out a tourist operator as commercial partner. The leader in Lovik formed an ongoing alliance with the CDA and later links to the national level. All these links were essential in the successful completion of the project. In a sense, the leaders were able to fill the 'structural holes' between the community and outside networks (Burt, 1998). However, they used these connections for public and not private gain. While it may be expected that the state, through the municipality, may be crucial in resourcing new developments, this was not the case in these three case studies. When the municipality was hostile as in Maleny and Lovik or indifferent as in Anapia, alternative paths to bridging were found through NGOs or other levels of government.

The leaders all had a broad vision for what was possible for the future for the community. They were able to articulate this vision and identify a path to achieve it. They were able to inspire others to follow that vision. That is, it was not simply a dream but one that could be actualised. This is the essence of visionary or transformational leadership (Avery, 2004). In all cases, the shared vision was one of ecological and social sustainability rather than economic expansion. While all the communities were concerned to maintain an adequate livelihood, this was only one consideration within a desire for a balanced development, one that put social and environmental issues in the forefront. However, in Anapia and Maleny the vision did include the potential for both improved wellbeing and an expanded economic base, albeit one firmly located within the ecological and cultural values of the community.

In the four cases, power belonged to the group rather than the leader. Change may have been slower than the leader wished, as in Anapia, because of the need for extensive consultation and wider participation and acceptance of new practices. But this collective approach was highly successful in leading complex change in a dynamic environment. All the leaders engaged in bridging to obtain the necessary resources and expertise, thus they could be seen as social entrepreneurs. The theme that does not appear in any theory of leadership except complexity theory is that the leaders were embedded in their communities and leadership action was emergent from the interaction of agents at that grassroots level (Chiles et al, 2004; Lichtenstein et al, 2006). Indeed, most theories emphasise the social distance between the leader and followers. However, it was the embeddedness in the community and shared decision making that helped maintain social capital during the community development process. The leaders were working with the community. They shared the problems and aspirations of their neighbours and the agreed actions were the result of collective agency and shared control by many people working together.

While the communities presented here have been analysed within a complexity theory framework, this also sits easily within a wider understanding of community development, which is often identified as a process of creative emergence of new solutions (Milofsky and Hunter, 1994; Gilchrist, 2009). As Gilchrist notes:

> The capacity of a community to respond creatively to change and ambiguity is to be found in its web of connections and relationships, rather than in the heads of individuals or the formal structure of voluntary bodies. (Gilchrist, 2009, p 171)

As Chapter Nine explained, social movements may be similarly mobilised and kept alive through their base of social networks, which act as 'social relays' making connections between different groups and communities, and promote common interest beyond the diversity (Ohlemacher, 1992; Tarrow, 1994).

The World Social Forum

The four cases presented in this chapter in some detail are all concerned with small rural communities, where everyone knows everyone and collective communication and action is therefore facilitated. However, the question remains as to whether the basic principles of emergence hold also for urban or even global network formation. The global case of the World Social Forum, referred to in Chapter Nine, may serve to address this question, at least in part.

The World Social Forum is perhaps best understood as a global social movement of civil society actors based on a commitment to open discussion of issues and the articulation of alternatives to dominant neoliberal policies. Initiated in 2001 in Porto Alegre. Brazil, it began with a conversation between a handful of local activists who, with the support of the municipality, formed a committee of local grassroots organisations and organised an international forum under the banner of 'Another World is Possible'. The municipality was led by the Brazilian Workers Party, which made use of open citizen forums. The first World Social Forum attracted 12,000 people from around the world and was followed by similar global forums each year. Four of the first five forums were held in Porto Alegre but others have since been held in different parts of the world, including Mumbai, Karachi, Nairobi, Dakar and Tunis. Numbers of registered groups attending have grown to between 50,000 and 60,000. In addition, hundreds of Social Forums have been established in various parts of the globe, all linked as loose networks.

The World Social Forum (WSF) presented itself as an alternative to the World Economic Forum, an annual meeting of neoliberal leaders, which meets annually in Davos, Switzerland. The World Social Forum is concerned, in contrast, with the wider social issues generated by globalisation and the advance of neoliberal policies. However, it has no specific social or political agenda beyond the provision of an open space for the free flow of ideas and debate.Following the first forum, the organising committee formulated a Charter of Principles, which has guided the operation of all forums since. However, there is no central governing body; each forum is managed locally by an organising committee.

The first and overarching principle is:

> The WSF is an open meeting place for reflective thinking, democratic debate of ideas, formulation of proposals, free exchange of experiences and interlinking for effective action, by groups and movements of civil society that are opposed to neoliberalism and to domination of the world by capital and any form of imperialism, and committed to building a planetary society directed towards fruitful relationships among Humankind and between it and the Earth. (World Social Forum, 2013)

Other principles elaborate on this, including for example the principle that no one will be authorised to speak on behalf of the forum and the forum cannot make decisions as a body. It was rather a process that encouraged its participant organisations and movements to situate their actions from the local level to the national and international level and seek to strengthen national and international links.

The case of the World Social Forum illustrates well the core principles of complexity theory and particularly of the principle of emergence. It arose out of a deep concern over the implications of neoliberalism for the peoples of the world. The Forum, seen as a continuing process, spread in a rhizomic pattern from Porto Alegre across the planet. It was and still is constantly changing, with no formal structure apart from the temporary organising committees and Charter of Principles. Leadership has been constantly forming and reforming, always in principle embedded in the grassroots organisations and movements that come together. The networks, and the World Social Forum itself, are self governing and self regulating. However, they are committed to coalesce around the central values of 'respect for human rights, and those of all citizens – men and women – of all nations and the environment and will rest on democratic international systems and institutions at the service of social justice, equality and the sovereignty of peoples' (Principle 5). In terms of its rapid growth, its global reach, the numbers of enthusiastic participants and its wider social and political impact, the World Social Forum has been seen as a remarkably successful social movement.

However, the very success of the World Social Forum has led to some serious problems and critiques. It has been criticised as 'too large, incoherent and more of a carnival than a space for serious engagement in ideas' (Foltz and Moodlier, 2005, p 1) and therefore limited in its capacity to strategise and mobilise, with little time between fora for action. Its governance and accountability structures have been criticised for being weak and open to abuse and its very inclusivity for permitting the participation of those allied to neoliberal projects (Foltz and Moodliar, 2005) and/or those in a position to afford international air travel. Nonetheless, as an ongoing process the World Social Forum raises significant questions about the impact of global civil society movements, issues and challenges that were explored in Chapter Nine.

Conclusions

The five cases reported here illustrate the complex process of emergence of new social formations within the local community but also within global civil society. Other cases could have been chosen to demonstrate much the same phenomena – with similar characteristics emerging as a result. These may be summarised as follows. The capacity to develop new community projects depended on existing bonding social capital, with common values, existing strong multiplex networks and good levels of trust. However, the process of development also generated new forms of bonding and bridging social capital. In all cases, the new social formation began with very little in the way of financial resources. However, good facilitative leadership created access to the necessary skills, knowledge and financial resources needed to complete the project. Above all, networks built trust, shared knowledge and made collective decisions that involved many participants. Out of the action and interaction of these emergent formations, new third sector organisations were created, either to manage a specific project, or as a side effect of the ongoing rhizomic movement.

The forms of active citizenship varied somewhat between and within cases. In nearly all cases, the new formations required some form of activism. Local citizens challenged existing vested interests, both within the community and outside. Yet the fundamental motivation was for collaborative action, where possible cooperating with formal authorities and being as inclusive as possible within the community itself. Once the new projects were in place, the third sector organisations that formed had a maintenance role and involved a commitment to preserving the new order.

None of this could have been predicted beforehand. As suggested by complexity theory, new, community-wide social formations arose from the actions and repeated interaction of lower level components; that is individuals and groups working within the community, but without the intervention of a centralised controller. There was no bureaucracy, no initial intervention by state or corporate power. The new forms were controlled by the grassroots community members, often in a dynamic process of creative learning, trial and error, mutual support and debate. Cooperative action produced positive feedback loops which enabled further learning and the courage to attempt more ambitious action. The studies demonstrated sustainable community development as a complex, emergent process. With regard to the relationship between the third sector and active citizenship, this chapter reverses the central question of this book. It is not (just) that civil society and its third sector organisations nurture active citizenship, but rather that active citizens together create and nurture the third sector and civil society.

ELEVEN

Shifting paradigms

Introduction

The third sector and the nature of active citizenship are both changing rapidly. Some argue that we are witnessing what appears to be a dramatic bifurcation of the third sector, although on closer examination, it is clear that the shifts are more complex than this would suggest. Indeed the sector may appear ever more confused as it moves simultaneously in opposite directions. With the increasing dominance of neoliberal, market-driven ideology, particularly in OECD countries, many third sector organisations, by choice or necessity, are turning to market-driven models of organisational structure and function and operating more like entrepreneurial businesses (see Chapter Five). However, as discussed in the previous chapter, much is also happening under the surface, often entirely out of the mainstream media gaze until a major crisis or event occurs to make the new types of third sector activity visible. There are the actions of social media, Facebook and Twitter, for example, but also, at least in their early stages, more targeted forms of civil activism such as GetUp, Avaaz and Wikileaks, referred to in earlier chapters. Such unruly, apparently unmanaged actions nonetheless have an (emergent) organisational base and indeed often operate through transnational networks. This chapter explores the implications of these dramatically different emergent new forms of organising. It examines how each to some extent serves to define the space of the other.

The growing dominance of neoliberal approaches

As Chapter Five reported, the move away from the welfare state in some countries was partly driven by the claim that intervention by the state simply perpetuates a welfare dependency, a kind of passive, learned helplessness by the community, which then has to wait for the government to fix everything. According to this view, people then lose their capacity to take action on their own account. The policies of neoliberalism turned attention from the state to the market. They championed privatisation and deregulation. Simply stated, neoliberal approaches rest on the free play of market forces. Through public policy, the state adopts the mechanisms and principles of the market. The basic assumptions are that individual citizens – now constructed as consumers – should exercise their free choice in accessing goods and services according to their capacity to pay; the providers of such goods and services will continue to provide them as long as demand is strong enough and the quality of their services are sufficiently attractive. Quality is ensured through competition between providers. All agents are motivated by rational self interest. The philosophical position that justifies all this is a form of neoliberalism which rests on the core value of individual choice and autonomy.

These basic tenets of neoliberalism have, in most OECD countries, been translated into bureaucratic regulations that emphasise standards of efficiency, performance and accountability in judging the performance of third sector organisations (Deakin, 1996). The impact of this ideology on the sector has been explored in more detail in Chapter Five. To summarise briefly, the shift in government approaches to funding and policy have led to the privatisation of public social services and increasing use of market mechanisms, the greater use of contracts in which the governments act as purchaser of services, the application of competition policy to third sector organisations with the expectation of consumer choice and greater emphasis on formal accountability and evaluation (usually in cost–benefit terms).

Social enterprise

The ultimate conclusion to the increasing move to neoliberal policies and values is the call for third sector organisations to become businesses or at least to operate more specifically according to the principles of the market. Social enterprise and social entrepreneurship are typically taken as synonymous, social entrepreneurship being the process by which social enterprise is formed. Both have contested definitions. However, in broad terms most commentators agree that at a minimum, social enterprise/social entrepreneurship consists of the following basic criteria (Dees, 1998; Dart, 2004; Paredo and McLean, 2006):

- adopting a mission to create and sustain social value, rather than private value;
- recognising and pursuing new opportunities to serve that mission, normally by identifying a need and articulating a new way of meeting that need;
- engaging in a process of continuous innovation, adaptation and learning;

- refusing to be constrained by a lack of existing resources;
- operating with a heightened sense of accountability to and embeddedness within the constituencies involved.

Debates around definition tend to focus on the centrality of resource generation or profit making (see Chapter Three for discussion of this issue). The five central criteria listed here do not focus on income generation or the requirement of distribution of profit to individuals and this is sometimes referred to as a 'soft' version of social enterprise. However, there is an alternative 'hard' version, which does make the specific requirement that the enterprise achieves its mission through an explicitly business focus, including the requirement for making a profit. Several reviews of the concept have developed some kind of typology to account for some of these differences in emphasis (Paredo and McLean, 2006; Neck et al, 2009; Casey, 2013). For example, Neck et al (2009) identify four quadrants, which they define as:

- social purpose: those with a predominantly social mission but an economic market orientation;
- traditional: those with a traditional market mission and an economic market orientation but who nonetheless produce some social benefit;social consequence: those with an economic mission but a predominant social market orientation often identified as corporate social responsibility;enterprising third sector organisations: those with both a social mission and social market orientation, with little regard to economic generation of income, beyond basic survival.

Paredo and McLean (2006) further explore the range of hybrid cases, in which social goals may be more or less central and commercial exchange can variously be out of the question, used directly for social benefit, or involve more or less profit making for the entrepreneur or investors. For example, at the more social end of the spectrum is Yunus's definition of social enterprise, which has been applied to microcredit programmes for the poor, particularly in Asia, as 'a non-loss, non-dividend company designed to address a social objective' (Yunus, 2010). This approach specifically limits the distribution of profit. However, in other cases, this is not so.

Regardless of the subtleties of social and economic mission, all versions of social enterprise tend towards a taken-for-granted acceptance of the language and techniques of business. So roles are described as 'CEO', the 'Board', and 'consumers'.

The organisation engages in 'strategic planning', provides 'annual reports' which focus on 'financial returns' and provide 'appropriate executive remuneration'. Dart (2004) explores this trend from the perspective of institutional theory and the centrality of moral legitimacy. As business has moved centre stage in neoliberal thought, government bureaucracies and nonprofit organisations are seen as nonproductive and burdensome. It follows that even social sector organisations can gain legitimacy by adopting the language, goals and structures of business. As Dart notes: 'Thus moral legitimacy of social enterprise can be understood because of the consonance between social enterprise and the pro-business ideology that has become dominant in the wider social environment' (Dart, 2004, p 419). Dart goes on to argue that, once social enterprise has gained this ideological legitimacy, it becomes somewhat immune to rational independent evaluation. Indeed the US literature on social enterprise is full of stories of heroic acts of achievement but very little in the way of hard evidence of outcome. One such preliminary assessment of outcome by Casey (2013) involved a follow-up of four high profile media cases. After some two and a half years following the initial media portrayal of these four 'heroes', all four enterprises had disappointing outcomes. This of course is not to say that all social enterprises are doomed to fail, only that there has been insufficient critical analysis of outcomes. As a direct result of this concern, there is a growing demand for objective measures of social impact of all projects, including social enterprise, of which the dominant example in the UK and Australia is Social Return on Investment. This is basically a cost–benefit analysis in which an attempt is made to identify the monetary value of actual social outcomes (Goodspeed et al, 2009; Maas and Liket, 2011).

Social enterprises may take various legal forms but basically they use business tools to meet a social mission. They may include cooperatives and community interest companies. The preferred business model, at least in the US, is one in which the organisation may make a profit, both in order to meet its social objectives but also to make a financial return to investors. The arguments in favour of this strongly business-centred approach have been recently demonstrated in a series of opinion pieces printed in *The Harvard Review* and widely disseminated within the business world. For example, Rottenberg and Morris (2013) argue that, while social enterprises face the dual task of creating financial value for their investors and social value for those they seek to serve, their advice is to always prioritise financial goals over social ones to maximise the long-term sustainability of the business. Their own case analysis of 50 social businesses around the world demonstrated that those who did prioritise financial goals over social goals were much more likely to experience high rates of growth and have greater social impact

Similarly, Pallotta (2013) argues that what he terms 'the humanitarian sector' has put itself at an enormous disadvantage by ignoring some basic rules of for-profit enterprises, including maximising salaries of CEOs, using professional paid advertising, building long-term plans for return on investment, allowing for risk of failure and raising massive capital in the stock market by offering investment returns. These rules he argues are just as effective for third sector organisations – or rather for social enterprises that are allowed to create profits.

Within the US, according to surveys done by Mirabella (2013), the major shift in higher education concerned with third sector studies has coincided with the rapid growth of social enterprise courses within business schools. She notes that in 1998 there were only four such courses, increasing to 21 and 26 in 2002 and 2006 respectively and almost 100 courses in 2013. At least 20 Universities offer a concentration in social entrepreneurship, of which 65% are in business schools (most leading to an MBA). Almost 55% of the content in the business school setting focuses on business skills, as opposed to those located in a public administration setting, where the majority of courses focused primarily on philanthropic and political skills. The same phenomenon is becoming evident in Australia and in the UK, where there is a parallel tradition of third sector managers seeking MBA qualification and large charities employing senior managers from the business sector, often people with little or no experience of the third sector.

The problem with this approach, as acknowledged for example by Rottenberg and Morris (2013) and Menasce and Dalsace (2011), is the inherent conflict of interest between profit generation and social good. While most nonprofits would acknowledge the importance of financial viability, many operational decisions made by an organisation are likely to find that the two objectives, that is, meeting social needs and financial needs, are noncommensurate. This can have dire consequences for the organisation's operation, including its human resource management (Green, 2009). It is also likely that as economic goals and the achievement of profit become paramount and as an organisation adopts the language of business then those intangible goals of social cohesion, trust and social justice become ever more invisible.

Some argue that this has been the case with some of the community development corporations (CDCs) set up in the United States during the government initiated War on Poverty in the 1960s. One review of the US literature concludes that many CDCs have lost contact with their roots and their ability to represent neighbourhood interests (Murphy and Cunningham, 2003, p 40), while de Filippis (2007, p 30) argues that, as they developed – in predominantly black neighbourhoods – community control became 'black capitalism'. 'The radical potential of demands for black power', he argues, 'became coopted into a debate about how best to reproduce capitalist practices in black urban neighbourhoods', becoming more and more part of the American tradition of individual entrepreneurship.

However, this may not always be the outcome. A UK study of community asset ownership identified the tension between economic and social objectives as one of the key challenges for many nonprofits who had taken on buildings or other assets (Aiken et al, 2011). However, there were some cases where organisations had achieved a successful balance, for example, by separating the business arm of the enterprise from the community development arm. The Baywind Energy Cooperative was one such case. It set up a separate but linked charity – the Energy Conservation Trust – into which it paid 0.5 percent of turnover to deliver local benefits. This provided an opportunity for local people to get involved as trustees without being involved in the more technical/financial focus of the Baywind board itself (Aiken et al, 2011). Community shares in the enterprise also combined social and economic benefit here and in other cases. As one participant said:

> 'One of the most satisfying events in my life took place when Westmill Wind Farm was hooked up to the national grid ... It would be hard to find a more valuable gift for my two grandchildren than shares in the project.' (Aiken et al, 2011, p 52)

The case of cooperatives

The European version of social enterprise within the 'social economy' provides an alternative model for combining economic and social goals, one not so entrenched in neoliberal thought. It applies specific forms of governance, especially the cooperative legal form, which represent a search for an alternative economic model based on solidarity rather than individualism. The cooperative form allows the generation and distribution of profits to individuals under certain circumstances but focuses on the protection and primacy of the social mission (Evers and Laville, 2004; Laville, 2011). Cooperatives and community enterprises all aim to generate profits – what is important is the way they are distributed.

European forms of social enterprise are concerned to preserve a democratic form of governance and participatory involvement of stakeholders. As such, they are more likely to attract government financial support and thus continue to focus on those who most need the service but are least likely to be able to afford market price (Defourny and Nyssens, 2010). In other words, European models of social enterprise begin to approximate the requirements of a community development approach to organisation. That is, the cooperative or community enterprise is designed first and foremost to assist the community to meet and grow its economic and social base.

Nonetheless, these cooperative businesses may be both socially and financially successful. Thus Euricse (European Research Institute on Cooperative and Social Enterprise) published a report about the effect of cooperatives in Italy throughout the financial crisis of 2008–11 (Euricse, 2014). The report concludes:

> During the course of the crisis, especially in the first years, the growth patterns of the various cooperative forms differed greatly from that of other forms of enterprise. The analyses presented confirm, especially in the case of those cooperatives for which valid data is available for the entire period from 2008 to 2011, the anti-cyclical function of cooperatives. Notwithstanding the crisis, in fact, higher positive growth rates can be seen in all the variables of interest both across and within most sectors. Overall in 2011 production increased by 8.2% and investments increased by 10.6%. (Euricse, 2014, p 3)

Employment within most cooperatives remained stable or increased during this period despite widespread unemployment across the nation.

As a single example of how cooperatives work in Italy, cooperative banks are created for the support of regional communities and are concerned with supporting local investment. According to traditional banking accounting, where the only criteria are absolute levels and growth of bank profits, they perform less well than commercial banks. However, an aggregate analysis of the overall direct and indirect impact of these cooperative banks, using satellite accounts to include, for example, the growth in employment and income from the local investments, demonstrates that these cooperative banks probably outperform commercial banks, certainly during periods of economic crisis.

A similar story comes from an analysis of cooperative housing in Sweden (McLean, 2011). Here, the legal provisions of tenant ownership have encouraged the formation of cooperation, reciprocity and trust. Member participation in planning a house or apartment cluster, as well as ongoing management and maintenance, all serve to lower costs. Improvements include: common facilities; a common meeting room for sharing cooking and meals; shared laundry, gym, childcare facilities, bicycle shed, gardens and/or other facilities on site. During the recession of the early 1990s no cooperative members lost their homes (McLean, 2011).

The social economy has been less apparent in the UK, at least until recently, although there have been exceptions in Scotland and Wales. But the founding of a Development Trusts Association in 1993 attested to the growth of interest in this field across the UK. One example of a successful development trust from Scotland is Fintry Development Trust (FDT), established in 2003 by two local people who wanted to 'do something with renewable energy' in the village. They set up Fintry Renewable Energy Enterprise (FREE) and, when plans were announced to build a wind farm in the vicinity, were able to negotiate the addition of one community-owned wind turbine. FDT has developed a range of activities to reduce energy use in the village with the aim of making the village a zero carbon, zero waste community. It has carried out energy surveys of each house in the village and is in the process of providing insulation for each surveyed home. The Trust has made the village amenities more energy efficient by installing a new heating system in the village hall and a biomass heating system in the local sports centre. It funded a 'woodland classroom' in the school and the refurbishment of an outside area. FDT has recently started a car sharing scheme as well as a growing project and community orchard. FDT not only looks at sustainable development, but also aims to provide employment to local people, provide affordable housing to young people and develop the skills of people in the village. It makes an effort to distribute the benefits of the wind turbine as equally as possible over the village. When there is a choice between two or more projects to support, FDT chooses the one that benefits the most people. If it is not possible for everyone in the village to benefit, FDT offers compensation to the others (Aiken et al, 2011). While there have been very positive experiences of cooperative development however, this is only one side of the story. Without developing the argument in detail here it is important to note the less positive experiences, including, for example, the problems encountered by the Cooperative Bank in UK in recent times, illustrating the potential scope for economic failure as well as the potential scope for loss of vision – possibly the worst of all outcomes.

Hybrid forms

Even within the US, where there is much greater emphasis on business techniques and profitability, there is nonetheless a recognition of the need for a diversity of funding, including that provided by foundations, as social enterprises will rarely if ever achieve breakeven income from their own enterprise without additional donor support (Austin et al, 2006). As Austin et al also note, social enterprises are much more likely to seek collaborative arrangements with competitors rather than seeking greater market share for themselves, thus distinguishing themselves from true business entrepreneurship.

One small Australian case illustrates the possibility of adopting some of the opportunities and associated language of social enterprise and business in the pursuit of old fashioned community development. Perhaps this is evidence of a creative hybrid used for quite different purposes than that usually proclaimed.

Warwick Farm is a small area of about 4,500 population and part of Liverpool Municipality. It is largely comprised of social housing for low income, single parent families, and has a reputation for drug dealing and prostitution. Warwick Farm Neighbourhood Centre is a pleasant building located in the centre of the suburb and this is a hive of local activity. Liverpool Neighbourhood Connections provides up to 60 community programmes each week, operating in seven locations across Liverpool. It services over 20,000 people across Liverpool each year. It has focused in particular on programmes for women, children and youth, and on the development of training and employment programmes for women. The coordinator of this organisation is a community worker – herself a local resident, a single mother, who struggled with much the same needs as the wider constituency, but who obtained formal qualifications in community management.

Recent programmes have included the development of entry-level courses as a stepping stone to further education and employment for women and a mentoring support program for teenage girls at risk of dropout from school. One such activity involved a major fashion show put on by the girls (including a number of Muslim girls in hijab).

To extend the impact of training/employment programmes for women and girls, Liverpool Neighbourhood Connections has established several social enterprises for women. The first of these enterprises was Pepper's Place, a café housed within the building, and (at the time of the study) operating almost every day, 21 hours a week. It generated a small annual income. Another was a lawn mower service, employing two people. The most recent enterprise to be opened was a beauty salon, housed in its own room within the Neighbourhood Centre complex. Again the aim was to provide initial training and employment experience within this incubation enterprise to assist local women to move on to more secure employment in the wider labour market.

Liverpool Neighbourhood Connections was first formed with the support of Liverpool Health Centre and with funding from the Western Sydney Area Assistance Scheme (WSAAS), a participatory planning and funding scheme with state funding, now defunct. It then became dependent on core funding from the Department of Community Services. However, the Department never fully funded the small enterprise incubation. Initial funding for the coffee shop came from Liverpool Municipality Community Donations programme, then from a larger grant from Clubs NSW (CDSE) plus a small grant from the Sydney Women's Fund (Sydney Community Foundation). These funds enabled the coffee shop to employ three part-time workers and three volunteers. The beauty salon received funding from Sydney Community Foundation. Recently, the organisation received funding from the Department to fund part of the salary of a worker to assist in the development of further employment initiatives.

This case demonstrates the capacity for a creative use of social enterprise within a traditional community development context. As the coordinator acknowledged, it was a matter of obtaining whatever resources were available to respond to the needs of her community. All projects were formed as collaborative projects drawing on the combined skills and resources of other local agencies: charities, foundations, local government, schools as well as more formal state government funding. None of the social enterprise projects was likely to generate a real profit but they were operating commercially and in doing so they were providing much needed work experience and training for local residents. The scale remained small and resources remained scarce. The hope though was that the combined efforts of all projects would catapult the whole local area into a new phase of social and economic development.

It could be argued that third sector organisations involved in community development have always been entrepreneurial, being opportunistic to new and alternative sources of income. This raises the question as to how far the current interest in social enterprise reflects new forms of organisation as opposed to an opportunistic rebranding of old practices in response to the promotion of the idea by successive governments. In the UK, for example, it could be argued that many third sector organisations involved in community development have been rebadging themselves as social enterprises in order to capture the current policy interest and identify new forms of income, but sometimes, it seems, in order to do much the same as they were doing before.

A different paradigm is emerging

While much of the world of the third sector is increasingly driven by neoliberal, business oriented demands, another alternative phenomenon is emerging, particularly among young people and largely out of the gaze of public scrutiny. It does appear that many of 'generation X' (those born roughly between 1963 and 1980) and even more so 'generation Y' (those born between 1981 and 1994) wish to avoid the formal world of organisations all together. This is not to say that they are antisocial, far from it, but rather that their sense of identity is shaped most strongly through friendship networks that may extend to a kind of 'tribe' identity. Communication and connectedness are maintained and nurtured as much online as face to face (Onyx et al, 2005; Yerbury, 2010). One obvious outcome in this shift in cultural approach is the very rapid development of such social media as Facebook and Twitter, both of which have now been coopted by the formal world of organisations as a means of reaching this demographic group. But originally, and still in the main, these new forms of communication are used by young people to form and maintain networks of 'friends' and acquaintances.

There is a paradox involved in forming community through online interactions, as Yerbury explains:

> ... the online community which only exists when we are interacting in it, gives the impression of always being there. This is because it is separated from place and time. The action of logging on creates the feeling of being somewhere where other people leave their traces – simultaneously a place and a non-place – but not where one is now. This "place" is always there for one to go to, its layout is familiar and one knows how to find the way around ... (Yerbury, 2009, p 224)

The largely online networks of 'friends' are not third sector organisations as defined in Chapter Three, though they may be 'emergent' as discussed in Chapter Ten. They do however have a loose membership, a set of informal norms of operation and they can lead to collective action. This collective action may often take the relatively private form of meeting for some form of entertainment. But it can also lead to broader action in the community, such as organising a charity run, seeking sponsorship for a charity purpose, or organising a public protest. The 'people power revolutions' of the Philippines were dramatic examples of almost instant mobilisation of mass people's demonstrations in the streets, achieved through the rapid transmission of text messages on mobile phones. Not a third sector organisation but very active citizenship! Nonetheless, this kind of ready online collective action does lead to some recognisable organisations. One such is Vibewire. The website of Vibewire proclaims:

> Vibewire was born on the streets of urban, inner city Sydney in 2000 as a dynamic connection point between young people and the arts, culture, business and ideas. A youth-led not for profit, we capture stories from within our urban communities transforming them into opportunities for young people to connect, create, innovate and grow. We ensure young people are included and can participate in conversations that matter. A team of energetic Vibewire volunteers drive our art, digital media, live performance and workspace projects. (vibewire.org)

Vibewire operates explicitly on the belief that 'young people should create the future, not just inherit it. Vibewire is a 'Launchpad for young change makers' (vibewire.org). Its aim, as the website description explains, is to engage young people in active citizenship through their involvement in local arts, culture, politics, current affairs, fiction and ideas. While it is very much an online organisation, it also organises regular face-to-face events in real time within the Sydney area and has developed a physical hub, known as Vibewire hub, which acts as a business incubator for young social entrepreneurs to develop new startup ventures. This model is also being rolled out in other states within Australia. As one member put it: "It's really important to have the online networks, but it's actually also really important to have those offline physical networks" (interview, coordinator, 2008). Within the Sydney region, Vibewire is part of a strong and integrated network of emergent organisations, all focused on youth, art and encouraging young entrepreneurs in a myriad of new projects. All struggle with minimal resources but gain strength from collaborating, sharing physical and online resources, and creating joint projects. As one of many examples, Vibewire hosted a creative Sydney networking night, which brought a range of creative people and organisations together and generated new opportunities and ideas. As its coordinator put it: "we provide residency for all these groups and organisations and young social entrepreneurs and the idea is that we come together, we all share resources, and we strengthen each other's networks and collaborations can grow out of that" (interview, coordinator, 2008). These emergent organisations exhibit an interesting paradox. On the one hand they represent the purist form of social entrepreneurship. They certainly exhibit all the criteria of social entrepreneurship identified earlier. That is, they:

- adopt a mission to create and sustain social value, rather than private value;
  recognise and pursue new opportunities to serve that mission;
- engage in a process of continuous innovation, adaptation and learning;
- refuse to be constrained by a lack of existing resources;
- operate with a heightened sense of accountability to, and embeddedness within, the constituencies involved.

On the other hand, they are far removed from the business model of entrepreneurship, showing little regard for profit or formal business tools. They are not competitive but explicitly collaborative in their operations. They largely avoid government funding beyond occasional local government assistance and they are highly democratic in their mode of operation, again with little regard to bureaucratic requirements.

Perhaps as a consequence of this phenomenon, new emergent activist organisations are also springing up which are very much part of the third sector though, again, they sometimes defy categorisation. These emergent organisations are driven by passion and not money but by making astute use of social media are able to operate with adequate though minimal financial resources. Wikileaks is a famous example of this at the international level. At a more mundane level we have the actions of more targeted local civil activism such as GetUp in Australia and Avaaz internationally, already referred to in previous chapters. Like its counterparts, GetUp may be taken as an exemplar emergent organisation that operates successfully entirely away from the realm of neoliberal ideology and state bureaucratic control. It may stand as an exemplar counter organisation to the prevailing hegemonic control of civil society.

About GetUp

GetUp operates primarily as an online organisation, although increasingly it also has a physical presence. Its website states clearly its mission:

> GetUp is an independent, grass-roots community advocacy organisation which aims to build a more progressive Australia by giving everyday Australians the opportunity to get involved and hold politicians accountable on important issues. (getup.org.au)

Using a variety of media and other actions, GetUp members take targeted, coordinated and strategic action to effect real change. GetUp does not support any particular party and does not accept government or political funding. It is based on broad progressive values of economic fairness, social justice and environmental sustainability and relies on small donations to fund its work and in-kind donations from the Australian public (getup.org.au).

The organisation began with a small number of young entrepreneurs. It was founded in 2005 by two young Australian graduates of Harvard University's Kennedy School of Government who had worked at the intersection of technology, new media and politics in the US. The two founders went on to cofound Avaaz, a new global online political community inspired by the success of GetUp. GetUp is operated by a small group of workers, interns and volunteers out of a Sydney office. In its incubation period it was housed and mentored by another grassroots organisation with premises in Sydney's central business district. It has a board of local activists. While it has no formal membership, members are those who sign up, make donations and sign petitions or otherwise engage with GetUp activities. There are an unknown number but estimated at more than 500,000 such members across Australia. Interestingly, while the organising energy is driven by young people, GetUp is mainly supported, both financially and in actions like signing petitions, by a growing band of older, professional people.

GetUp has been involved in many campaigns over time. The most spectacular was its involvement during the 2013 Federal election in Australia. Prior to the election, GetUp campaigned heavily to have young people enrol to vote and saw enrolment shoot up by over 30%. It engaged in TV and newspaper ads (funded by supporter donations) to highlight key social/environmental issues. When these ads were blocked by the Murdoch press, they pursued a highly successful online headline-making campaign to call the Murdoch press to account. During election day, an estimated 6,000 volunteers of all ages and demographics, in bright orange T shirts, handed voters some 2.4 million independent party scorecards. These scorecards rated the major political parties on each of 14 issues relating to the environment, social justice, a fair economy, and human rights, scores being based on survey responses of the parties themselves.

While the election involved a number of policy issues, most GetUp campaigns are much more targeted. For example some 165,000 members signed a petition in support of saving the Great Barrier Reef. When the new Environment Minister took office, one of the first things he saw was a hand delivered petition signed by 165,000 GetUp members. More recently, GetUp organised a major protest rally in several cities in Australia concerning the harsh treatment of refugees under the new government policy of 'stop the boats'. Tens of thousands of ordinary citizens attended these protests. It would be hard therefore to characterise GetUp as a 'clicktivist' organisation.

GetUp is one of a growing number of grassroots activist organisations that have emerged without any clear external agent beyond a small number of committed individuals who see the need for social action and who find ways of mobilising many citizens who similarly are concerned for action to be taken. At a time of disillusionment in many countries with formal politics, it offers a way for citizens to have their voice heard.

Discussion

It would appear that we are witnessing in the early decades of the 21st century an ideological struggle within the OECD-based third sector. On the one hand there is clear evidence of an increased dependence on business values and technology, and on social enterprise as a means to tackle entrenched social problems. This has clearly influenced government funding regimes, which increasingly emphasise strict protocols of performance and accountability. With others, this book has argued that such neoliberal regimes can have a very negative effect on the capacity for individuals to exercise active citizenship within civil society except in the individualistic role of consumer or agent of state policy.

On the other hand, and clearly as a form of resistance to the hegemony of this economistic regime, there is a strong emergent culture of online activism, particularly among the younger generations. Much of this activism appears to occur outside prevailing forms of governance, with little or no funding apart from public donations and without regard to, or in opposition to, government policy and bureaucratic regimes of control. The US and UK support several similar organisations, such as 'MoveOn' and 38 Degrees. 38 Degrees 'is the angle at which an avalanche happens. In the UK, 38 Degrees will enable people to act together, to create an avalanche for change' (38degrees.org.uk). We are not aware to what extent other countries in Asia and South America have developed similar online networks, although examples are emerging.

The question is, then, to what extent do these new ways of being active citizens replace older, established forms? Up until the 1990s, the dominant forms of active citizenship in the third sector were the traditional charities and community welfare organisations on the one hand and activism on the other (see Parts 1 and 2 of this book). These two forms with their supporting ideologies were strong throughout the advanced capitalist world but also dominant in other parts of the globe. Charities fostered a commitment to service to the disadvantaged and poor, often within an institutional religious context and supported by donations and volunteers. More activist approaches, such as community development, fostered a commitment to empowerment and the development of skills and new opportunities as well as engagement in social action. Each generated a different kind of active citizenship as discussed in previous chapters. Both forms continue to exist today, though perhaps neither is as dominant as before.

The newer versions of these different approaches to active citizenship appear to differ radically both from each other and from their historical roots. In fact the reality is much more messy and dynamic than such a simplistic categorisation would suggest. Traditional charities still survive – although sometimes in varying forms, including social enterprise formats, such as providing a service under government contract. So too does community development, albeit with varying strategies. The case study of Warwick Farm is illustrative of one kind of blending of old and new paradigms. Here, social enterprises are specifically developed with the support of charitable foundations as part of a larger community development scheme that focuses on 'place-based planning'. They are modelled on business practices and do generate income but for the primary purpose of providing training and work experience for the disadvantaged women and young people of the area. They will never break even, nor is that the intention. There is a high level of engaged citizenship involving workers, volunteers and programme participants.

Vibewire presents a different kind of blending, again using the form of social enterprise but this time with virtually no charitable foundation funding or indeed any kind of state support. These are young people with passion and energy who want to do things their own way without state intervention or management. They are highly creative and by working collaboratively and using online technology are able to generate new projects, develop skills and form new enterprises. These new enterprises may or may not prove financially profitable but they are constantly breaking new ground. They also generate a high level of engaged citizenship moving well beyond the bounds of any specific organisation.

Meanwhile new alliances are being developed across former divides, bringing different forms of third sector organisations and activities together for common purposes. Building on previous experiences of building trade union and community alliances in a number of contexts, including Australia (Watkins, 1979), activists in Britain have been developing new forms of resistance to neoliberal austerity (TUC, 2010). Supported by community organisers, they are bringing vulnerable groups, such as migrant workers and longer established communities together, as well as service providers and service users, identifying common interests in differing situations and localities. Similar trends can be identified internationally, as public service workers link up with communities to defend and improve public services (Wainwright and Little, 2009; Wainwright, 2014) – a form of the cosmopolitanism discussed in Chapter Four.

It seems therefore, at the time of writing at least, that old forms of organising and active citizenship continue to operate but that new, largely hybrid forms are also being created, both in response to wider political and social constraints and opportunities, and as a creative search for new and more effective ways of meeting community needs. We are witnessing both an expansion and a diversification of what it is to be an active citizen within civil society, with a concomitant expansion in forms of third sector organising.

TWELVE

W(h)ither the third sector?

Introduction

Over the past 50 years or so, civil society – and particularly the third sector within it – has attracted growing attention as a key site for nurturing the active citizenship that is seen by many as the bedrock of a democratic society.

A number of factors have contributed to this current interest. Revolutions against authoritarian regimes, particularly in the 1980s and 1990s, and more recently, were hailed at the time as demonstrating that citizens were taking power to themselves. Meanwhile, falling turnouts at elections and evidence of growing apathy or mistrust of formal politics have led governments in the more established democracies to look for ways of reinforcing their legitimacy and revitalising their own democratic systems. The spread of neoliberalism to many parts of the globe found in civil society and the third sector an opportunity to roll back the frontiers of the state. In contrast, those alarmed at the rise of neoliberalism and the market turned to civil society more generally as a means of countering the market's worst excesses. Against this background, concepts of communitarianism and social capital also found a ready audience. After a decade or so of structural adjustment, even global financial institutions, such as the World Bank and the International Monetary Fund, stressed the need 'to engage the energies and enthusiasm of those at the grass-roots' (Salamon, 1995, p 257).

In this book, we set out to unpack a number of the central assumptions that lay behind this current interest in civil society and the third sector. We started by asking how the concepts of active citizenship, civil society and the third sector have been constructed, dissected and reconstructed, both internationally and more locally. We then discussed the differing claims that can be made about the way in which third sector organisations nurture active citizenship: as a vehicle for agency, association, democracy and cosmopolitanism. The first part of the book ended by exploring the varying roles that the third sector plays in relation to market and state, taking account of differing ideologies, and sociopolitical contexts, as well as the scope for human agency within wider structural constraints. We have paid particular attention throughout to the ways in which neoliberal globalisation has framed the relationship between the third sector and active citizenship in different contexts.

The second part of the book then set out to explore these questions further, on the basis of empirical research (using both the authors' own research and the research of others). We considered the extent to which the third sector has been engaged in promoting active citizenship across different world regions, using the examples of community-based volunteering, processes of reconstruction after natural disasters, engagement with policy processes at varying levels and advocacy and campaigning for human rights and social justice. In the third part of the book we then looked at the ways that citizens have come together to create new forms of action. First, we explored how action emerges at a micro level and then we examined some of the newer forms of action that are emerging on the world stage, including the possibilities that are opened up by new and constantly changing active citizenship communications technology.

In Chapter One, we set out the values that we bring to this task. However, the relationship between the third sector and active citizenship is complex, changing and context specific. So, while we have identified the positive contributions third sector organisations can make in these respects, we are only too well aware of the potential 'dark side' too. We have therefore explored the extent to which third sector organisations can live up to the varying expectations placed upon them – as well as the constraints that they face in doing so (some unique to our contemporary world; others more constant through time and space). Here too we have not assumed that the third sector is the sole, or even the preeminent, means of promoting active citizenship for human rights and social justice agendas. Rather our aim has been to make a critical and, where possible, empirical assessment of the contributions that it can make and the conditions that either help or constrain it in doing so.

The original research that the book draws on to support our assessments was mostly conducted in the UK and Australia, but also includes studies carried out in Central and South America, Indonesia, Russia and the Middle East. It has also drawn on the wider literature to incorporate examples from other countries, particularly the US. But this remains a partial picture. A central issue for much of the analysis has been that civil society – and even citizenship – can have quite different meanings and potentialities in different parts of the globe – and that the terminology of the third sector is by no means universal. While these concepts need to be understood in their own terms, therefore, they also need to be understood within the economic, cultural and political context within which they operate. The 'West' has dominated much of the discourse in this field. In other contexts the links between the third sector and active citizenship can be quite different.

These differences between contexts and cultures across time and space emerge as a central theme in a number of chapters. Nonetheless, there are common themes too in relation to the processes that foster active citizenship as well as the structural constraints and challenges faced by both the third sector and citizens in the contemporary world. Globalisation, changing migration patterns and the digital age, for example, have each posed common challenges: in relation to the new hegemonies created by the rise of neoliberalism and the increasing dominance of the market; and in relation to the local, national and regional identities that citizens are creating for themselves. But they have also spawned fresh opportunities in relation to the development of new forms of citizenship that can cross cultural and national divides and innovative forms of organisation – in virtual spaces in and across continents.

Does the third sector facilitate and promote active citizenship?

What, then, does this mean for the book's central questions: what is the relationship between the third sector and active citizenship? Does the third sector facilitate and promote active citizenship and, if so, how and in what circumstances, taking account of the varying degrees of scope for human agency within wider structural constraints? The foregoing chapters demonstrate that there is no one way to be an active citizen. For many, as Chapter Six illustrated, it is a matter of civil commitment, for example, supporting those in need as a volunteer. For others, it entails some form of civil or political engagement, either within or outside state structures, including advocacy and campaigning at international as well as national and local levels (Chapters Eight and Nine). Then again, as Chapters Ten and Eleven illustrate, it may be neither as such, but rather a collective endeavour to create something new. These forms of active citizenship are not mutually exclusive, though. They can inform and support each other. The demands of active citizenship and the forms this takes may also change as circumstances and opportunities vary. Thus, what may begin as a strongly political act may become a collaborative act of construction, eventually developing a maintenance function. Demands and opportunities may require action 'on the street' or virtually, just as they may demand long-term administrative commitment to a third sector organisation, caring for others or establishing a mutual endeavour.

Previous chapters have highlighted the importance of being cautious about some of the claims that have been made for civil society and its third sector organisations. As Chapters Three and Four demonstrate, champions of the third sector tend to stress its value base, rooted in commitments to solidarity and cooperation, together with its democratic nature, its concern with social justice goals, even its cosmopolitanism. Other chapters in the book have shown, however, that although its organisations can live up to these claims they do not always do so. This undermines any attempt to promote third sector organisations as providing magic bullets to tackle society's wider ills.

At their best, we have argued, third sector organisations can indeed nurture active citizenship. This means that the third sector can be the source of innovative processes and structures. It has been the persistent activism of citizens over the centuries, working through third sector organisations, that has led to the development of many institutions and services that have been seen as essential to a healthy society. The third sector can also maintain a watching brief on existing systems and structures, constantly looking to defend and improve, as well as to identify gaps in, public service provision, for example, and to hold other actors in society to account. And from within the wider civil society social movements can be mobilised to address and seek social justice and social change, building alliances in the process and creating networks that can often lead to the development of third sector organisations in their turn.

On the other hand, however, as we have also argued, the third sector can create opportunities for citizens to organise collectively around narrow agendas of self-interest, exclusion and even hatred. This is not simply a question of separating out a few 'darker' tendencies from the mainstream. Even in their more benign forms, third sector organisations can at times be patronising, insular, competitive, paternalistic and oppressive just as much as they can be egalitarian, democratic, cooperative and empowering. They can be a source of fragmentation as well as a source of cohesion and social solidarity.

Earlier in the book, we described how attempts are sometimes made to categorise the sector in terms of market-led public service contractors, contrasting these with 'citizens movements' or value-based organisations and redrawing the boundaries to contain only those who have remained true to their associational roots. But, as Edwards and Hulme have argued (1995), these attempts do less than justice to the complexity of operating in this diverse and sometimes contradictory territory. The evidence would seem to point to more complex and dynamic realities. Boundaries may well continue to shift as third sector organisations find their own ways of managing the tensions inherent in their varying contexts. And the forms of active citizenship that are produced seem likely to shift in parallel. Indeed, it is this very diversity and its ability to release a range of energies to address common needs and mobilise diverse constituencies that enables the sector to act as a channel for active citizenship.

Also, earlier in this book, we described the territory in which third sector organisations operate as a tension field between the state, the market and the informal, community sphere. An even wider view would see it, and the civil society of which it is a part, as an ambiguous arena where many tensions within society are played out: between universalism and particularism, the individual and the collective, public and private, diversity and equality among them. This position has made it a potential barometer of the feasibility and consequences of change, the 'canary in the coalmine' – as the welfare state has been receding and neoliberalism advancing (Taylor, 1996). Its experiences of trying to make sense of the dilemmas inherent within the intermediate space that it occupies – dealing with uncertainty and ambiguity, reconciling different interests around common dilemmas, releasing resources in new ways – are what makes the third sector so fascinating and important as an area of study.

To summarise, then, this book has presented evidence to suggest that third sector organisations are essential ingredients for any healthy society, an important locus of active citizenship within civil society more widely. While the actions of active citizens may be driven by the values of social justice, however, they may, on occasion, be driven by very different values, or passions driven by considerations of power and dominance. Nor does the sector have a premium on values – or even civility – which can be found in all parts of society. Thus, while the third sector is a necessary condition for the development of active citizenship, even at its most vibrant, it is by no means sufficient.

Although, as these pages have shown, authoritarian states can act as a trigger to active citizenship, through stirring up oppositional activity, to thrive, we might argue that the third sector requires the kind of overarching infrastructural framework that an effectively democratic state can provide. It has been only too understandable for activists to resist such a conclusion, given their experiences of the state as a power which itself inhibits and excludes. However, Evers reminds us that the state 'has a fundamental role in helping civil society to develop' and that 'a bigger society does not necessarily mean a smaller state, but a different, more responsive state' (2013, pp 153, 154). Just as a healthy democracy requires a vibrant third sector, a vibrant third sector needs to operate within an effectively democratic state. Rather than rolling back the state, therefore, what is perhaps required is a revitalisation of the notion of the democratic state and the public sphere, based on a shared understanding that an effectively democratic and genuinely accountable state is the responsibility of us all. This, perhaps, represents the most significant finding of all.

Is the sector reinventing itself?

At the outset, this book set out to consider whether and how the third sector might survive and move forward into the future – whether, for example, formalised third sector structures were in the process of being replaced by other forms of civil society organisations. In the current context, neoliberal market forces dominate the policies of many governments and, through them, exert control over many established third sector organisations. Although these processes have been occurring most commonly in OECD countries, they have also achieved a global reach including via humanitarian aid policies, the World Bank and multinational corporations. The risk is that a compliant, consumer-oriented third sector, lacking the will or incentives to engage in more active participation, will become part of the machinery of increasingly marketised states, working through third sector organisations that essentially deliver state agendas.

Against this trend, previous chapters have described a continuing resurgence of citizen action. New alliances are being developed. And new third sector organisations are being created, whether to meet new needs or to readdress existing problems. This is exemplified as much in the formation of a new collective enterprise in an island of Lake Titikaka in Peru as in a Lock the Gate action by farmers in Australia, trying to block the development of coal seam gas, or a global internet campaign to protest against state indifference towards violence against women. This process of emergence has been a feature of the third sector over the centuries, defying or at least eluding effective control by either the market or the state.

These new formations may have leaders and they may form relatively stable structures. But they do not necessarily begin that way. They typically emerge through grassroots action, as a handful of passionate individuals share their vision, exercise agency, challenge the status quo, find effective ways to work collectively, and build alliances, as Chapter Nine on social movements demonstrated, communicating with others who join and grow the action. Nor do all new networks go on to form stable, sustainable organisational forms. Many, if not most, do not. Some, like the Occupy movement, seem to become less visible over time, even if many of their activists move on to different struggles. Others are explicitly intended as temporary formations from the outset, designed to achieve a specific outcome and then to disband. Whether temporary or stable over time, however, these new forms of activism demonstrate the continuing vitality of active citizenship in practice.

While it contains large and relatively stable bureaucratic charities, therefore, the sector also contains a myriad of moving, growing, creative entities, often forming briefly out of informal networks only to disappear again, sometimes shaping creative new social forms, which eventually become major institutions. Between these two extremes, other organisations ebb and flow, responding to the pressures they find around them. Some fragment and some fail. But others manage to thrive, staying light on their feet without succumbing to the tyrannies of structurelessness or the dysfunctions of bureaucratisation, offering new models of organisation more widely. And as some organisations become coopted into what Habermas called the 'systems world', others emerge to challenge them, developing new forms of dialogue as they create alternative approaches.

In this analysis, the third sector seems to emerge as extremely fluid, even chaotic. This testifies to the potential dynamism that may be associated with active citizenship, a dynamism that needs to be explored through continuing research. For while previous chapters have engaged with theoretical discourse, they have also underlined the importance of empirical understandings, drawing upon the evidence of experiences on the ground. This approach can lead to a more nuanced understanding of how the third sector's different constituents organise and operate in practice, with varying meanings and assumptions in different contexts. It can also lead to a more complex understanding of the competing pressures on third sector organisations locally, regionally, nationally and internationally in the context of increasing globalisation and the changing roles and boundaries between the state, the market and civil society more generally.

This points to the need for caution when it comes to attempting to make predictions about future trends for the third sector in the 21st century. The Arab Spring, greeted as a celebration of a burgeoning civil society in many quarters, has, in some cases, been ruthlessly suppressed, in other cases falling prey to processes of fragmentation that are only too frequently observed in civil society. Similarly, the Occupy movement, hailed by some as the advent of a new form of resistance to neoliberalism, has, thus far, proved a more temporary phenomenon, although it remains to be seen how it will develop in future.

Rather than attempting to predict future trends then, we would emphasise the scope for varying outcomes. People have the capacity for agency, engaging with third sector organisations and making choices, even if in circumstances not of their own choosing, in this contested terrain. As we explained in the introduction, we set out to unpack contested concepts and critically examine empirical evidence, rather than setting out to develop blueprints for the coming period.

This was in no way to imply that we have had no positions ourselves, however, as Chapter One made clear. Far from being totally neutral, as the introduction also explained, we share commitments to the values of equality, social solidarity, human rights and social justice, together with respect for diversity and differences, within, as well as between, communities. These shared commitments have underpinned our varying approaches to researching the third sector and active citizenship.

We conclude therefore by summarising the developments that we should most welcome for the future. Rather than operating as an arm of government, providing services on the cheap, third sector organisations would be innovating, engaging citizens in collectively developing new ways of identifying and meeting emerging needs inclusively. Rather than spearheading further marketisation, third sector organisations would be working in partnership with local communities, service users and service providers and through transnational and transcultural networks. Within states, they would work to improve the forms of governance and the quality as well as the cost effectiveness of public services and reinvigorating the public sphere through transsectoral networks and alliances. Rather than promoting particular interests or working in exclusive ways, third sector organisations would be promoting increasing inclusivity. Building alliances between those active via new forms of social mobilisation and those active within longer established organisations and social movements, including traditional village cooperatives, humanitarian aid organisations and the labour and trade union movement, third sector organisations would be continuing to work for equality, social solidarity, human rights and social justice, locally, nationally and internationally.

References

6, P. and Kendall, J. (eds) (1997) *The contract culture in public services*: *Studies from Britain, Europe and the USA,* Aldershot: Arena.

6, P. and Leat, D. (1997) 'Inventing the British voluntary sector by committee: from Wolfenden to Deakin', *Nonprofit Studies,* 1(2): 33–46.

ABS (Australian Bureau of Statistics) (2001) *Voluntary work, Australia,* Canberra: AGPS.

ABS (Australian Bureau of Statistics) (2002) *Australian social trends 2002,* Canberra: AGPS.

Acheson, N. and LaForest, R. (2013) 'The expendables: community organizations and governance dynamics in the Canadian settlement sector', *Canadian Journal of Political Science,* 46(3): 597–616.

Aiken, M., Cairns, B., Taylor, M. and Moran, R. (2011) *Community organisations controlling assets: A better understanding,* York: Joseph Rowntree Foundation.

Alessandrini, M. (2010) 'Towards a fourth sector? Australian community organisations and the market', *Third Sector Review,* 16(1): 125–43.

Alexander, J. (2006) *The civil sphere,* Oxford: Oxford University Press.

Alinsky, S. (1969) *Reveille for radicals,* New York: Vintage Books.

Alinsky, S. (1971) *Rules for radicals,* New York: Random House.

Almond, G. and Verba, S. (1963) *The civic culture: Political attitudes and democracy in five nations,* Princeton NJ: Princeton University Press.

Anderson, M. (1996) 'Humanitarian NGOs in conflict intervention' in C. Crocker, F. Hampsen and P. Aall (eds) *Managing global chaos,* Washington, DC: United States Institute of Peace Press, pp 343–54.

Anheier, H. (2007) 'Bringing civility back in: reflections on global civil society', *Development Dialogue,* 49: 41–50.

Anheier, H. and Seibel, W. (eds) (1990) *The third sector: Comparative studies of nonprofit organisations,* Berlin and New York: Walter de Gruyter, pp 5–44.

Antlov, H., Ibrahim, R. and van Tuij, P. (2005) 'Indonesia: Challenges in a newly democratizing country', www.icnl.org/research/library/files/Indonesia/Peter_NGO%20accountability%20in%20Indonesia%20July%2005%20version.pdf.

Aouragh, M. and Alexander, A. (2011) 'The Arab Spring, the Egyptian experience: Sense and nonsense of the internet revolution', *International Journal of Communication,* 5: 1344–58.

Archibugi, D. (2008) *The global commonwealth of citizens,* Princeton, NJ: Princeton University Press.

Arnstein, S. (1969) 'A ladder of citizen participation', *Journal of the American Institute of Planners*, 35(4): 216–24.

Atkinson, R. (1999) 'Discourses of partnership and empowerment in contemporary British urban regeneration', *Urban Studies*, 36(1): 59–72.

Atkinson, R. (2003) 'Addressing urban exclusion through community involvement in urban regeneration', in R. Imrie and M. Raco (eds) *Urban renaissance? New Labour, community and urban policy*, Bristol: Policy Press.

Atkinson, R. and Carmichael, L. (2007) 'Neighbourhood as a new focus for action in the urban policies of West European states', in I. Smith, E. Lepine and M. Taylor (eds) *Disadvantaged by where you live? Neighbourhood governance in contemporary urban policy*, Bristol: Policy Press, pp 43–64.

Austin, J., Stevenson, H. and Wei-Skillern, J. (2006) 'Social and commercial entrepreneurship: same, different or both?' *Entrepreneurship Theory and Practice*, 1042–2587: 1–22.

Avery, G. (2004) *Understanding leadership: Paradigms and cases*, London: Sage Publications.

Ayittey, G., (1991) 'Why structural adjustment failed in Africa', *TransAfrica Forum*, 8(2): 43.

Baker, E., Onyx, J. and Edwards, M. (2011) 'Emergence, social capital and entrepreneurship: understanding networks from the inside', *E:CO*, 13(3): 21–38.

Baldock, C. (1998) 'Feminist discourses of unwaged work: the case of volunteering', *Australian Feminist Studies*, 13(27): 19–34.

Barber, B, (1992) *Strong democracy: Participatory politics for a new age*, Berkeley, CA: University of California Press.

Barnes, M., Newman, J. and Sullivan, H. (2007) *Power, participation and political renewal: Case studies in public participation*, Bristol: Policy Press.

Baring Foundation (2014) 'Independence undervalued: The voluntary sector in 2014', Report of the Panel on the Independence of the Voluntary Sector, London: The Baring Foundation.

Barraket, J. and Archer, V. (2010) 'Social inclusion through community enterprise? Examining the available evidence', *Third Sector Review*, 16(1): 13–28.

Batliwala, S. (2002) 'Grassroots movements as transnational actors', *Voluntas*, 13(4): 393–409.

Bauman, Z. (1999) *In search of politics*, Cambridge: Polity Press.

Bauman, Z. (2000) *Liquid modernity*, Cambridge: Polity Press.

Bauman, Z. (2001) *Community: Seeking safety in an insecure world*, Cambridge: Polity Press.

Beatty, C. and Fothergill, S. (2013) *Hitting the poorest places hardest: The local and regional impact of welfare reform*, Sheffield: Centre for Regional Economic and Social Research.

Bebbington, A., Hickey, S. and Mitlin, D. (2008) 'Introduction: Can NGOs make a difference? The challenge of development alternatives', in A. Bebbington, S. Hickey and D. Mitlin (eds) *Can NGOs make a difference?* London: Zed Books, pp 3–37.

Beck, D. and Purcell, R. (2013) *International community organizing: Taking power, making change*, Bristol: Policy Press.

Beck, U. (1992) *Risk society: Towards a new modernity*, London: Sage.

Beck, U. (1993) *Die Erfindung des politischen: Zu einer Theorie reflexiver Modernisierung*, Frankfurt: Suhrkamp-Verlag.

Beck, U. (1999) *World risk society*, Cambridge: Polity Press.

Beck, U. (2000) *The brave new world of work*, Cambridge: Polity Press.

Beck, U. (2006) *The cosmopolitan vision*, Cambridge: Polity Press.

Beck, U. and Sznaider, N. (2006) 'Unpacking cosmopolitanism for the social sciences: a research agenda', *British Journal of Sociology*, 57(1): 1–23.

Bedford, J., Gorbing, S. and Hampson, S. (2010) 'The five Cs: confident, challenging, co-operative, constructive and critical women' in M. Mayo and J. Annette (eds) *Taking part?* Leicester: NIACE, pp 186–210.

Benson, A. (2014) ' 'The devil that has come amongst us': The impact of commissioning and procurement practices', Working paper no. 6, NCIA Inquiry into the Future of Voluntary Services, London: National Coalition for Independent Action.

Benthall, J. and Bellion-Jourdan, J. (2003) *The charitable crescent*, London: IB Tauris.

Bhatnagar, B. and Williams, A. (1992) 'Participatory development and the World Bank: Potential directions for change', World Bank Discussion Papers, 183, Washington DC: World Bank.

Billante, N. and Saunders, P. (2002) 'Why civility matters', *Policy*, 18(3): 32–6.

Billis, D. (ed) (2010) *Hybrid organisations and the third sector: Challenges for practice, theory and policy*, Basingstoke: Palgrave Macmillan.

Blake, G., Robinson, D. and Smerdon, M. (2006) *Living values: A report encouraging boldness in third sector organisations*, London: Community Links.

Bob, C. (2005) *The marketing of rebellion: Insurgents, media and international activism*, Cambridge: Cambridge University Press.

Bode, I. and Evers, A. (2004) 'From institutional fixation to entrepreneurial mobility? The German third sector and its contemporary challenges', in A. Evers and J-L. Laville (eds) *The third sector in Europe*, Cheltenham: Edward Elgar, pp 101–21.

Boje, T. (2009) 'Organised civil society: volunteering and citizenship', in B. Enroljas and K. Siveskind (eds) *Comparative social research (26): Civil society in comparative perspective*, Bingley: Emerald Books, pp 243–62.

Bonoli, G. (1997) 'Classifying welfare states; A two dimension approach', *Journal of Social Policy*, 26(3): 351–72.

Bourdieu, P. (1977) *Outline of a theory of practice*, Cambridge: Cambridge University Press.

Bourdieu, P. (1986) 'The forms of capital', in J. Richardson (ed) *Handbook of theory and research for the sociology of education*, New York: Greenwood, pp 241–58.

Bourdieu, P. (1990) *In other words: Essays towards a reflexive sociology*, Stanford, CA: Stanford University Press.

Bourdieu, P. and Wacquant, L. (1992) *An invitation to reflexive sociology*, Chicago, IL: University of Chicago Press.

Bradley, J. (2012) *After the Arab Spring: how Islamists hijacked the Middle East revolts*, New York: Palgrave Macmillan

Brenton, M. (1985) *The voluntary sector in British social services*, Harlow: Longman.

Brodie, E., Hughes, T., Jochum, V, Miller, S., Ockenden, N. and Warburton, D. (2011) *Pathways through participation: What creates and sustains active citizenship?* London: NCVO.

Brown, C. (2000) 'Cosmopolitanism, world citizenship and global civil society', *Critical Review of International Social and Political Philosophy*, 3(1): 7–26.

Brown, K., Kenny, S. and Turner, B. (2000) *Rhetorics of welfare: Uncertainty, choice and voluntary associations*, London: Macmillan.

Browne, J., Jochum, V. and Paylor, J. (2013) *The value of giving a little time: Understanding the potential of micro-volunteering*, London: Institute for Volunteering Research.

Bunyan, P. (2010) 'Broad-based organizing in the UK: reasserting the centrality of political activity in community development', *Community Development Journal*, 45(1): 111–27.

Burt, R. (1998) 'The gender of social capital', *Rationality & Society*, 10(1): 5–42.

Butcher, M. and *Harris*, A. *(2010)* 'Pedestrian crossings: young people and everyday multiculturalism', *Journal of Intercultural Studies*, 31(5): 449–53.

Cairns, B., Hutchison, R. and Aiken, M. (2010) ' "It's not what we do; it's how we do it": managing the tension between service delivery and advocacy', *Voluntary Sector Review*, 1(2): 193–207.

Calhoun, C. (2000) 'The virtue of civility', *Philosophy and Public Affairs*, 29: 251–75.

Caniglia, B. and Carmin, J. (2005) 'Scholarship on social movement organisations: classic views and emerging trends', *Mobilization*, 10(2): 201–12.

Cantle, T. (2012) *Interculturalism: The new era of cohesion and diversity*, Basingstoke: Palgrave Macmillan.

Carmel, E. and Harlock, J. (2008) 'Instituting the 'third sector' as a governable terrain: partnership, procurement and performance in the UK', *Policy and Politics*, 36(2): 155–71.

Casey, J. (2013) 'Hybrid discourses on social enterprise: Unpacking the zeitgeist', in T. Lyons (ed) *Social Entrepreneurship*, Santa Barbara, CA: Praeger.

Castello, G., Lavalle, A. and Houtzager, P. (2007) 'Civil organizations and political representation in Brazil's participatory institutions', in A. Cornwall and V. Coelho (eds) *Spaces for change*, London: Zed Books, pp 114–30.

Chambers, R. (1983) *Rural development: Putting the first last*, London: Longman.

Chanan, G. (1991) *Taken for granted: Community activity and the crisis in the voluntary sector*, London: Community Development Foundation.

Chandler, D. (2002) *From Kosovo to Kabul and beyond: Human rights and international intervention*, London: Pluto Press.

Chaves, M., Stephens, L. and Galaskiewicz, J. (2004) 'Does government funding suppress nonprofits' political activity?', *American Sociological Review*, 69(2): 292–316.

Chia, R. (1999) 'A rhizomic model of organizational change and transformation: perspective from a metaphysics of change', *British Journal of Management*, 10: 209–27.

Child, C. and Gronbjerg, K. (2007) 'Nonprofit advocacy organizations: their characteristics and activities', *Social Science Quarterly*, 88(1): 259–81.

Chiles, T., Meyer, A. and Hench, T. (2004) 'Organizational emergence: The origin and transformation of Branson, Missouri's musical theaters', *Organization Science*, 15(5): 499–519.

Clark, J. (2003) 'Introduction: civil society and transnational action', in J. Clark (ed) *Globalizing civic engagement: Civil society and transnational action*, London: Earthscan, pp 1–28.

Clary, G., Snyder, M. and Stukas, A. (1996) 'Volunteers' motivations: findings from a national survey', *Nonprofit and Voluntary Sector Quarterly*, 25(4): 485–505.

Cleaver, F. (2004) 'The social embeddedness of agency and decision making', in S. Hickey and G. Mohan (eds) *Participation: From tyranny to transformation*, London: Zed Books, pp 271–7.

Clegg, S. (2010) 'The state, power and agency: missing in action in institutional theory?', *Journal of Management Inquiry*, 19(1): 4–13.

Coelho, V. and von Lieres, B. (2010) 'Mobilizing for democracy: citizenship engagement and the politics of public participation', in V. Coelho and B. von Lieres (eds) *Mobilising for Democracy*, London: Zed Books, pp 1–19.

Cohen, J. (1999) 'Trust, voluntary association and workable democracy: the contemporary American discourse of civil society', in M. Warren (ed) *Democracy and trust*, Cambridge: Cambridge University Press, pp 208–48.

Cohen, J. and Arato, A. (1994) *Civil society and political theory*, Cambridge MA: MIT Press.

Cohen, J. and Rogers, J. (1992) 'Secondary associations and democratic governance', *Politics & Society*, 20(4): 393–472.

Cohen, J. and Rogers, J. (1995) *The Real Utopias Project vol. 1: Associations and democracy*, New York: Verso.

Cooke, B. and Kothari, U. (2001) *Participation: The new tyranny?* London: Zed Books.

Cornwall, A. (2004) 'New democratic spaces? The politics and dynamics of institutionalised participation', *IDS Bulletin*, 3(2): 1–10.

Cornwall, A. (2008) 'Unpacking "participation": models, meanings and practices', *Community Development Journal*, 43(3): 269–83.

Cornwall, A. and Coelho, V. (eds) (2007) *Spaces for change? The politics of participation in new democratic arenas*, London: Zed Books.

Cornwall, A. and Coelho, V. (2007) 'Spaces for change? The politics of participation in new democratic arenas', in A. Cornwall and V. Coelho (eds) *Spaces for change*, London: Zed Books, pp 1–29

Corry, O. (2011) 'Defining and theorizing the third sector', in R. Taylor (ed) *Third sector research*, New York: Springer, pp 11–20.

Craig, G., Taylor, M. and Parkes, T. (2004) Protest or partnership? The voluntary and community sectors in the policy process, *Social Policy & Administration*, 38(3): 221–39.

Crossley, N. (2002) *Making sense of social movements*, Buckingham: Open University Press.

Crossley, N. (2003) 'From reproduction to transformation: social movement fields and radical habitus', *Theory, Culture and Society*, 20(6): 43–68.

Dagnino, E. (2008) 'Challenges to participation, citizenship and democracy: perverse confluence and displacement of meanings', in A. Bebbington, S. Hickey and D. Mitlin (eds) *Can NGOs make a difference? The challenge of development alternatives*, London and New York: Zed Books, pp 55–70.

Dahl, R. (1989) *Democracy and Its critics*, New Haven: Yale University Press.

Dahrendorf, R. (2001) *The Arnold Goodman lecture*, Tonbridge: Charities Aid Foundation.

Dart, R. (2004) 'The legitimacy of social enterprise', *Nonprofit Management & Leadership*, 11(4): 411–24

Davis, M. (2006) *Planet of slums,* London: Verso.

Deakin, N. (1996) 'The devil's in the detail: some reflections on contracting for social care by voluntary organisations', *Policy & Administration*, 30(1): 20–38.

Deci, E. and Ryan, R. (2000) 'The 'what' and 'why' of goal pursuits: human needs and the self-determination of behavior,' *Psychological Inquiry*, 11(4): 227–68.

Dees, J. (1998) 'Enterprising Nonprofits', *Harvard Business Review*, Jan-Feb.

de Filippis, J. (2007) 'Community control and development: the long view', in J. de Filippis and S. Saegert (eds) *The community development reader*, New York: Routledge.

de Filippis, J., Fisher, R. and Shragge, E. (2009) 'What's left in the community? Oppositional politics in contemporary practice', *Community Development Journal*, 44(1): 38–52.

Defourny, J. and Nyssens, M. (2010) 'Conceptions of social enterprise and social entrepreneurship in Europe and the United States: convergences and divergences', *Journal of Social Entrepreneurship*, 1(1): 32–53.

Dekker, P. (2002) 'On the prospects of volunteering in civil society', *Voluntary Action*, 4(3): 31–48.

Dekker, P. (2004) 'The Netherlands: from private initiatives to non-profit hybrids and back?', in A. Evers and J-L. Laville (eds) *The third sector in Europe*, Cheltenham: Edward Elgar.

Dekker, P. (2009) 'Civicness: from civil society to civic services?', *Voluntas*, 20(3): 217–9.

Dekker, P. and Halman, L. (eds) (2003) 'Volunteering and values: an introduction', in Dekker, P. and Halman, L. (eds) The values of volunteering: cross-cultural perspectives', New York: Kluwer Academic, pp 1–16.

Delanty, G. (1999) *Social theory in a changing world: Conceptions of modernity*, Cambridge: Polity Press.

Delanty, G. (2000) *Citizenship in a global age: Society, culture, politics*, Buckingham: Open University Press.

Delanty, G. (2006) 'The cosmopolitan imagination: critical cosmopolitanism and social theory', *British Journal of Sociology*, 57(1): 25–47.

Delgado, G. (1986) *Organizing the movement: The roots and growth of ACORN*, Philadelphia: Temple University Press.

Della Porta, D. (2013) *Can democracy be saved*? Cambridge: Cambridge University Press.

Della Porta, D. and Diani, M. (1999) *Social movements*, Oxford: Blackwell.

Della Porta, D. and Rucht, D. (2013) *Meeting democracy: Power and deliberation in global justice movements*, Cambridge: Cambridge University Press.

Della Porta, D. and Tarrow, S. (2005) 'Transnational processes and social activism: an introduction', in D. Della Porta and S. Tarrow (eds) *Transnational protest and global activism*, New York and Oxford: Rowman and Littlefield.

de Tocqueville, A. (1969) *Democracy in America*, edited by J.P. Mayer, New York: Knopf Publishing Group.

de Tocqueville, A. (2003) *Democracy in America and two essays on America*, translated by G. Bevan, London: Penguin Books.

Diani, M. (1997) 'Social movements and social capital: a network perspective on movement outcomes', *Mobilization*, 2, 129–48.

Dietz, M (1987) 'Context is all: Feminism and theories of citizenship', *Daedalus*, 116(4): 1–24.

DiMaggio, P and Powell, W, (1983) 'The iron cage revisited: institutional isomorphism and collective rationality in organizational fields', *American Sociological Review*, 48: 459–62.

Dryzek, J. (2002) Deliberative democracy and beyond: Liberals, critics, contestations, Oxford: Oxford University Press.

Duffield, M. (2005) *Global governance and the new wars*, London: Zed Books.

Durkheim, E. (1957) *Professional ethics and civil morals*, London: Routledge and Kegan Paul.

Eade, D. and Williams, S. (1995) *The Oxfam handbook of development and relief*, Oxford: Oxfam.

Easterly, W. (2003) 'IMF structural adjustment programs and poverty', in M. Dooley and A. Frankel (eds) *Managing currency crises in emerging markets*, National Bureau of Economic Research, Chicago, IL: University of Chicago Press.

Easterly, W. (2006) *White man's burden: Why the west's efforts to aid the rest have done so much ill and so little good*, New York: Penguin Books.

Edwards, M. (1999) *Future positive: International co-operation in the 21st century*, London: Earthscan.

Edwards, M. (2004) *Civil society*, Cambridge: Polity Press.

Edwards, M. (2008) *Small change: Why business won't save the world*, San Francisco, CA: Berrett-Koehler and London: Demos.

Edwards, M. and Hulme, D. (1995) *Non-governmental organizations - performance and accountability: Beyond the magic bullet*, London: Earthscan.

Edwards, M. and Onyx, J. (2007) 'Social capital and sustainability in a community under threat', *Local Environment*, 12(1): 17–30.

Escobar, A. (1992) 'Reflections on "development": Grassroots approaches and alternative politics in the third world', *Futures*, June: 211–27.

Escobar, A. (1995) Encountering development: The making and unmaking of the third world, Princeton, NJ: Princeton University Press.

Escobar, A. and Alvarez, S. (1992) 'Introduction: theory and protest in Latin America today', in A. Escobar and S. Alvarez (eds) *The making of social movements in Latin America: Identity, strategy and democracy*, Boulder, CO: Westview Press, pp 1–15.

Esping Andersen, G. (1990) *The three worlds of welfare capitalism*, Cambridge: Polity Press and Princeton, NJ: Princeton University Press.

Etzioni, A. (1973) 'The third sector and domestic missions', *Public Administration Review*, 33(4): 314–23.

Etzioni, A. (1996) 'The responsive community: A communitarian perspective', *American Sociological Review*, 6(1): 1–11.

Etzioni, A. (1998) *The essential communitarian reader*, Lanham, MD: Rowman and Littlefield.

Euricse (2014) 'Cooperation in Italy during the crisis years', Second Eurice Report, European Research Institute on Cooperative and Social Enterprises, http://euricse.eu/en/node/2494

Evers, A. (1990) 'Shifts in the welfare mix: introducing a new approach for the study of transformations in welfare and social policy', *Eurosocial*, 57/8, pp 7–8.

Evers, A. (1995) 'Part of the welfare mix: the third sector as an intermediate area', *Voluntas*, 6(2): 159–82.

Evers, A. (2009) 'Civicness and civility: their meanings for social services, *Voluntas*, 20(3): 239–59.

Evers, A. (2013) 'The concept of "civil society": different understandings and their implications for third sector policies', *Voluntary Sector Review*, 4(2): 149–64.

Evers, A. and Laville, J-L. (eds) (2004) *The third sector in Europe*, Cheltenham: Edward Elgar.

Evers, A. and Guillemard, A. (eds) (2013) *Social policy and citizenship: The changing landscape*, Oxford: Oxford University Press.

Eyerman, R. and Jamison, A. (1991) *Social movements: A cognitive approach*, Cambridge: Polity Press.

Fairclough, N. (1992) *Discourse and social change*, Cambridge: Polity Press.

Falk, R. (1997) 'Resisting "globalisation-from-above" through "globalisation-from-below"', *New Political Economy*, 2(1): 17–24.

Fanany, I. (2010) 'Towards a model of constructive interaction between aid donors and recipients in a disaster context: the case of Lampuuk', in M. Clarke, I. Fanany and S. Kenny (eds) *Post-disaster reconstruction: Lessons from Aceh*, London : Earthscan, pp 107–125.

Favoreto, A., Galvanese, C., Menino, F., Coelho, V. and Kawamura, Y. (2010) 'How styles of activism influence social participation and democratic deliberation', in V. Coelho and B. von Lieres (eds) *Mobilising for democracy*, London: Zed Books, pp 243–63.

Ferrera, M. (1996) 'The 'Southern model' of welfare in social Europe', *Journal of European Social Policy*, 6(1): 17–37.

Florini, A. (2000) *The third force: The rise of transnational civil society*, Washington, DC: Carnegie Endowment for Peace.

Foley, G. (1999) *Learning in social action*, London: Zed Press.

Foley, M. and Hodgkinson, V. (2003) *The civil society reader*, Lebanon, NH: University Press of New England.

Foltz, K. and Moodliar, S. (2005) *The future of the World Social Forum Process*, www.nadir.org/agp/wsf/portoalegre.

Foucault, M. (1980) *Power/Knowledge*, edited by C. Gordon, Brighton: Harvester Press.

Fowler, A. (2008) 'Development and the new security agenda: w(h)ither(ing) NGO alternatives', in A. Bebbington, S. Hickey and D. Mitlin (eds) *Can NGOs make a difference?* London: Zed Press, pp 111–30.

Fowler, A. (2012) 'Measuring civil society: perspectives on Afro-centrism', *Voluntas,* 23(1): 5–25.

Fox Piven, F. (2011) *Who's afraid of Frances Fox Piven? The essential writings of the professor Glenn Beck loves to hate,* New York: New Press.

Fraser, N. (1992) 'Rethinking the public sphere: a contribution to the critique of actually existing democracy', in C. Calhoun (ed) *Habermas and the public sphere,* Cambridge, MA: MIT Press, pp 109–42.

Fraser, N. (2008) *Adding insult to injury,* London: Verso.

Freire, P. (1976) *Education: The practice of freedom,* London: Writers and Readers.

Frohlich, C. (2012) 'Civil society and the state intertwined: the case of disability NGOs in Russia', *East European Politics,* 28(4): 371–89.

Fukuyama, F. (1995) *Trust: The social virtues and the creation of prosperity,* London: Penguin.

Fuller, S., Kershaw, P. and Pulkingham, J. (2008) 'Constructing "active citizenship": single mothers, welfare and the logics of voluntarism', *Citizenship Studies,* 12(2): 157–76.

Fung, A. and Wright E. (2003) *Deepening democracy: Institutional innovations in empowered participatory governance,* London: Verso.

Furial, P. (2005) 'Global citizenship, anyone? Cosmopolitanism, privilege and public opinion', *Global Society,* 19(4): 331–59.

Gallopín, G., Funtowicz, S., O'Connor, M. and Ravetz, J. (2001) 'For the twenty-first century: from social contract to the scientific core', *International Journal of Social Science,* 168, 219–29.

Gamble, A. (1996) *Hayek: The iron cage of liberty,* Cambridge: Polity Press.

Gaventa, J. (2001) 'Global citizen action: lessons and challenges', in M. Edwards and J. Gaventa, (eds) *Global Citizen Action,* London: Earthscan, pp 275–87.

Gaventa, J. (2004) 'Towards participatory governance: assessing the transformative possibilities', in S. Hickey and G. Mohan (eds) *Participation: From tyranny to transformation,* London: Zed Books, pp 25–41.

Gaventa, J. (2007) as summarized in: Economic and Social Research Council (ESRC) 'From local to global', Report from the ESRC/NCVO series: Mapping the public policy landscape, London: NCVO.

Gaventa, J. (2010) 'Foreword' in J. Gaventa and R. Tandon (eds) *Globalising citizens: New dynamics of inclusion and exclusion*, London: Zed Books, pp x-xii.

Gaventa, J and Mayo, M, (2010) 'Spanning citizenship spaces through transnational coalitions; the Global Campaign for Education' in J. Gaventa and R. Tandon (eds) *Globalizing citizens*, London: Zed Press, 140–62.

Gaventa, J. and Tandon, R. (2010) 'Citizen engagements in a globalizing world', in J. Gaventa and R. Tandon (eds) *Globalizing citizens*, London: Zed Press, pp 3–30.

Gaynor, N. (2011) 'In-active citizenship and the depoliticization of community development in Ireland', *Community Development Journal*, 46(1): 27–41.

Gelvin, J. (2012) *The Arab uprisings: What everyone needs to know*, Oxford: Oxford University Press.

Giddens, A. (1982) *Profiles and critiques in social theory*, London: Macmillan.

Giddens, A. (1990) *The consequences of modernity*, Cambridge: Polity Press.

Giddens, A. (1994) *Beyond left and right: The future of radical politics*, Cambridge: Polity Press.

Giddens, A. (1998) *The third way: The renewal of social democracy*, Cambridge: Policy Press.

Gidron, B. Kramer, R. and Salamon, L. (eds) (1992) *Government and the third sector*, San Francisco: Jossey Bass.

Gilchrist, A. (2009) *The well connected community* (2nd edn), Bristol: Policy Press.

Gilchrist, A. and Taylor, M. (2011) *The short guide to community development*, Bristol: The Policy Press.

Gitlin, T. (2012) *Occupy Nation*, New York: Harper Collins.

Glaeser, E. Laibson, D. and Sacerdote, B. (2002) 'An economic approach to social capital', *Economic Journal*, 112 (483): 437–58.

Goldstein, J. (2011) 'Emergence in complex systems', in P. Allen, S. Maguire and B. McKelvey (eds), *The Sage handbook of complexity and management*, pp 65–78.

Goodspeed, T., Lawlor., E., Neitzert. E. and Nicholls, J. (2009) *A guide to social return on investment*, London: Office of the Third Sector.

Gramsci, A. (1971) *Selections from the Prison Notebooks*, edited by Q. Hoare, translated by G. Nowell, London: Laurence & Wishart.

Green, J. (2009) 'The business of values and value of business: The role of organisational values in the recruitment and selection of nonprofit community service managers and executives', PhD thesis, University of Technology, Sydney.

Griffin, D. and Stacey, R. (eds) (2005) *Complexity and the experience of leading organizations*, New York: Routledge.

Gutmann, A. (ed) (1998) *Freedom of association*, Princeton, NJ: Princeton University Press.

Habermas, J. (1989) *The structural transformation of the public sphere*, translated by T. Burger and F. Lawrence, Cambridge, MA: MIT Press.

Hahn, T., Olsson, P., Folke, C., and Johansson, K. (2006) 'Trust building, knowledge generation and organizational innovations: the role of a bridging organization for adaptive comanagement of a wetland landscape around Kristianstad, Sweden', *Human Ecology*, 34: 573–92.

Hall, P.D. (1992) *Inventing the nonprofit sector and other essays on philanthropy, voluntarism and nonprofit organisation*, Baltimore, MD: Johns Hopkins University Press.

Halpern, D. (2005) *Social capital*, Cambridge: Polity Press.

Hammack, D. and Young, D. (eds) (1993) *Nonprofit organizations in a market economy*, San Francisco, CA: Jossey-Bass.

Hanieh, A. (2013) *Lineages of revolt: Issues of contemporary capitalism in the Middle East,* Chicago, IL: Haymarket.

Harvey, D. (2007) *A brief history of neoliberalism*, Oxford: Oxford University Press.

Haugh, H. and Kitson, M. (2007) 'The third way and the third sector: New Labour's economic policy and the social economy', *Cambridge Journal of Economics*, 31: 973–94.

Hefner, R. (2000) *Civil Islam, Muslims and democratization in Indonesia*, Princeton, NJ: Princeton University Press.

Held, D. (ed) (1995) *Cosmopolitan democracy: An agenda for a new world order*, Cambridge: Cambridge University Press.

Held, D. and McGrew, A. (eds) (2002), *Governing globalization: Power, authority and global governance*, Cambridge: Polity Press.

Hickey, S. and Mohan, G. (eds) (2004) *Participation: From tyranny to transformation?*, London: Zed Press.

Hirst, P. (1994) *Associative democracy: New forms of economic and social governance*, Cambridge: Polity Press.

Hoi Ok Jeong (2013) 'From civic participation to political participation', *Voluntas*, 24(4): 1138–53.

Holst, J. (2002) *Social movements, civil society, and radical adult education*, London: Bergin and Garvey.

Home Office (1998) 'Compact: Getting it right together', Cm 4100, London: The Home Office.

Honneth, A. (1992) 'Integrity and disrespect: principles of a conception of morality based on the theory of recognition', *Political Theory*, 20(2): 187–201.

Howard, J. and Lever, J. (2011) 'New governance spaces: what generates a participatory disposition in different contexts?', *Voluntary Sector Review*, 2(1): 77–95.

Howard, J. and Taylor, M. (2010) 'Hybridity in partnership working: managing tensions and opportunities', in D. Billis (ed) *Hybrid organizations and the third sector: Challenges for practice, theory and policy*, Basingstoke: Palgrave Macmillan, pp 175–96.

Hulme, D. and Edwards, M. (eds) (1997) *NGOs, states and donors: Too close for comfort?*, Basingstoke: Palgrave Macmillan.

Isakhan, B, Mansouri, F and Akbarzadeh, S. (2012) 'Introduction: people power and the arab revolutions: towards a new conceptual framework of democracy in the Middle East' in B. Isakhan, F. Mansouri and S. Akbarzadeh (eds) *The Arab revolutions in context*, Melbourne: Melbourne University Press, pp 1–20

Isin, E. and Turner, B. (2007) 'Investigating Citizenship: an agenda for citizenship studies', *Citizenship Studies*, 11(1): 5–17.

Isin, E. and Nielsen, G. (2008) *Acts of citizenship*, London: Zed Books.

Jepson Grassman, E. and Svedberg, L. (2007) 'Civic participation in a Scandinavian welfare state: Patterns in contemporary Sweden', in L. Trägårdh (ed) *State and civil society in Northern Europe: the Swedish model reconsidered*, New York: Berghahn, pp 126–64.

Jochum, V. Pratten, B. and Wilding, K. (2005) *Civic renewal and active citizenship: A guide to the debate*, London: NCVO.

Johannisson, B. and Olaison, L. (2007) 'The moment of truth: reconstructing entrepreneurship and social capital in the eye of the storm', *Review of Social Economy*, 65 (1), 55–78.

Johnson H. and Bernstein, H. (eds) (1982) *Third world lives of struggle*, London: Heinemann.

Joppke, C. (2007) 'Transformation of citizenship: status, rights, identity', *Citizenship Studies*, 11(1): 37–48.

Kabeer, N. (2005) 'Nijera Kori and social mobilization in Bangladesh', in N. Kabeer (ed) *Inclusive citizenship*, London: Zed Press, 181–98.

Kaldor, M. (2003) *Global civil society: An answer to war*, Cambridge: Polity Press.

Kane, D. and Allen, J. (2011) *Counting the cuts: The impact of spending cuts on the UK voluntary and community sector*, London: NCVO.

Keane, J. (2005) 'Eleven theses on markets and civil society', *Journal of Civil Society*, 1(1): 25–34.

Kellner, D. (1999) 'Globalization from below? Toward a radical democratic technopolitics'. *Angelaki,* 4(2): 101–13.

Kendall, J. and Knapp, M. (1995) 'A loose and baggy monster: boundaries, definitions and typologies', in J.D. Smith, C. Rochester and R. Hedley (eds) *An introduction to the voluntary sector*, London and New York: Routledge: pp 66–95.

Kendall, J. and Knapp, M. (1996) *The voluntary sector in the UK*, Manchester: Manchester University Press.

Kendall, J. and Knapp, M. (2000) 'The third sector and welfare state modernization', Civil Society Working Paper 4, Personal Social Services Research Unit PSSRU and the Centre for Civil Society CCS, London: London School of Economics and Political Science.

Kenny, S. (2002) 'Tensions and dilemmas in community development: new discourses, new Trojans?' *Community Development Journal*, 37(4): 284–99.

Kenny, S. (2010) 'Reconstruction through participatory practice?' in M. Clarke, I. Fanany and S. Kenny (eds) *Post-disaster reconstruction: Lessons from Aceh*, London: Earthscan, pp 79–106.

Kenny, S., Fanany, I., and Rahayu, S. (2013) '*Community development in Indonesia: Westernization or doing it their way?*', Community Development Journal, 48(2): 280–97.

Kenny, S., Clarke, M., Fanany, I. and Kingsbury, D. (2010) 'Deconstructing Aceh's reconstruction', in M. Clarke, I. Fanany and S. Kenny (eds) *Post-disaster reconstruction: Lessons from Aceh*, London: Earthscan, pp. 3–25.

Kiai, M. (2014) Coalition's lobbying bill threatens to leave a stain on British democracy, Guardian, 12 January, www.theguardian.com/commentisfree/2014/jan/12/lobbying-bill-stain-on-democracy

Kirby, P. (2003) *Introduction to Latin America*, London: Sage.

Klein, N. (2007) *The shock doctrine: The rise of disaster capitalism*, London: Penguin.

Knight, B. (1993) *Voluntary action*, London: Home Office

Kooiman, M. (2003) *Modern governance: New government-society interactions*, London: Sage.

Kramer, R. (1981) *Voluntary agencies in the welfare state*, Berkeley, CA: University of California Press.

Kramer, R. (2000) ' A third sector in the third millennium?', *Voluntas*, 11(2): 25–44.

Kropotkin, P. (1902) *Mutual aid: A factor in evolution*, edited by C. Alorando, Public Domain Book.

Kymlicka, W. (1998) 'Ethnic associations and democratic citizenship', in A. Gutmann (ed) *Freedom of association*, Princeton, NJ: Princeton University Press, pp 177–213.

Kymlicka, W. (2002) *Contemporary political philosophy: An introduction*, Oxford: Oxford University Press.

LaForest, R. (2013) *The recession and beyond: Taking stock of government nonprofit relations*, Toronto: McGill-Queen's University Press.

Langan, M. and Ostner, I. (1991) 'Gender and welfare: towards a comparative framework', in G. Room (ed) *Towards a European welfare state*, Bristol: SAUS, pp 127–50.

Larner, W. and Butler, M. (2005) 'Governmentalities of local partnerships: the rise of a "partnering" state', *Studies in Political Economy*, 75: 85–108.

Latouche, S.(1993) *The westernization of the world*, Cambridge: Polity Press.

Laville, J-L. (2011) 'What is the third sector? From the non-profit sector to the social and solidarity economy: Theoretical debate and European reality', European Research Network Working Paper, 11/01.

Lawrence, R. (1982) 'Voluntary action: a stalking horse for the right?', *Critical Social Policy*, 2(6):14–30.

Ledwith, M. (2005) *Community development: A critical approach*, Bristol: The Policy Press.

Leibfried, S. (1992) 'Towards a European welfare state? On integrating poverty regimes in the European Community', in Z. Ferge and J. Kolberg (eds) *Social policy in a changing Europe*, Boulder, CO: Westview Press.

Leitch, D. (1997) 'Society in motion: Russia's emerging voluntary sector', *Nonprofit Management & Leadership*, 7(4): 421–33.

Leonard, R. (1997) 'Theorizing the relationship between agency and communion', *Theory and Psychology*, 7(6): 823–835.

Leonard, R. and Onyx, J. (2004) *Spinning straw into gold: Social capital in practice*, London: Janus.

Leonard, R., Onyx, J. and Hayward-Brown, H. (2004) 'Volunteer and coordinator perspectives on managing women volunteers', *Nonprofit Management & Leadership*, 15(2): 205–19.

Lewis, D. (2001) 'Civil society in non-Western contexts: Reflections on the 'usefulness' of a concept', Civil Society Working Paper 13.

Lewis, D. (2010) 'Encountering hybridity: lessons from individual experience', in D. Billis (ed) *Hybrid organizations and the third sector: Challenges for practice, theory and policy*, Basingstoke: Palgrave Macmillan, pp 219–39.

Lewis, D. (2014) 'Heading South: time to abandon the "parallel worlds" of international non-governmental organization (NGO) and domestic third sector scholarship?', *Voluntas*, 25(5): 1132–51.

Lewis, D. and Kanji, N. (2009) *Nongovernmental organisations and development*, Abingdon, UK: Routledge.

Lichtenstein, B., Uhl-Bien, M., Marion, R., Seers, A., Orton, J. and Schreiber, C. (2006) 'Complexity leadership theory: an interactive perspective on leading in complex adaptive systems', *Emergence: Complexity and Organization*, 8(4): 2–12.

Linklater, A. (1998) 'Cosmopolitan citizenship', *Citizenship Studies*, 2(1): 23–41.

Lipsky, M. and Smith, R. (1989) 'Nonprofit organizations, government, and the welfare state', *Political Science Quarterly*, 104(4): 625–48.

Lischer, S. (2005) *Dangerous sanctuaries: Refugee camps, civil war, and the dilemmas of humanitarian aid*, Cornell Studies in Security Affairs, Ithaca, NY: Cornell University Press.

Lister, R. (1997) *Citizenship: Feminist Perspectives*, New York: New York University Press.

Longland, T. (1994) 'Development in conflict situations: the occupied territories' in *Community Development Journal*, 29(2): 132–40.

Lorentzen, H. (2010) 'Sector labels', in R. Taylor (ed) *Third Sector Research*, New York: Springer, pp 21–36.

Lyons, M. (2001) *Third sector: The contribution of nonprofit and cooperative enterprises in Australia*, Crows Nest, NSW: Allen & Unwin.

Maas, K. and Liket, K. (2011) 'Social impact measurement: classification of methods', in R. Burritt et al (eds) *Environmental management accounting and supply chain management*, Eco-efficiency in industry and science 27, DOI: 10.1007/978–94–007–1390–1_8.

Macmillan, R. (2013) 'Decoupling the state and the third sector? The 'Big Society' as spontaneous order', Working Paper 101, Birmingham: Third Sector Research Centre.

Mann, M. (1987) 'Ruling class strategies and citizenship', *Sociology*, 21: 339–54.

Marshall, T. (1992) 'Citizenship and social class', in T. Marshall and T. Bottomore (eds) *Citizenship and social class*, London: Pluto Press, pp 2–51.

Marris, P. and Rein, M. (1967) *Dilemmas of social reform*, New York: Atherton Press.

Mason, P. (2013) *Why it's still kicking off everywhere: The new global revolutions*, London: Verso.

Mayo, M. and Anastacio, J. (1999) 'Welfare models and approaches to empowerment: competing perspectives from area regeneration programmes', *Policy Studies*, 20(1): 5–21.

Mayo, M. and Annette, J. (2010) *Taking part: Active learning for active citizenship and beyond*, Leicester: National Institute for Adult and Continuing Education.

Mayo, M., Mendiwelso-Bendek, Z. and Packham, C. (eds) (2013) *Community research for community development*, Basingstoke: Palgrave Macmillan.

McCabe, A. and Phillimore, J. (2012) 'All change? Surviving 'below the radar': community groups and activities in a Big Society', Working Paper 87, Birmingham: Third Sector Research Centre

McFaul, M. (2000) 'Russia's stalled democracy: Russia's political system lacks many features of a liberal democracy but also lacks those of a dictatorship', *World and I*, 5i(3): 16–26.

McLean, S. (2011) *Creating green, affordable housing: Social and cultural issues, implications solutions*, Sydney: Nextgen Housing Project, University of Technology, Sydney.

Meade, R. and Shaw, M. (2007) 'Community development and the arts: reviving the democratic imagination', *Community Development Journal*, 42(3): 413–21.

Melucci, A. (1989) *Nomads of the present*, Philadelphia, PA: Temple University Press.

Melucci, A. and Lyyra, T. (1998) 'Collective action, change and democracy', in M. Giugni, D. McAdam and C. Tilly (eds) *From contention to democracy*, New York and Oxford: Rowman and Littlefield, pp 45–58.

Menasce, D. and Dalsace, F. (2011) 'Getting involved: BoP vs Social Business', *Journal of Social Business*, 1(1): 117–25.

Mendelson, S. (2002) 'Conclusion: the power and limits of transnational democracy networks in postcommunist societies', in S. Mendelson and J. Glenn (eds) *The power and limits of NGOs*, New York: Columbia University Press, pp 232–51.

Merrifield, J. (2010) 'Putting the learning into citizenship', in M. Mayo and J. Annette (eds) *Taking Part?*, Leicester: NIACE, pp 261–73.

Milbourne, L. (2013) *Voluntary sector in transition*, Bristol: Policy Press.

Miller, C., Taylor, M. and Howard, J. (2013) 'Surviving the 'civil society dilemma': critical factors in shaping the behaviour of non-governmental actors', in J. Howell (ed) *Nongovernmental public action and social justice*, Basingstoke: Palgrave Macmillan, pp 136–58.

Miller, M. (2010) 'The role of Islamic Law Sharia in post-tsunami reconstruction', in M. Clarke, I. Fanany and S. Kenny, (eds) *Post-disaster reconstruction: Lessons from Aceh*, London: Earthscan, pp 29–60.

Miller, P. and Rose, N. (2008) *Governing the present*, Cambridge: Polity Press.

Milofsky, C. and Hunter, A. (1994) 'Where non-profits come from: a theory of organisational emergence', paper presented to 24th ARNOVA conference, San Francisco.

Minkoff, D. (2002) 'The emergence of hybrid organizational forms: combining identity-based service provision and political action', *Nonprofit & Voluntary Sector Quarterly*, 31(3): 377–401.

Mirabella, R. (2013) University-based education programs in nonprofit and nongovernmental administration and philanthropic studies: a global overview, personal communication.

Morison, J, (2000) 'The government-voluntary sector compacts: governance, governmentality and civil society', *Journal of Law & Society*, 27(1): 98–132.

Mosley, J. (2011) 'From skid row to the statehouse: how nonprofit homeless service providers overcome barriers to policy advocacy involvement', paper presented at the Nonprofits and Advocacy conference, Georgetown University, March.

Moyo, D. (2009) *Dead aid: Why aid is not working and how there is a better way for Africa*, London: Penguin.

Mullins, D. and Pawson, H. (2010)' Housing associations: agents of policy or profits in disguise?' in D. Billis (ed) *Hybrid organizations and the third sector: Challenges for practice, theory and policy*, Basingstoke: Palgrave Macmillan, pp 197–218.

Murphy and Cunningham (2003) *Organizing for community controlled development: Renewing civil society*, London: Sage

Nair, G. (2003) 'Nurturing capacity in developing countries: from consensus to practice', *Capacity Enhancement Briefs*, 1/2003: 1–4.

Narushima, M. (2005) 'Payback time: community volunteering among older adults as a transformative mechanism', *Ageing & Society*, 25: 567–84.

NCVO (National Council for Voluntary Organisations) (2014) *The UK civil society almanac*, London: NCVO.

Neck, H., Brush, C., and Allen, E. (2009) 'The landscape of social entrepreneurship', *Business Horizons*, 52: 13–19.

Neveu, C., Clarke, J., Coll, K. and Dagnino, E. (2011) 'Introduction: questioning citizenships/questions de citoyennetes', *Citizenship Studies*, 15(8): 945–64.

Newman, J. (2001) *Modernising governance: New Labour, policy and society*, Bristol: The Policy Press.

Nugroho, E (2013) 'Bill on Societal Organizations (RUU Ormas) and Freedom of Association in Indonesia', *The International Journal of Not-for-Profit Law*, 15 (1), www.icnl.org/research/journal/vol15iss1/special_2.htm.

Obadare, E. (2012) 'Introduction to special issue: Civil Society in Africa', *Voluntas,* 23(1): 1–4.

Obama, B. (1988) 'Problems and promise in the inner city', *Illinois Issues*, http://illinoisissues.uis.edu/archives/2008/09/whyorg.html.

Ohlemacher, T. (1992) 'Social relays: micro-mobilisation via the meso-level', Discussion paper FS III 92–104, Berlin: Wissenschaftzentrum

Onyx, J. and Bullen, P. (2000) 'Measuring social capital in five communities',. *Journal of Applied Behavioral Science*, 36(1): 23–42.

Onyx, J. and Bullen, P. (2001) 'The different faces of social capital in NSW Australia', in P. Dekker and E. Uslaner (eds) *Social capital and participation in everyday life*, London: Routledge, pp 45–58.

Onyx, J. and Dovey, K. (1999) 'Celebration in the time of cholera: praxis in the community sector in the era of corporate capitalism', *Community Development Journal*, 34(3): 179–90.

Onyx, J. and Leonard, R. (2000) 'Women, volunteering and social capital', in J. Warburton and M. Oppenheimer (eds) *Volunteers and volunteering*, Sydney: Federation Press, pp 113–24.

Onyx, J. and Leonard, R. (2010) 'Complex systems leadership in emergent community projects', *Community Development Journal*, 46(4): 493–510.

Onyx, J., Edwards, M. and Bullen, P. (2007) 'The intersection of social capital and power: an application to rural communities', *Rural Society*, 17(3): 215–30.

Onyx, J, Kenny, S. and Brown, K. (2011) 'Active citizenship: an empirical investigation', *Social Policy & Society*, 11(1): 55–66.

Onyx, J., Leonard, R., and Hayward-Brown, H. (2003) 'The special position of volunteers in the formation of social capital', *Voluntary Action,* 6(1): 59–74.

Onyx, J., Wood, C., Bullen, P. and Osburn, L. (2005) 'Social capital: a rural youth perspective', *Youth Studies Australia*, 24(4): 21–7.

Osler, A. and Starkey, H. (2003) 'Learning for cosmopolitan citizenship: theoretical debates and young people's experiences', *Educational Review*, 55(3): 243–54.

Ostrander, S. (2013) 'Agency and initiative by community associations in relations of shared governance: between civil society and local state', *Community Development Journal*, 48 (4): 511–24.

Ostrom, E. (1990) *Governing the commons*, Cambridge: Cambridge University Press.

Owen, D, (1964) *English philanthropy 1660–1960*, Cambridge, MA: Harvard University Press.

Pallotta, D. (2013) 'Business can't solve the world's problems: but capitalism can', *Harvard Business Review*, 15 January, https://hbr.org/2013/01/business-cant-solve-the-worlds/.

Paredo, A. and McLean, M. (2006) 'Social entrepreneurship: a critical review of the concept', *Journal of World Business*, 41: 56–65.

Parkes, T., Taylor, M. and Wilkinson, M. (2004) 'From protest to partnership? Voluntary and community organisations in the democratic process', in M. Todd and G. Taylor (eds) *Democracy and participation: Popular protests and new social movements*, London: Merlin Press, pp 307–25.

Pestoff, V. (2004) 'The development and future of the social economy in Sweden', in A. Evers and J-L. Laville (eds) *The third sector in Europe*, Cheltenham: Edward Elgar, pp 63–82.

Peters, B. and Pierre, J. (2001) 'Developments in intergovernmental relations: towards multi-level governance', *Policy & Politics*, 29(2): 131–5.

Pfeffer, J. and Salancik, G. (1978) *The external control of organizations: A resource dependence perspective*, New York: Harper and Row.

Phillips, A. (2004) 'Identity politics: have we now had enough?', in J. Anderson and B. Siim (eds) *The politics of inclusion and empowerment*, Basingstoke: Palgrave Macmillan, pp 36–48.

Piper, L. and Nadvi, L. (2010) ' Popular mobilization, party dominance and participatory governance in South Africa', in L. Thompson and C. Tapscott (eds) *Citizenship and social movements*, London: Zed Press, pp 212–38.

Plowman, D., Solansky, S., Beck, T., Baker, L., Kulkarni, M., Travis, D. (2007) 'The role of leadership in emergent, self-organization', *The Leadership Quarterly*, 18(4): 341–56.

Portes, A. (1998) 'Social capital: its origins and applications in modern sociology', *Annual Review of Sociology*, 24(1): 1–24.

Portes, A. and Sensenbrenner, J. (1998) 'Embeddedness and immigration: notes on the social determinants of economic action', *American Journal of Sociology*, 98: 1320–50.

Powell, F. (2007) *The politics of civil society: Neoliberalism or social left?* Bristol: Policy Press.

Powell, W. (1991) 'Extending the scope of institutional analysis', in P. DiMaggio and W. Powell (eds) *The new institutionalism in organizational analysis*, Chicago, IL: University of Chicago Press, pp 183–203.

Purdue, D., Razzaque, K., Hambleton, R., Stewart, M. with Huxham, C. and Vangen, S. (2000) *Community leadership in area regeneration*, Bristol: The Policy Press.

Purkis, A. (2012) 'Big Society contractors? Big questions for voluntary organisations', *Voluntary Sector Review*, 3(1): 93–101.

Putnam, R., Leonardi, R. and Nanetti, R. (1993) *Making democracy work: Civic traditions in modern Italy,* Princeton, NJ: Princeton University Press.

Putnam, R. (2000) *Bowling alone: The collapse and revival of American community*, New York: Simon and Schuster.

Recknagel, G. and Holland, D. (2013) ' How inclusive and how empowering? Two case studies researching the impact of active citizenship learning initiatives in a social policy context', in M. Mayo, Z. Mendiwelso-Bendek and C. Packham (eds) *Community research for community development*, Basingstoke: Palgrave Macmillan, pp 19–39.

Rees, J., Mullins, D. and Bovaird, T. (2012) 'Third sector partnerships for service delivery: An evidence review', Working Paper no. 60, Birmingham: Third Sector Research Centre.

Rhodes, R. (1997) *Understanding governance*, Buckingham: Open University Press.

Riddell, R. (2007) *Does foreign aid really work?,* Oxford: Oxford University Press.

Rist, G. (2008) *The history of development: From Western origins to global faith* (3rd edn), London: Zed Books.

Robertson, G. (2011) *The politics of protest in hybrid regimes: Managing dissent in post-communist Russia*, New York: Cambridge University Press

Robins, S., Cornwall, A. and von Lieres, B. (2008) 'Rethinking 'citizenship' in the postcolony', *Third World Quarterly*, 29(6): 1069–86.

Rochester, C. (2013) *Rediscovering voluntary action: The beat of a different drum*, Basingstoke: Palgrave Macmillan.

Rochester, C., Ellis Paine, A. and Howlett, S. (2010) *Volunteering and society in the 21st century*, London: Palgrave Macmillan.

Rooke, A. (2013) 'Contradiction, collaboration and criticality: researching empowerment and citizenship in community-based arts context', in M. Mayo, Z. Mendiwelso-Bendek and C. Packham (eds) *Community research for community development*, Basingstoke: Palgrave Macmillan, pp 150–69.

Rose, N. (1999) *Powers of freedom: Reframing political thought*, Cambridge: Cambridge University Press.

Rosenblum, N. (1998) *Membership and morals: The personal uses of pluralism in America*, Princeton, NJ: Princeton University Press.

Rosenblum, N. and Post, R. (2002) 'Introduction ' in N. Rosenblum and R. Post (eds) *Civil society and government*, Princeton, NJ: Princeton University Press, pp 1–5.

Rothman, J. and Tropman, J. (1993) 'Models of community organizations and macro practice perspectives: their mixing and phasing', in F. Cox, J. Erlich, J. Rothman and J. Tropman (eds) *Strategies of community organization* (4th edn), Itasca, IL: F.E.Peacock

Rottenberg, L. and Morris, R. (2013) 'If you want to scale impact, put financial results first', *Harvard Business Review*, 9 January, https://hbr.org/2013/01/new-research-if-you-want-to-sc.

Roy, A. (2005) *Gendered citizenship: Historical and conceptual explorations*, Chennai, India: Orient Blackswan.

Roy, O. (2002) *Globalised Islam: The search for a new ummah*, London: Hurst and Company.

Ryan, L. (2014) 'Outsourcing and the voluntary sector', Working Paper no. 5, NCIA Inquiry into the Future of the Voluntary Sector, London: National Coalition for Independent Action.

Russell, J. and Scott, D. (1997) *Very active citizens: The impact of the contract culture on volunteers*, University of Manchester; Department of Social Policy and Social Work.

Sakwa, R. (2002) *Russian politics and society* (3rd edn), Buckingham: Open University Press.

Salamon, L. (1987) 'Of market failure, voluntary failure, and third-party government: toward a theory of government-nonprofit relations in the modern welfare state', *Journal of Voluntary Action Research*, 16(1–2): 39–49.

Salamon, L. (1995) *Partners in public service*, Baltimore, MD: Johns Hopkins Press.

Salamon, L. and Anheier, H. (1998) 'Social origins of civil society: explaining the nonprofit sector', *Voluntas*, 9(3): 213–48.

Salamon, L. and Sokolowski , W. (2004) *Global civil society: Dimensions of the nonprofit sector*, Bloomfield: Kumarian Press.

Salamon, L., Anheier, H., List, R., Toepler, S., Sokolowski, W. and Associates (1999) *Global civil society: Dimensions of the nonprofit sector*, Baltimore: The Johns Hopkins Center for Civil Society Studies.

Sampson, R. (2006) 'Collective efficacy theory: lessons learned and directions for future inquiry', in F. Cullen, J. Wright and K. Blevins (eds) *Taking Stock: The status of criminological theory*, Advances in Criminological theory, 15. London: Transaction Publishers, pp 149–68.

Sampson, R. (2007) 'What community supplies', in J. de Filippis and S. Saegert (eds) *The community development reader*, New York: Routledge, pp 163–73.

Saward, M. (2005) 'Governance and the transformation of political representation', in J. Newman (ed) *Remaking governance: Peoples, politics and the public sphere*, Bristol: The Policy Press, pp 179–96.

Schattle, H. (2008) *The practices of global citizenship*, Lanham MD: Rowman and Littlefield.

Schattschneider, E. (1960) *The semi-sovereign people,* New York: Holt, Rinehart and Winston.

Schein, R. (2012) 'Whose occupation? Homelessness and the politics of park encampments', *Social Movement Studies*, 11 (3–4): 335–41.

Schmitter, P. (1974) 'Still the century of corporatism', *The Review of Politics*, 36(1): 85–131.

Schneider, J. (2009) 'Organizational social capital and nonprofits', *Nonprofit & Voluntary Sector Quarterly*, 38(4): 643–62.

Scholte, J. A. (2005) 'Civil society and democracy in global governance', in R. Wilkinson (ed) *The global governance reader*, London: Routledge.

Schuller, T. (2001) 'The complementary roles of human and social capital', *Canadian Journal of Policy Research*, 2(1): 18–24.

Schuller, T. (2007) Reflections on the use of social capital, *Review of Social Economy*, LXV(1): 11–28.

Schuurman, F. (2000) 'Paradigms lost, paradigms regained? Development studies in the twenty-first century', *Third World Quarterly*, 21(1): 7–20.

Scott, R. (1995) *Institutions and organizations*, Thousand Oaks: Sage.

Seligman, A. (1992) *The idea of civil society*, New York: Free Press.

Sen, A (1999) *Development as freedom*, Oxford: Oxford University Press.

Simpson, N. and Waldman, L. (2010) 'Mobilization through litigation: claiming health rights on asbestos issues in South Africa', in L. Thompson and C. Tapscott (eds) *Citizenship and social movements*, London: Zed Press, pp 87–109.

Skrbis, Z. and Woodward, I. (2013) *Cosmopolitanism uses of the idea*, London: Sage.

Smith, C., Castaneda, E. and Heyman, J. (2012) 'The homeless and Occupy el Paso: creating community amongst the 99%', *Social Movement Studies*, 11(3–4): 356–66.

Smith, S. and Pekkanen, R. (2012) 'Revisiting advocacy by non-profit organisations', *Voluntas*, 3(1): 35–50.

Smith, V. (1996) 'Contracting for social and welfare services: the changing relationship between government and the voluntary sector in New Zealand', *Third Sector Review*, 2.

Smock, K. (2003) *Democracy in action: Community organizing and urban change*, New York: Columbia University Press.

Snow, E. and Benford, R. (1998) 'Ideology, frame resonance, and participant mobilization', in B. Klandermans, H. Kriesi and S. Tarrow (eds) *From structure to action: Social movement participation across cultures*, Greenwich, CT: JAI Press, pp 197–217.

Snowdon, C. (2014) 'The sock doctrine: What can be done about state-funded political activism?', IEA Discussion Paper no. 53, London: Institute for Economic Affairs.

Sowa, T. (2014) 'Philanthropy and giving: some myths we should explore', keynote address given to International Society for Third Sector Research, 11th International Conference, Muenster, July.

Sperling, V. (1999) *Organising women in contemporary Russia: Engendering transition*, Cambridge: Cambridge University Press.

Stevenson, N. (ed) (2001) *Culture and citizenship*, London: Sage, pp 167–179.

Stiglitz, J. (2002) *Globalization and its discontents*, New York: W.W. Norton & Company.

Stoker, G. (1998) 'Governance as theory: five propositions', *International Social Science Journal*, 155: 17–28.

Stokes, G. (2000) 'Global citizenship' in W. Hudson and J. Kane (eds) *Rethinking Australian citizenship*, Cambridge: Cambridge University Press, pp 231–42.

Suarez, D. and Hwang, H. (2008) 'Civic engagement and nonprofit lobbying in California', *Nonprofit & Voluntary Sector Quarterly*, 37(1): 92–112.

Surie, G. and Hazy, J. (2006) 'Generative leadership: nurturing innovation in complex systems', in J. Hazy, J. Goldstein and B. Lichtenstein (eds) *Complex systems leadership theory: New perspectives from complexity science on social and organizational effectiveness*, Mansfield, MA: ISCE Publishing, pp 349–66.

Tam, H. (1998) *Communitarianism: A new agenda for politics and citizenship*, Basingstoke: Macmillan.

Tamir, Y. (1998) 'Revisiting the civil sphere', in A. Gutmann (ed) *Freedom of association*, Princeton, NJ: Princeton University Press, pp 214–38.

Tarrow, S. (1994) *Power in movement: Social movements, collective action and politics,* Cambridge: Cambridge University Press.

Tarrow, S. (2011) *Power in movement: Social movements and contentious politics* (4th edn), Cambridge: Cambridge University Press.

Taylor, M. (1996) 'The canary in the coalmine: issues facing the voluntary sector', in M. May, E. Brunsden and G. Craig, (eds) *Social policy review 8*, Social Policy Association, pp 40–61.

Taylor, M. (2007) 'Community participation in the real world: opportunities and pitfalls in new governance spaces', *Urban Studies*, 44(2): 297–317.

Taylor, M. (2011) *Public policy in the community* (2nd edn), Basingstoke: Palgrave Macmillan.

Taylor, M. (2012a) 'The changing fortunes of community', *Voluntary Sector Review*, 3(1): 15–35.

Taylor, M. (2012b) 'Surviving over time and space: the experience of the English Compact', *Nonprofit Policy Forum*, 3(2), DOI: 10.1515/2154-3348.1050.

Taylor, M. and Kendall, J. (1996) 'History of the voluntary sector', in J. Kendall and M. Knapp (eds) *The voluntary sector in the UK*, Manchester: Manchester University Press, pp 28–30.

Taylor, M. and Lewis, J, (1997) 'Contracting: what does it do to voluntary and nonprofit organisations?', in P. 6 and J. Kendall (eds) *The contract culture in public services: Studies from Britain, Europe and the USA*, Aldershot: Arena.

Taylor, M., Howard, J. and Lever, J. (2010) 'Citizen participation and civic action in comparative perspective', *Journal of Civil Society*, 6(2): 145–64.

Taylor, M., Langan, J. and Hoggett, P. (1995) *Encouraging diversity: voluntary and private organisations in community care*, Aldershot: Arena/Joseph Rowntree Foundation.

Taylor, M., Howard, J., Harris, V., Lever, J., Mateeva, A., Miller, C., Petrov, R. and Serra, L. (2009) 'Dilemmas of engagement; The experience of non-governmental actors in new government spaces', Non-Governmental Public Action Working Paper 31, London: London School of Economics.

Taylor, R. (2011) 'Moving beyond empirical theory' in R. Taylor (ed) *Third Sector research*, New York: Springer, pp 1–10.

Telford, J., Cosgrave, J. and Houghton, R. (2006) *Joint evaluation of the international response to the Indian Ocean tsunami: Synthesis report*, London: Tsunami Evaluation Coalition.

Terry, F. (2003) 'Reconstituting whose social order? NGOs in disrupted states', in W. Maley, C. Sampford and R. Thakur (eds) *From civil strife to civil society: Civil and military responsibilities in disrupted states*, Tokyo: United Nations University, pp 279–99.

Thompson, E.P. (1963) *The making of the English working class*, London: Victor Gollancz.

Thompson, L. and Tapscott, C. (2010) 'Introduction: mobilization and social movements in the South: the challenges of inclusive governance', in L. Thompson and C. Tapscott (eds) *Citizenship and social movements*, London: Zed Press, pp 1–32.

Touraine, A. (1988) *Return of the actor: Social theory in post-industrial society*, Minnesota, MN: University of Minnesota Press.

Touraine, A. (2000) *Can we live together? Equality and difference*, Cambridge: Polity Press.

TUC (Trades Union Council) (2010) *Swords of justice and civic pillars*, London: TUC.

Turner, B. (1992) 'Outline of a theory of citizenship' in C. Mouffe (ed) *Dimensions of radical democracy: Pluralism, citizenship, community*, London: Verso, pp 33–62.

Turner, B. (1999) 'McCitizens: Risk, coolness and irony in contemporary politics', in B. Smart (ed) *Resisting McDonaldization*, London: Sage, pp 83–100.

Turner, B. (2001) 'The erosion of citizenship', *British Journal of Sociology*, 52(2): 189–210.

Turner, B. (2006) 'Classical sociology and cosmopolitanism: a critical defence of the social', *British Journal of Sociology*, 57(1): 133–51.

UNDP (United Nations Development Programme) (2005) 'Survivors of the tsunami: One year later', UNDP's Bureau for Asia and the Pacific, www.asia-pacific.undp.org/content/rbap/en/home/library/crisis_prevention_and_recovery/survivors-of-the-tsunami.html.

Unsworth, S. (2005) 'Focusing aid on good governance', University of Oxford Working Paper no 18, Global Economic Governance Programme, Department of Politics and International Relations, Oxford: Oxford University Press.

Uphoff, N. (1995) 'Why NGOs are not a third sector: a sectoral analysis with some thoughts on accountability, sustainability and evaluation', in M. Edwards and D. Hulme (eds) *Non-governmental organizations - performance and accountability: Beyond the magic bullet*, London: Earthscan, pp 17–30.

van der Meer, T. and van Ingen, E. (2009) 'Schools of democracy? Disentangling the relationship between civic participation and political action in 17 European countries', *European Journal of Political Research*, 40(2): 281–308.

Vanderwoerd, J. (2004) 'How faith-based organizations manage secular pressures associated with government funding', *Nonprofit Management & Leadership*, 14 (3): 289–304.

van Til, J. (2000) *Growing civil society: From nonprofit sector to third space*, Bloomington: Indiana University Press

Vertovec, S. and Cohen, R. (eds) (2002) *Conceiving cosmopolitanism*, Oxford: Oxford University Press.

Wagner, A. (2000) 'Reframing 'social origins' theory: the structural transformation of the public sphere', *Voluntary & Nonprofit Sector Quarterly*, 29 (4): 541–53.

Wainwright, H. (2014) *The tragedy of the private: The potential of the public*, Ferney-Voltair Cedex, France: Public Services International and Amsterdam: Transnational Institute.

Wainwright, H. with Little, M. (2009) *Public service reform: But not as we know it*, Compass and UNISON with support from the Transnational Institute and the International Centre for Participation Studies, University of Bradford, distributed by Picnic Publishing, Hove.

Walzer, M. (1995) 'The civil society argument', in R. Beiner (ed) *Theorizing citizenship*, New York: Albany State University of New York Press, pp 153–74.

Warren, M. (2001) *Democracy and association*, Princeton, NJ: Princeton University Press.

Watkins, R. (1979) 'The Green Ban Movement', in G. Craig, M. Mayo and N. Sharman (eds) *Jobs and Community Action*, London: Routledge and Kegan Paul.

Weisbrod, B. (1998*) To profit or not to profit: The commercial transformation of the nonprofit sector*, New York: Cambridge University Press.

Weiss, T. (1999) 'Principle, politics and humanitarian action', *Ethics and International Affairs*, 13: 1–21.

White, S. (1996) 'Depoliticising development: the uses and abuses of participation', *Development in Practice*, 6(1): 6–15.

White, S. (2002) 'Ten years on, what do the Russians think?' in R. Fawn and S. White (eds) *Russia after communism*, London: Frank Cass Publishers, pp 35–50.

Wieviorka, M. (2012) 'Multiculturalism: a concept to be redefined and certainly not replaced by the extremely vague term of interculturalism', *Journal of Intercultural Studies*, 33(2): 225–31

Williams, K. and Guerra, N. (2011) 'Perceptions of collective efficacy and bullying perpetuation in schools', *Social Problems*, 58(1): 126–43.

Wilson, J. (2000) 'Volunteering', *Annual Review of Sociology*, 26: 215–40.

Wilson, J. and Musick, M. (1997) 'Who cares? Toward an integrated theory of volunteer work', *American Sociological Review*, 625: 694–713.

Wise, A. and and Velayutham, S. (2009) *Everyday multiculturalism*, Basingstoke: Palgrave Macmillan.

Winyard, P. (2011) *The Work Programme: Initial concerns from civil society organisations*, London: NCVO.

Wollebaek, D. and Strømsnes, K. (2008) 'Voluntary associations, trust, and civic engagement: a multilevel approach', *Nonprofit & Voluntary Sector Quarterly*, 37(2): 249–63.

Woodward, V. (2004) *Active learning for active citizenship*, London: Home Office.

Woolcock, M. (2001) 'The place of social capital in understanding social and economic outcomes', *Canadian Journal of Policy Research*, 2(1): 11–17.

Woolcock, M. and Narayan, D. (2001) 'Social capital: implications for development theory, research and policy', *World Bank Research Observer*, 15(2): 225–50.

World Bank (2011) 'The World Bank and Civil Society', http://go.worldbank.org/PWRRFJ2QH0.

World Bank (2013) 'Governance and Public Sector Management', http://go.worldbank.org/36UKIEBEK0.

World Social Forum (2013) 'World Social Forum Charter of Principles', www.forumsocialmundial.org.br/main.php?id_menu=4&cd_language=2

Yaln-Heckman, L. (2011) 'Introduction: claiming social citizenship', *Citizenship Studies*, 15: 3–4

Yerbury, H. (2009) 'Creating community: Theorising on the lived experience of young people', PhD thesis, University of Technology, Sydney.

Yerbury, H. (2010) 'Who to be? Generations X and Y in civil society online', *Youth Studies Australia*, 29(2): 25–32.

Young, D. (2001) 'Organizational identity and the structure of nonprofit umbrella associations', *Nonprofit Management & Leadership*, 11(3): 289–304.

Young, I. (1990) *Justice and the politics of difference*, Princeton, NJ: Princeton University Press.

Yunus, M. (2010) *Building social business: The new kind of capitalism that serves humanity's most pressing needs*, New York: Public Affairs Books.

Zdravomyslova, E. (2002) 'Overview of the feminist movement in contemporary Russia', *Diogenes*, 49(194): 35–9.

Ziai, A. (2004) 'The amblivalence of post-development: between reactionary populism and radical democracy', *Third World Quarterly*, 25(6): 1045–60.

Zimmeck, M. (2010) 'The Compact ten years on: government's approach to partnership with the voluntary and community sector in England', *Voluntary Sector Review*, 1(1): 125–33.

Index